Access Control Systems

Security, Identity Management and Trust Models

Access Control Systems

Security, Identity Management and Trust Models

by

Messaoud Benantar
IBM Corp, Austin, TX, USA

 Springer

Dr. Messaoud Benantar
IBM Corp.
Austin, TX, USA

Library of Congress Cataloging-in-Publication Data

A C.I.P. Catalogue record for this book is available
from the Library of Congress.

Access Control Systems:
Security, Identity Management and Trust Models
by Messaoud Benantar

e-ISBN-10: 0-387-27716-1
ISBN-13: 978-1-4419-3473-4   e-ISBN-13: 978-0-387-27716-5

Printed on acid-free paper.

Printed in the United States of America.

9 8 7 6 5 4 3 2 1

springeronline.com

"To my little world – Elyes, Aicha and Houda. To my elementary school teachers – Abdelmadjid Bouanane and Messaoud Berrou."

Preface

Secure identification of users, programming agents, hosts, and networking devices is considered the core element of computing security. Rarely is anonymity a desired goal of systems, networks, and applications. This aspect is dictated largely by the extent in which computing has evolved to automate many facets of critical human activities, such as in businesses and even in processes that can have direct effects on human lives. To that end every unit of computing in modern systems with a relative level of security is attached to an authenticated identity associated with it. This enables deterministic accountability and lays the foundation for responsible and secure computing, as we present in chapter 1. We emphasize the major aspects relating to identification and access control and define the basic concepts that collectively form the foundation for computing security.

An identity in computing reflects real-life entities in that its level of granularity can be coarse (such as representing an organization; a group of people) or can represent a specific individual or a particular computing device. The premise of achieving deterministic accountability is centered on the processes that support coherent and consistent identity management where a one-to-one correspondence of an identity to a real entity, its owner, can be achieved. Assurance in identity, referred to as *identity trust*, is established through authentication. In computing security trust is computable. The authentication process is based on providing what is called the *proof of identity possession*, while uniqueness of an identity is generally parameterized by referencing a well defined naming space. The latter can be as simple as a local registry of a centralized system or as wide and global as the Internet. The level of trust in an identity varies depending on the proof presented to establish it. Although trust in computing spans all elements that contribute to enforcing system and networking controls including the integrity of identity repositories and that of governing policies, evidently it is all predicated on the trust that a system or a network establishes in an identity.

The Evolution of computing—from centralized to distributed systems and now well into the global era of the Internet—has tremendously increased the complexity associated with identity management and trust. Chapter 2 introduces the reader to the elements of identity management.

We provide a taxonomy of various existing schemes based on the defining scope of an identity and discuss the benefits and limitations of each. We present the elements of federated identity and show how identity has moved from being simply a concept and a manipulated data construct that has little effect on processing to becoming, by its own right, the object of systems management in what is known as *identity provisioning*.

The simplistic view in the centralized computing era is characterized by the scope of identity being limited to a locally managed user registry. The naming space from which an identity is drawn is generally flat and implicitly qualified by the computer system in which it is defined. It ceases to exist uniquely outside this limited boundary. Since the proof of identity possession remained in the confines of an organization's computing infrastructure, it largely relied on the use of passwords.

The network-computing era raised the scope of an identity to the network level, thereby becoming visible to all computing systems attached to a network. It pushed the limits into network wide identity registries and authentication protocols that are based on various encryption schemes, most notably secret key. When multiple registries are used, consistency and synchronization of identity attributes became a necessity. This era also highlighted the need for network wide single sign-on and presented eloquent solutions to it. The network wide scope increased the functional requirements needed for securely establishing and maintaining trust in an identity. The network-security context came into existence to represent this trust.

The era of Internet computing is seeing an unprecedented need for reliable identity-management and trust mechanisms. Conducting business transactions over public networks requires secure processes for establishing a security context before it is attached to a particular transaction, verifying it, propagating it from end point to end point, and managing its life cycle. The multitude of Web services that can potentially collaborate behind the scene of a single-end-user transaction requires secure propagation of identity trust and interoperable models of profiling attributes. Several models of trust propagation have emerged.

The Web model of computing necessitates a Web model of identity management. Identity attributes, known as *profiles*, need to be consistently interpreted and exchanged across organization boundaries in arbitrary ways. Profiles that are associated with the same entity may need to maintain a mapping to each other and be kept synchronized. Privacy concerns have emerged to an extent never seen before. Remedies to these issues need to apply to every level of profile attributes from coarse to finer components and should be based on individual concerns, organizational policies, and emerging standards. To facilitate and ease collaboration, organizations may find the need to be federated together to form entities whose boundaries are seamless to users. The transparency provided by these federations allows entities to undergo a single registration process and experience the benefits of single sign-on throughout a virtually larger organization.

Chapter 3 is concerned with the elements of identity trust. We survey exist-ing models as they relate to assurance in an identity. We begin with the sim-plistic method of sharing secrets and subsequently delve into the public-key aspect of trust. Various public-key-based trust models are presented. Identity-management processes alone are not sufficient if they are not cou-pled with a strong foundation of trust, particularly across organizations. The ultimate need for the secure establishment of an identity is to impose controls over the entitlements, which can be granted or denied to the associated entity. The goal is to base access-control decisions on secure foundations.

Trust in an identity and its associated profile attributes is generally intended as a prerequisite for a secure determination of entitlements. Access control is founded on the establishment of secure identity contexts. Assurance in that foundation is a key element in secure access-control implementations. Other important aspects include the processes enabling access decision mak-ing and the adoption of access policies that are based on well-defined mod-els. Management of access-control supporting constructs (such as policy maintenance) and of the provisioning of entitlements to various entities is also an important element. Subsequent to the initial introduction of existing paradigms of information access control in Chapter 1, we discuss the details of the mandatory-access-control (MAC) model in Chapter 4. We demon-strate the ease of information-flow analysis in this model and present a few of its variants. In Chapter 5 we delve into the access-matrix model and focus on all aspects of discretionary access control (DAC). We introduce the reader to the elements of safety and show the complexity of analyzing access-con-trol systems in a generalized form. Chapters 6 and 7 present the take-grant and the schematic models, respectively. These schemes are of lesser general-ity than the access-matrix model but have computable safety properties. Chapter 8 presents the details of role-based access control (RBAC) beginning with the basic concepts to the complex aspects of mapping DAC and MAC onto RBAC. Information-flow analysis of RBAC is discussed and the RBAC standard is highlighted.

Models help elevate access-control management to a level that is concise and in some cases even formal. Modeling is an important tool for attempting to define the bounds of information flow in any given computing environ-ment. Access-control models follow along existing paradigms of information flow. Two major such paradigms are known to date, discretionary and mandatory. *Discretionary access control* empowers resource owners in divulging access to others. The flexibility of this paradigm, however, removes any possibility for defining the limits that can be reached by a given protec-tion state. Such states are unbounded, and the flow of information is gener-ally unpredictable. Nevertheless, DAC is the most widely adopted access-control paradigm. It naturally fits many of real-life processes that govern access to resources based on ownership.

Mandatory access control leaves no powers to end entities in deciding the flow of information. Instead, select administrators of an organization grant or deny access by assigning security classifications to resources and active entities (such as computing devices and programming subsystems and users, referred to as labels and clearances, respectively). Access decisions are then made in accordance with a partially ordered relationship between labels and clearances in what is known as *dominance* or the lack thereof. Contrary to DAC, dissemination of information in MAC is predictable as it follows a lattice structure that accurately determines the bounds of information flow. MAC lends itself well to military environments, while it is generally regarded as a handicapping measure in commercial environments.

Role-based access control has emerged in recent years as a generalized access model that although it encapsulates more of discretionary flavor than mandatory, it theoretically applies to DAC as well as MAC policies. RBAC seems to fit naturally into modeling access control. Its main advantage is in the simplification of management and administrative tasks of governing security policies. Additionally, it lends itself well to the *separation-of-duty* (SoD) principle. SoD can be viewed in many respects as a bridge between DAC and MAC policies. Like in MAC, the administrative tasks play an important role in how information is disseminated in RBAC. Like DAC, RBAC is capable of maintaining the concept of resource ownership.

Although the elements surrounding RBAC are interpreted with relative uniformity across the computing industry, interoperability of implementations remains elusive. The absence of common-role semantics and unified policy representations makes it difficult to switch from one environment to another. Nevertheless, a recent attempt by the National Institute of Standards and Technology (NIST) at standardizing some of the RBAC aspects can be an important step forward. We devote chapter 8 to this important topic.

This book is a modest attempt at discussing these elements of computing security. I hope you find it enjoyable to read and that it clarifies these concepts for you.

Messaoud Benantar
Austin, Texas, USA

Contents

Chapter 1

Foundations of Security and Access Control in Computing

Introduction

Access control in computing is motivated by the need to divulge access to information and available computing resources and services to authorized entities only. An *entity* is a generic term that refers to an active agent capable of initiating or performing a computation of some sort (for example, an end user invoking a command or a program, a programming agent acting on behalf of a user, a running daemon process, a thread of execution, a hosting system, or a networking device). Access modes can be broadly categorized into the ability to read or write information whether in the address space of an executing process, on a secondary storage, or on a network or a peripheral device. This ability can be explicitly expressed by a direct privilege possessed by the acting entity or indirectly through services and computing tasks that the entity is allowed to execute. A purist may pose the question of whether temporarily modifying computer information without having to read it and in a way that leaves its final state unchanged is consistent with the definition of access control. The likely answer is that such activity constitutes a breach to access control and thus it should be guarded against. Otherwise, one of the fundamental security tenets of resource availability becomes at risk of being compromised. Availability of computing resources has indeed stood as a system and network security concern of its own. Furthermore, concurrent access to information that is being modified even temporarily by authorized or unauthorized entities is clearly unacceptable.

Evolution of computing systems from single-user to multiuser machines led to the necessity of shielding users and running processes from one another. Early protection mechanisms consisted of hardware and operating systems components. Subsequently, policy-based authorization subsystems have emerged. Controlling access to computing systems is the first defense against disclosing information to unauthorized entities. Systems and network access is based on trusted methods for identifying users and programming agents. Secure identification is the cornerstone of modern computing security. The advent of networking and distributed computing has led to the proliferation of computing identities. Consequently, identity management has evolved as a discipline of its own. The goal is to mitigate the cost of maintaining identity repositories that may exist in the potentially a myriad of systems used by a single enterprise, enforcing consistency and achieving unambiguous mapping of identities representing the same entity or multiple entities collaborating together. Automation of interenterprise exchanges has further necessitated the drive for federated identity systems. As a result, the scope of an identity is extending well beyond the confines of an organization. With all the associated complexities, a purist perspective seeks a unified model of secure identification. Although this is far from being achieved in the real world, any such attempts can only benefit computing security.

Real-world examples of access control are abundant and vary according to the needs and policies dictated by the circumstances. At a basic level, users of the same organization are granted access to shared computing resources based on the roles each user is entitled to within the organization. An enterprise may be concerned over losing its competitive edge should its trade secrets become known to its competitors. A financial institution has every need to confine updates in its records to legitimate transactions only and to protect them from exposure to unauthorized individuals and institutions. While a patient's medical records may not be of any immediate financial gain, one cannot put a price to their privacy.

Access control is evolving from its traditional host-centric paradigm to resources and entities that transact over large networks as wide as the Internet. The low-level access-control privileges of the basic read and write of information are now moving up a level higher to include attributes that make up a profile for an entity. These are the elements that mimic real-life user entitlements such as the privilege of having a banking account, having a credit-card number, or being assigned a well-defined role. The processes needed to maintain entity profiling gave rise to what is referred to as identity management, which is indeed a prelude to any access-control mechanism. It is concerned with the trusted methods of managing and exchanging entity entitlements on various computing systems and resource managers. Identity management forms the foundation on which access control is based.

In this chapter we introduce the main concepts behind computing security. We begin with a brief overview of security threats. We then elaborate on the major elements of systems security, in particular the aspects surrounding identification and authentication. We highlight the importance of system integrity as a prelude to secure computing. We define what is meant by a security context and discuss its propagation along the units of computing work. Subsequently, we delve into the paradigms of access control and outline the elements surrounding trust and assurance, including an introduction to the confinement problem. We conclude with an overview of the major security-design principles.

Elements of Systems Security

A threat by definition is a situation in which any protection mechanisms that govern access to a computing system may become subject to harm. Such protection mechanisms are driven by what is called a *security policy*. We discuss the concept of a security policy in further detail later in the chapter. Security threats are analogous to harmful activities that are bound to happen and thus convey the meaning of a pending attack. The latter makes the threat a reality. Threats are made possible due to *vulnerabilities*, also referred to as *weaknesses*, either in the mechanisms enforcing a particular security policy or in the operational controls of that policy (such as those having to do with configuration parameters). Mechanism-related vulnerabilities can be due to design or implementation flaws. Dormant vulnerabilities represent a risk. A *risk* is a measure of potential harm that can be realized when a threat is executed. Some of the known categories of security threats include identity theft through masquerading or spoofing, unauthorized access to resources, unauthorized disclosure or modification of data, and denial of service attacks.

Security in computing can be viewed as having the following elements:

☐ Secure entity identification, known as *authentication* and which we refer to as *identity establishment*;

☐ Confining actions of an established identity to its designated entitlements for services and computing resources, known as *resource access control*;

☐ Data integrity, confidentiality, and origin authenticity, broadly referred to as *data and message security*;

☐ Prevention from denial of taking part in a transaction, whether as an initiating or a receiving party, known as *nonrepudiation*;

☐ Resource *availability* to thwart against the denial of service attacks.

The fundamental prerequisite for the integrity and soundness of any access-control or other security mechanisms is the secure establishment of identities. For example, the lack of enforcement for secure establishment of identities, makes all attempts to enforce an access policy virtually useless.

Identity Establishment

Identity establishment is concerned with the methods by which a user, a running process, or a thread of execution is securely associated with a legitimate entity. Recall that an entity may represent a single user, a group of users, an entire organization, a host system, or some networking device. Establishing an identity is the means of concluding that indeed the identity in use corresponds to the entity that it claims to be and thus is said to be authentic. *Authentication* is the secure identification of entities in which a proof of possessing an identity is verified. An entity's access to a system is encapsulated in what has become known as an *account*. Engaging in an act of authentication can take place on every attempt to access a controlled computing system, known as a *login*, when a service from an application is requested, or each time a network access is performed. Varying system and network security policies as well as application requirements can dictate the frequency of entity authentication.

The evidence resulting from an established identity is maintained by the computing device in what is referred to as a *security context*. The latter remains securely attached to every unit of work requested by the corresponding entity. A security context can be exchanged locally across address spaces and may be transmitted over a network embodied in the request with which it is associated.

Resource Access Control

Access control, one of the central themes of this book, is also referred to as *access authorization* or simply *authorization*. It is about enforcing a predefined access policy. The goal is to confine the actions of an entity only to the services and to the computing resources that it is entitled to. To prevent an access policy from subversion, the controls that enforce it should be foremost capable of binding computing activities to authenticated identities at any fine level of computation, the scope of which may be an entire address space or at the task and thread level. These bindings are known as *secure associations*. A safe access-control policy prevents leakage of access to unauthorized users directly or indirectly in any state of the underlying computing system. As we have already mentioned, identity establishment is the cornerstone of enforcing any resource access-control policy.

Data and Message Security

Although the term *data security* is generic, its use is mainly concerned with modification detection, origin authenticity, and confidentiality of data that is being processed in-memory, or while residing on a storage medium or during transmission over a computer network (i.e., a message). Modification detection or simply data integrity alone is not of value to data security unless it is combined with origin authenticity. An eavesdropping entity may apply the same data-integrity procedures after having intercepted and modified data items, leading the receiving entity to successfully verify the integrity of the breached data but without realizing it was modified. Thus, data integrity is usually combined with some form of origin authenticity, ensuring that an integrity-check sum is indeed generated by a legitimate entity, the original source of the data. Secure data integrity, one combined with origin authenticity, protects against an unauthorized update of data.

Confidentiality is the process of sealing data using a keyed data-scrambling algorithm so that only a designated entity, one with knowledge of the key, is able to apply the reverse transformation and retrieve the data in its original form. The goal is to prevent disclosure of information to unauthorized entities. In a sense, data confidentiality can be used as a mechanism for enforcing access to information. The underlying cost, however, can be prohibitive so that access-control mechanisms are generally not based on data confidentiality. Data confidentiality remains a discipline of its own in security. It is selectively applied to sensitive information that when disclosed results in measurable or un-measurable loss of some kind.

Nonrepudiation

Nonrepudiation of action is the process by which an entity is prevented from denying participation in a transaction either as an initiating/sending or a receiving end. The definition is ultimately applicable to preventing any process or a thread of execution running on behalf of an end user to circumvent the binding of the acting identity with the legitimate entity. Although one might argue that nonrepudiation can be accomplished simply by producing audit and transaction trails in a secure and a controllable fashion, a purist would assert that a legally binding nonrepudiation can be very hard to realize. Denial may always take one form or another. Nevertheless, digital signatures based on public key cryptography and a combination of tamper-proof hardware and software modules have come a long way toward establishing verifiable nonrepudiation services, particularly for initiating entities (i.e., those generating information).

Availability

Availability addresses the issue of disrupting access to computing resources and services. The type of disruption may range from compromising the functions of a particular service or a system to completely denying access to it. Under all circumstances, it is natural for users of any computing service to expect reasonable response times that are comparable to or much better than human-to-human interactions (over a telephone line, for instance) to attain the same service.

Protecting computing resources from extreme degradation of performance or from deliberate denial of service takes priority over the enforcement of any access-control policy. A denial-of-service (DOS) attack is one in which a deliberate high volume of bogus requests are sent to a service provider. The intent is to keep legitimate users of the service from using it. An attack as such may bring the service to its threshold capacity, leaving it dedicated to handling malicious requests instead of legitimate ones. The manifestation may result in extremely slow response times and potentially may lead to a complete inhibition of service and ultimately a shutdown due to the exhaustion of runtime resources, such as real or secondary storage or network sockets. Powerful attacks as such may further bring down an entire network as wide as the Internet to a crawl.

When authorized users are not able to send requests or reach a service, it becomes a secondary concern to have that service enforce an access-control policy. Furthermore, the mere existence of the service is entirely threatened. Security mechanisms that protect the availability of computing resources guard against various threats of interruption and deliberate actions of slowing down a service or rendering it completely inaccessible. Detection and prevention of DOS attacks have emerged as among the leading security issues in this era of computing over public networks.

It should be noted that disruptions leading to denial of service may occur at different locations along the path between a client and a server, including the following:

- ❐ *In the environment of the service* Here the service is prevented from obtaining resources needed for its proper execution. The attacker focuses on exhausting computing resources of the system in which the service is hosted.
- ❐ *In the environment of the client* The target service is diverted from responding to legitimate requesters and dealing with useful communications by way of attempting to respond to a massive bombardment of random client messages instead.
- ❐ *Along the path between clients and the server* The attacker intercepts and then discards useful requests to the service.

Cost of Security

Security in computing, as in anything else, comes with cost and overhead. That cost should be put in perspective with the value of the protected resources. The cost of security has to be proportionate to the losses incurred from any security breaches. Insignificant losses do not require significantly higher security costs. Measuring potential loss is not a deterministic process; worst-case scenarios therefore are to be assumed. In quantifiable terms, the cost of security should be less than that of entirely replacing a protected computing asset including its data and functionality. Being able to quantify various elements of risk enables the development of informed policies that balance the cost of security with the benefits of increased safety. Threats have to be considered even in highly secure environments. The probability of ruin in a computing infrastructure, even when relatively low, should be the driving factor behind the provision of security. However, one cannot always put cost to security. Invasion of privacy (such as publicly exposing a person's medical records) can be detrimental to the person, even when seemingly no quantifiable physical harm is inflicted on the person and the health-care provider.

System Integrity: A Prelude to Security

Integrity of information processing was the focus of attention in early stages of the developments in information technology (IT). First, the need for a strict separation between a running control program and user or application programs was addressed even in basic single-user systems. Operating systems and hardware advancements such as those pioneered by the IBM System/360 and System/370 family have led to multiuser systems that accommodate a large number of users. The execution of multiple processes addressing a common memory meant that one process must be prevented from overwriting memory locations that are assigned to another process. Address-space separation, therefore, had to be maintained in both the virtual storage assigned to a process and the real memory blocks used at runtime. In early IBM systems this problem was addressed with storage-protection keys where a particular process and the storage assigned to it are associated with a unique storage key that must match if the process is allowed to access the storage. Any attempt by a process to store data outside of its assigned blocks of memory is recognized by the hardware due to mismatched storage-protection keys.

In IBM's System/360 through System/390 and beyond, the control program defining the operating system is isolated from user programs by means of a two-state instruction execution environment. These two states are called *supervisor state* and *problem-program state*. A special set of machine instructions, including input/output (I/O) commands to the I/O channels and memory as well as address-space-management instructions are operable only when the system is running in supervisor state. The control program typically executes in supervisor state while user programs always execute in the problem-program state. When an application requests the services of the control program (such as performing I/O), a request is issued to the control program. The control program, executing in the supervisor state, first examines the request to make sure that it will not exceed the logical boundaries of the problem program before the request is executed.

The assurance provided by modern operating systems in isolating concurrently running user applications and control programs is the key to enforcing the security controls that a computer system provides. Such isolation is further extended to finer levels of computing units—that of execution threads. The needs for isolation equally apply to the threads executing in a single address space. Figure 1.1 illustrates the concept of isolation across operating system and user processes as well as threads. A classical example of the benefits from well-designed isolation mechanisms are found in the features that are embedded in the control program of the System/390 and its derivative platforms. These mechanisms are extended to cover new software components that are tightly related to the control program. One of these components is the security service layer, which is invoked by various resource managers and also by system components to mediate access to system resources.

Trusted Computing Base

A *trusted computing base* (TCB) is defined as the totality of protection mechanisms within a computer system, including hardware, firmware, and software, the combination of which is responsible for enforcing a security policy

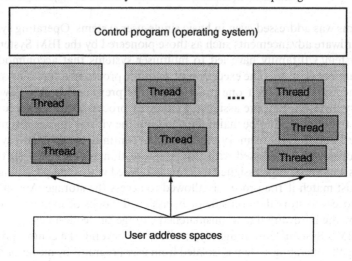

FIGURE 1.1 Isolation of program execution in modern operating systems

[ABRA95]. The ability of a trusted computing base to enforce a security policy correctly depends foremost on the integrity, correctness, and protection of
the mechanisms implementing the elements of the TCB itself. Similarly, a *network trusted computing base* (NTCB) is defined as the totality of protection
mechanisms within a network including hardware, firmware, and software,
the combination of which is responsible for enforcing a networkwide security
policy. A *mechanism* is the term used to refer to a specific paradigm, model,
or a construct that is used in the implementation of a particular service.
A security service enforcing a policy is therefore a combination of security
mechanisms. Trust in a TCB means the components and mechanisms implementing the enforcement of controls dictated by a security policy behave in
an expected manner. The expectation here is that the TCB should not subvert
the policy that it is designed to enforce. Basic to the element of trust in the
TCB is its correctness and overall system integrity.

The general method of defining the boundaries of a TCB is that any software, firmware, or a hardware component that has the ability to subvert a
security policy is considered to be part of an applicable TCB or NTCB.
Breaching a TCB is usually accomplished by carrying an attack that the
designer of the TCB had not anticipated. Building an ideal TCB, therefore,
requires exhausting all possible attacks. While it may seem that the elements
of network TCB are scattered and disjoint, in practice trust is a continuous
concept throughout that follows the information flow. Applicable trust properties should remain invariant when information is residing on a storage system, within a thread of execution, during an exchange of data across address
spaces, or while in transmission over a network.

Users, Principals, Subjects, and Objects

The term *user* in computing has been traditionally equated with a human being. Its use conveys a unique association between a computing system and an entity that can be a human being or some programmable agent. User information is generally encapsulated in an *account*, sometimes referred to as a *profile*. A user account contains information about authentication as well as authorization credentials and may contain a set of attributes describing the user (such as a name, a serial number, an organization name, and so forth). Each user account is associated with an identifier that must be unique in the naming space of the underlying computing system.

While a user represents an entity external to a computing system, a *principal* generally refers to an entity's internal representation to a computing system. Each user may have several principals associated with it. Each principal, on the other hand, is associated with one user only. The principal construct defines the runtime association between a computing task and a particular user and generally encapsulates a subset of the entitlements of that user. The scope of entitlement is dependent on the application to which the user signs in. For instance, besides being an employee of Zeta, Inc., user Aicha is participating in two projects within her company codenamed Green and Blue. Each of these projects requires special privileges. In the absence of a dynamic policy that constraints the entitlements of an entity based on its role, Aicha may be assigned three principal identities, all of which point to the same user. The first is Aicha, being the basic identity in the system; AichaB and AichaG correspond to projects Blue and Green, respectively. The relationship of the secondary identities AichaB and AichaG to the main identity Aicha should be well maintained in the system to establish an accurate binding between a physical entity, such as a user and all of its principal identities. A profile representing the primary identity of a user should point to all principal identities associated with that user.

A *subject* is the term used to identify a running process, a program in execution. Each subject assumes the identity and the privileges of a single principal. A principal may launch several processes within a single login session and thus will be associated with multiple subjects, each of which inherits the identity of the login session. Figure 1.2 illustrates the relationships between a user, a principal, and a subject.

An *object* generally refers to a passive entity (i.e., one that is an information receptacle such as a file, or a record in a database). An object, however, may indicate an active device from the system's resource pool (such as a network printer, or further can be a programmable service that is managed as a resource).

It is worth noting that in many cases we simply encounter the basic scenario in the relationships among a user, principal and subject where the user, the principal, and the subject are all the same. In the security literature the term *principal* is generally used to mean an active entity that is capable of.

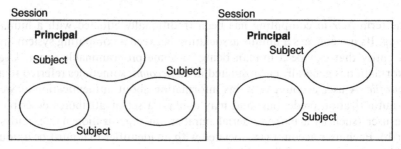

FIGURE 1.2 Relationships between a user, a principal, and subject

causing information to be retrieved, changed or flown between controlled objects of a computing environment. These three terms are in many cases interchangeably used to underscore the abstraction for "who".

Identification and Authentication

The process of establishing a user identity is known as *identification and authentication* (I&A). The goal is to have only authorized users access a computer system, a network or a particular service. Users are assigned identities from the naming space of the underlying authentication system. Each identity is associated with an authentication credential that is known only to the user and that can be verified by the system. The premise that an entity maintains secrecy of its credential except sharing it with a designated computing system yields authenticity of the identity associated with that entity. Three methods of producing and presenting a secret to a computing system are in use:

◻ *Presenting something the user knows* A password, a personal identification number (PIN), and a pass-phrase are the common schemes in this category. Secret codes in the form of passwords are extensively used on various computing devices. Widespread use of passwords is, to a great extent, due to their simplicity and perhaps to their being inherently the natural approach. Passwords are generally chosen by users but can be system generated as well. Policies can put various constraints on passwords for instance, restricting the alphabet of the password, its syntax, its length, or its lifetime. As much as they are simple to use and present to a computing system, passwords present users with a number of management challenges. Foremost is the need to memorize a password. The proliferation of systems and applications that use passwords generally leave a single user handling multiple passwords. Unfortunately, to mitigate such challenges users resort to adopting weak passwords that are easy to recall. The result is an increased exposure risk.

◻ *Presenting something that the user has* This authentication scheme consists of storing credential information in a device that generally is portable and as small as a credit card. This device, commonly known as a *token*, is presented as an input to a reader attached to the underlying computing system. The credential stored in the token is used to authenticate the user to the system based on a predefined protocol. Smart cards are a common example of such authentication technique.

◻ *Presenting something that the user is* This scheme relies on biometrical traits that reliably distinguish users. Examples include fingerprints, hand geometry, eye shape, voice, and face recognition as well as hand signature. Fingerprints are steadily gaining acceptance. This method has remained limited in use partly due to the extra cost it incurs and perhaps to the inaccuracies of the related technologies.

Authentication Factors: A Comparison

The three authentication factors that are described in the previous section are fundamentally different from one another. Certainly, the biometrics approach has nothing in common with secret codes or physical tokens. The trust elements in each of these schemes are completely different. The computational aspects of asserting each of these authentication factors have no commonality. Passwords rely on secretive information, while physical tokens are based on the premise that the token is safely kept and guarded by its owner. Biometrics, on the other hand, depends on the uniqueness of biological properties among humans. Although a functional comparison between these schemes may seem useless, we set them side by side as shown in Table 1.1 and contrast them in terms of benefits and disadvantages.

Regardless of which authentication factor is used, remote authentication requires a secure channel for the transmission of secrets or the distinguishing biometric attributes or some derivative thereof. Such a secure channel generally requires end-to-end encryption of exchanged information. To prevent interception at any level, the interacting end points may be required to be the direct participants in the encrypted channel. For instance, a channel that connects a client with a brokering service such as a proxy or a Web server may leave the path from the Web server or the proxy to the target application exposed to interception.

In the absence of an end-to-end secure transmission channel, the password technique becomes the most vulnerable and the easiest to breach. An attacker will need only to spoof the communication to learn about the passwords exchanged in clear text. Similarly, token and biometric methods become subject to replay attacks that at least can be limited in time. Damage from password interception, however, can go undetected for a long period of time.

Multiple-Factor Authentication

The majority of programmable systems adopt a single authentication factor in supporting identity establishment. In some situations, however, the risk of

TABLE 1.1. Authentication factors: Advantages and disadvantages.

Passwords	Tokens	Biometrics
Are easy to implement and low cost	May require special skill to interface with the device reader; can be expensive to implement	Require special skill to interface with the equipment; expensive to implement
Need to be memorized	Need to be carried around so the size of the token can be a factor	Are naturally present with the user
Are susceptible to guessing and compromise by others	Duplicated only by the manufacturer	User compromised only when victimized; generally very hard to compromise
User unaware of an active compromise for some time, perhaps until damage is done	User immediately aware of potential for compromise when realizing that the token is missing	User immediately aware of compromise
Require secure communication channels	Generally intended for use with a local system or device but a resulting authentication context still requires protection from replay attacks by imposters	Same as for tokens
Can be easily reused across multiple systems and applications	Require special-purpose input devices on all systems	Require special-purpose equipment on all systems
Provide accurate implementations	Accurate but device is prone to wear and loss of information	Are prone to confusion and error
Are perfect for users connecting from unpredictable remote locations	Require special-purpose input devices and thus may be a limitation to roaming users	Same as for tokens
Can be shared across users and systems	May be replicated by the manufacturer but generally are not shared across users	Cannot be shared across users

an authentication compromise can have a lasting and a damaging effect. Systems operating under stringent security constraints (due to the high value of information they contain) employ multiple-factor authentication schemes. The paradigm here follows that of adopting multiple lines of defenses in which the defeat or failure of one defense line may be stopped by the next line of defense. The common example is found in the financial area, where access to automatic teller machines (ATM) requires two factors at the same time, a card and a PIN. The first line of defense here is the token, while the second one is the secret information in the form of a PIN shared between the card holder and the banking institution. The PIN factor protects the user in that when the card is lost or stolen, the next hurdle for the illegitimate user of the card requires cracking the PIN. Although the use of distinct multiple factors is appealing, any one particular factor may be applied multiple times. For instance, a system may require two or more different passwords to authenticate a user.

Passwords: The Prevalent Authentication Method

Use of passwords is without a doubt the most prevalent form of authentication. Because of the simplicity involved, passwords offer a great advantage to system and application developers. Typically, systems prompt users with the login information that consists of a *user identifier* (UID) and a password. The UID is uniquely mapped into the user registry of the underlying system so that a comparison between the password, or a derivative of it, as provided by the user and that stored in the user entry of the registry is performed without ambiguity. A match is required, generally with case sensitivity enforced.

Approaches to Reliable Password Management

Password-based authentication is expected to remain in widespread use for at least the foreseeable future. To mitigate some of the weaknesses associated with passwords, one should adopt the best practices available. In the following, we outline some of the common practices for managing passwords [BISH02].

Password Encoding

Passwords are rarely stored as readable plaintext. Reliable user registries maintain passwords in some scrambled form. Furthermore, the scrambled form is generally such that it is irreversible. One-way hash functions that are easy to compute in one direction but intractable to reverse are the choice for storing passwords in encoded forms [SCHN96]. The underlying trust in user authentication is based on the fact that a plaintext password is provided when requesting system or service access by an identified entity. The password is then encoded using a known one-way digest algorithm, and the resulting stream is compared with the stored value of that identity credential. The following is a list of common one-way encoding functions:

- ❑ *MD4* A one-way hash function that produces a 128-bit digest of its input message;
- ❑ *MD5* An improved, and more complex, version of MD4 that also produces a 128-bit hash;
- ❑ *Secure hash algorithm* (SHA-1) This produces a 160-bit hash, longer than MD5, slightly slower than MD5, but the larger message digest makes it more secure against brute-force collision and inversion attacks;
- ❑ *Unix crypt* The well known UNIX hashing algorithm.

It is worth noting that host security systems such as IBM's Resource-Access Control Facility (RACF) do not compute the one-way transform of a password; rather, the identity of a user is encoded using a one-way transform keyed by the password.

One-way transformed passwords are sometimes further encoded into a readable base64 form. Base64 is a method for encoding arbitrary binary data as american standard code for information interchange (ASCII) text. This is particularly useful when communicating information via Internet email protocols, which can handle only 7-bit ASCII text. The resulting base64 encoding is slightly larger than its input.

Adding Salt to Password Encoding

Storing and using only one-way cryptographic transforms of passwords is not enough to prevent intruders from carrying dictionary attacks against a password. A *dictionary attack*, also referred to as *precomputation attack*, is one in which an attacker, knowing the details of the one-way transform, precomputes the one-way encoding of a dictionary of likely passwords, obtains a password in its encoded form, and looks it up in the dictionary for a possible match. Brute-force attacks that do not depend on a prebuilt dictionary can be used to crack encoded passwords as well.

A minute change in the input of a one-way digest algorithm yields a different digest. The *salt* is a value that is incorporated into the calculation of the password transform to thwart dictionary attacks. By digesting the password with a salt, a dictionary attack becomes harder to achieve. The attacker needs to search through the entire dictionary for each value of the salt. Pseudo-random generation of salt values makes them harder to guess. When salt is added, users who happen to select the same passwords will end up with different transforms of those passwords because each is likely to use a different salt value. Thus the use of salt helps avoid password collision and potentially limits the number of user accounts that can be simultaneously compromised. Another practice that helps deter attacks on passwords is to apply a high enough number of iterations of the scrambling algorithm to make exhaustive search attacks impossible to achieve.

Password Syntax Rules

A key preventive measure in protecting against password attacks is to force users into selecting hard-to-guess passwords. Users generally tend to compose passwords out of easy-to-remember words yielding weak passwords that are susceptible to dictionary attacks. Enforcing lexicographic as well as syntactic rules on passwords can be a strong defense against password attacks. Some or all of the following rules are widely adopted:

◻ Require a minimum password length (the longer a password is, the harder a brute-force attack becomes);
◻ Require mixed case for systems that are case sensitive;

- Require the use of digits or special characters;
- Require a particular syntax for combining alphanumeric as well as special characters and avoid obvious combinations;
- Require a minimum number of inside digits or special characters;
- Prohibit passwords based on user identifiers or words from a dictionary and permutations thereof;
- Offer the user the possibility of randomly generated passwords.

Password Aging

The longer a password remains in use, the more likely is to become subject of attack. *Password aging* refers to the requirement of changing passwords frequently by imposing a period of time after which a password must be changed. Implementation of a password-aging scheme requires keeping the history of passwords for every user. The following practices are in common use:

- Require a maximum lifetime for each password after which a password automatically expires;
- Avoid recycling old passwords by maintaining the history of N previous passwords for each user;
- Require a time limit that should pass before a password can be reused (a good measure against users changing passwords N times just to reuse a recent password and thus defeat the practice of not reusing N previous passwords);
- Old and new passwords must differ by at least a certain number of prescribed characters.

Auditing

Auditing was first proposed by Anderson [ANDE80] as a tool for monitoring threats. *Auditing* in the traditional sense consists of logging security-related events, analyzing them for potential breaches, and notifying concerned parties accordingly. This definition applies to past as well as to real-time or nearly real-time events. Auditing is starting to take a different shape in recent years, that of vulnerability assessment and intrusion detection or prevention. Intrusion prevention attempts to predict security incidents and attacks before they take place. Auditing is a key security element of systems and networks. It maintains evidence of attempts to compromise the security controls put in place by an organization. Furthermore, audits that are regularly performed can be used to determine system and resource usage and to identify the parties involved. Past protection states of a system can thus be intermittently reviewed to provide answers to investigative activities. Active audits can also be used to determine abnormal behavior and potentially detect system or network intrusion attacks [GLIG85]. Auditing is founded on three elements:

- ❏ *Logging* A precursor to auditing, logging provides the ability to record security events. Logging should be flexible enough to be driven by various parameters, including time and date, use of a particular resource, success or failure of access, and so forth. Logging builds audit records that make up audit trails, also referred to as *audit logs*. A key element of an audit record is its secure association with the entity causing the record to be logged (the subject of the action being logged). This association is the main difference between recording security events and logging general system activities. It identifies the responsible entities to enable accountability. Audit trails must be tamper proof and should be updated only by authorized security components of the system.
- ❏ *Analysis* Once an audit record is collected, it must be analyzed to determine any attempt to violate applicable security policies. Key information gathered from this analysis is the object and type of access attempted and the identity of the entity associated with the attempt.
- ❏ *Notification* An attempt to violate a security control should be communicated to the entities concerned with that particular event, including a system administrator and the resource owner. Notification should be configurable and may not necessarily be driven by unauthorized accesses.

Although the mechanisms above are logically separated, they cooperate to form an integral part of an auditing subsystem. Security-relevant information that should be part of an audit record may include the following:

- ❏ Identity of the entity requesting the access,
- ❏ Type or mode of access,
- ❏ Time of attempted access,
- ❏ Identification of the system or subsystem from which the request is made,
- ❏ Status as to success or failure,
- ❏ Keyed integrity check sum.

Integrity of an audit trail is an important safeguard against modification. A particularly important aspect of an auditing subsystem is recording actions initiated by privileged users, such as system administrators and security officers. A key motivation for that is due to the power and capability of such user in inflicting damage. Auditing privileged users may serve as a deterrent to costly violations and misuse of authoritative powers. Separation of duty between a system administrator and an auditor is an important aspect of reliable auditing subsystems. Violations of security controls caused by an administrator should always be communicated to the system or the network auditor.

Auditing can be best implemented by performing it under the covers of authentication and access-control mechanisms. This tight integration increases the reliability of the auditing subsystem, provides transparency, and relieves applications from programming directly to the auditing functions.

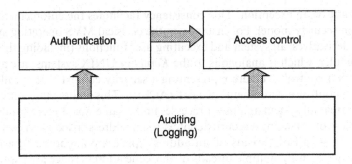

FIGURE 1.3 Elements of a secure access-control subsystem

Instead, auditing becomes driven primarily through configuration proce-dures; such is the case with RACF subsystems of the IBM MVS.

Auditing functions may also be embedded at the middleware layer and within runtime execution containers. Other approaches may choose to imple-ment an auditing subsystem as a stand-alone service. This approach requires each application to enable auditing on its own. Due to its sensitivity, an audit-ing subsystem requires strict controls that prevent users and programming agents from circumventing its activities. To this end, it is desirable to embed auditing functions within reference monitors enforcing system wide access control. Auditing is the third key foundation of access-control systems, the other two being authentication and access policy enforcement. Figure 1.3 is an illustration of the three pillars of access control.

The Security Context

The establishment of an identity as a result of a successful authentication process remains a valid fact that is associated with that identity and generally persists throughout a session. The *security context* is the term that refers to the embodiment of an established identity as represented by the memory control blocks and constructs of a system runtime. Attaching a security con-text to the units of work in a system must be performed securely and reliably. This context is used to confine actions of an entity in accordance with its assigned privileges and entitlements and becomes an anchor for tracing user activities for accountability purposes. Due to its sensitivity, a security context is always protected from modification by users and system subcomponents. While some systems may not put any time limit on the use of a security con-text, others limit its lifetime to a relatively short period of time after which the context is required to be refreshed if it is to remain in use. The security context of an entity is sometimes referred to as an *authentication credential*.

Security contexts should apply uniformly to all of the processes and address spaces that may be active in a system. Trusted-computing-bases components should not be an exception. This consistency facilitates the enforcement of a common security model. For instance, in the classical MVS operating system and its derivatives, all system and executing user functions (including the master scheduler, which is analogous to the *Kernel* in UNIX systems) are associated with a control structure representing a security context that is called an accessor control environment element (ACEE). This uniformity allows the TCB to treat all system and user processes in the same way. Figure 1.4 depicts the process of attaching a security context to an address space or an execution thread. In A, all of threads of an address space are anchored to a single context, while in B, multiple threads of the same address space are associated with different security contexts. The first scenario applies to an application that serves each request in a separate address space. In the second case, each request is served by a separate thread of a single address space in which the service executes.

Content of a Security Context

A security context carries the user's roles and group membership within the set of entities defined to the system. It encapsulates the identity of its principal as it is known in the user registry of the system. This identity must be uniquely identifiable. The group membership enumerates any user groups in which the authenticated entity is a member. The entity as such is automatically assigned the entitlements associated with each group. A security context may also anchor the user's roles and capabilities to access system and

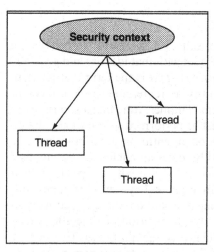
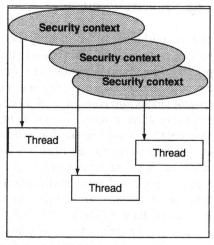

A. Address space   B. Address space

FIGURE 1.4 Anchoring computing tasks with security contexts

network resources. Other non-persistent forms of identification such as an internally used unique identifier may also be part of the security context.

The Flow of a Security Context

Components of a system's or a network's TCB are responsible for the creation and lifecycle management of a security context. Units of computing work performed by the system can be anchored to security contexts in various ways, based on the security policy and the controls implemented by the system. As computation proceeds, it is desirable that downstream services are seamlessly invoked without having the user explicitly reauthenticate. This characteristic is provided as a core functionality of modern operating environments. For example, the system authorization facility (SAF), a major component of the TCB in MVS, provides support for the creation, modification, transfer, or deletion of a security context by trusted operating system components such as resource managers. This capability supports two important security aspects:

❏ A new process that is initiated by an existing process can be forced to inherit the authenticated identity of the parent user process. In this case, the newly created process remains associated with its parent address space.

❏ A trusted service can initiate a new process with an associated security context of any other identity known to the system.

It is important to note that the authority of attaching a security context to user address spaces is accomplished without having to access the user's secret authentication information. Therefore, this can be achieved only in a highly reliable and trusted environment, such as one analogous to the classical environment of the MVS operating system.

Delegating Security Contexts

Identity delegation is the term commonly used when referring to the inheritance of security contexts along a chain of processes or threads of execution in response to a service request. Delegating security contexts can be achieved with various semantics. The following are a few of these:

❏ *The adoption of the security context of an originating entity by downstream processes and threads without changes* This is known as *impersonation*, where from the security perspective there is no distinction observed between the processes or threads directly initiated by a user and those that are downstream. Impersonation presents the advantage of ease of implementation. An audit trail of an executing chain of delegated processes as such will account only for one identity.

❏ *Use of an inherited security context along with a new security context representing the identity in control of the newly created address space or*

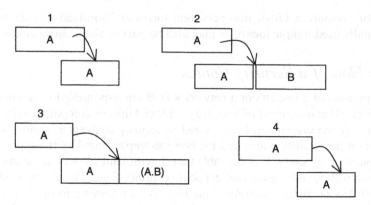

FIGURE 1.5 Some variations of delegating security contexts between an entity A and entity B

    spawned thread This can be complex to implement but enables the construction of detailed and more accurate audit trails. It also allows the underlying system to switch from one security context to another as needed. We call this method a *controlled impersonation*. Each unit of work is associated with either of the security contexts but not with both.

❐ *Augmenting the inherited security context with that of the identity associated with the new address space* This allows the extension of the privileges of the initial user with those associated with downstream processes. Managing the chain of all security contexts can be complex. Units of work are associated with one single context, that representing the originating entity, but with entitlements that are the union of privileges of original entity and those of the inheriting user.

❐ *Retracting the delegated security context to a lesser level of entitlement* This delegation method is intended to downgrade security credentials along the chain of processes or execution threads.

Impersonation is widely used in various programming systems. Figure 1.5 illustrates these forms of delegation.

Access Control

At the core of an access-control system is the secure evaluation of whether an established identity has access to a particular computing *resource*, also referred to as an *object*. A resource can be a service of some kind, an information receptacle such as a file or a Web resource such as a uniform resource identifier (URI). Access control is decided over an existing security context and a controlled resource. Modern access-control mechanisms are based on the *reference monitor* concept introduced in early 1970s by Lampson [LAMP74]. A reference monitor is the TCB component of a computing system that mediates every access of a subject to a resource in accordance with a security policy that governs such access. The policy may be implemented in the form of rules and attributes associated with a registry of subjects and a registry of objects. The rules can be static access rights (permissions), roles, or dynamically deduced rights. Figure 1.6 illustrates the concept of an access-control reference monitor.

In addition to the mediation of access, a reference monitor should not be bypassed at all times, should support isolation of the security services from un-trusted processes, maintain system integrity, and prevent from tampering by users or system processes. The reference-monitor footprint should be kept small enough to be susceptible to rigorous verification methods. The gate-keeper approach of the reference monitor makes it an ideal component for the generation of audit trails reflecting access attempts to the resources within its confines.

In the next sections, we describe various topologies of the reference monitor and show the merits of each. Subsequently, we discuss the access-control paradigms known to date.

Reference-Monitor Topology

The reference-monitor concept can be implemented using various topologies. We distinguish two important factors of reference monitors. The first is access-control enforcement, and the second is the computation of an access-control decision. Enforcement of the reference-monitor paradigm is concerned with the responsibility of invoking the interface to the component

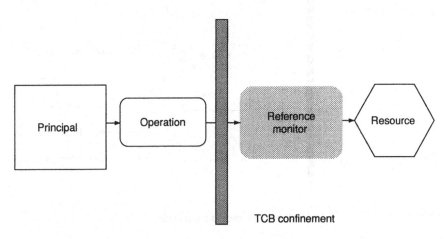

FIGURE 1.6 The reference monitor concept of access control

providing access-control decisions. A division along the enforcement and the access decision making in the reference monitor yields three categories:

☐ *Systemwide enforcement of the reference monitor* In this case, a single instance of a reference-monitor implementation is running system or networkwide providing access-control enforcement to all applications and system processes. Each time an entity attempts to access a resource, the monitor automatically intercepts the request and either allows or denies access based on the policy enforced and the security context of the requesting entity. An example of this category is the classical SAF component of the MVS system that provides the ability to plug into external resource access-control managers such as IBM's RACF. In MVS it is the combination of system integrity, the SAF authorized interfaces, and the external-to-MVS access-control component that constitutes the Lampson reference monitor. Advantages of this method are exhibited mainly by the security and reliability that it offers due to the enforcement being part of the operating system's kernel. Access-control elements that define the system's TCB in this case are centralized, can be isolated, and have a single interface to all system processes and resource managers. This approach provides the advantage of transparency to application developers in controlling access. A disadvantage can be the single point of failure that the monitor represents. Add to that a possible performance bottleneck that may occur under system-overloading conditions. Figure 1.7 illustrates the concept of a systemwide reference monitor.

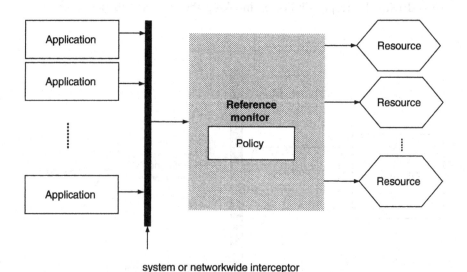

system or networkwide interceptor

FIGURE 1.7 A centralized reference monitor topology

❑ *Enforcement of the reference monitor at the resource manager level* In this case, various resource managers that may exist in a system or that are accessible over a network are responsible for the invocation of underlying access-control components. Access attempts to resources are automatically intercepted by the respective resource manger in order to decide whether to grant or deny access. Examples include database management systems such as IBM's DB2, transaction monitors, Web servers, and more recently Web application servers (WAS) such as IBM's Websphere as well as various network file systems. Advantages of this method include the ease of portability of such programming systems to different operating-system platforms as well as the transparency of access-control functionality to application developers. Redundancy in the implementation of reference monitors by various middleware systems when the access decision in itself is performed through the resource manager or the middleware represents a disadvantage. This approach may also lead to managing various user and resource registries separately by each middleware. Some middleware implementations, however, bridge directly into the underlying system's single reference monitor, thereby leveraging existing and in many cases proven and reliable access-control mechanisms. The TCB of a system in this case becomes scattered throughout the middleware subsystems. Figure 1.8 depicts the approach to middleware-based reference-monitor enforcement.

❑ *Application-based reference monitor* Each application is the sole responsible for the invocation of access-control services. Application developers are required to program to the mechanisms implementing the reference monitor. The latter may be provided by an underlying middleware subsystem or can be a system wide reference monitor. Although not so widely adopted, in some cases the reference monitor is also part of the application. Each reference monitor may be using different interfaces, programming models, and policies. Hence switching among multiple providers of reference-monitor implementations can be costly. This approach can be implemented to leverage existing system or network-wide access-control mechanisms. But it may result in redundancy, inhibits scalability, and increases the cost of deploying applications. Figure 1.9 shows the direct interactions of each application with the reference-monitor enforcement layer. Note how the access-control providers used by the application at the bottom use separate interfaces.

About Access-Control Policies, Models, and Mechanisms

A security policy from an access-control perspective is the set of rules that an organization adopts to govern who can have access to what resource. In broader terms, a security policy is a statement of what is allowed to happen

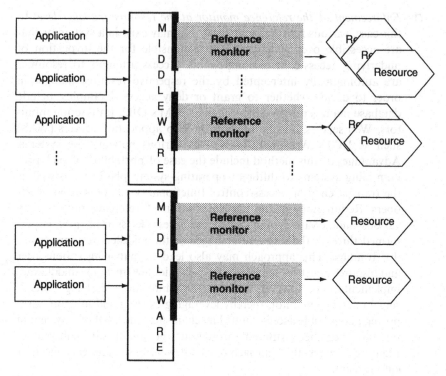

FIGURE 1.8 Middleware-based reference monitors

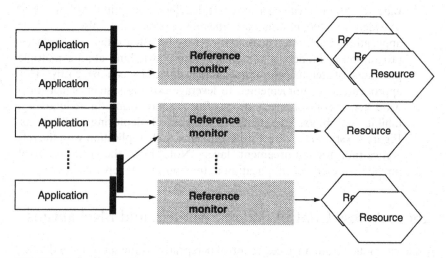

FIGURE 1.9 Application-based reference monitors

and what is not allowed to happen within the realms of an organization. It describes acceptable protection states in a computing system. Defining a security policy requires a thorough analysis of the information flow required in the day-to-day activities of an organization. Although some security policies can be described using formal specifications, a great deal of real-world policies are defined using a variety of controls that are not amenable to a unified description or can be formally described and specified. At a broad level, we note the existence of two main access-control policies:

❏ Discretionary policy and
❏ Mandatory policy.

A *discretionary access control* (DAC) *policy* is owner-centric in that each system resource is assigned ownership by one or more entities. The owner of a resource has complete discretion over who else can access the resource and in what mode access is accomplished. The DAC policy is so widely adopted that virtually most implemented policies are related to it in one form or another. The resource-ownership paradigm of access control is more prevalent and naturally corresponds to the real world. The advantages offered by DAC include simplicity, flexibility, and to a great extent ease of implementation. The drawback, however, is that DAC does not provide any formal assurance concerning the flow of information. Propagation of access rights in discretionary policies is unbounded and hard to predict for all systems.

Contrary to DAC, a *mandatory access-control* (MAC) *policy* does not make use of the resource-ownership concept. Access to information is predefined through administrative procedures and remains invariant thereafter. System entities have no control over disseminating access to information. Instead, access capabilities are mandated by a trusted information-flow officer who sets the rule on who has access to what based on the sensitivity of information contained in each resource. To access a resource, one must hold the proper security clearance. MAC naturally fits with the military policies. It has evolved within the United States Department of Defense (DoD). Access control here yields a predictable information flow that is unidirectional.

A security model is a tool that can be used to describe one or more security policies. A model has systematic features, is precise, and can be formal. The most important aspect of a security model is that it allows one to reason about the behavior of the policy being modeled. Access-control models define the formalism for specifying and implementing security policies and are concerned with studying the implications from dynamic changes affecting the protection states of a computing system. Analysis of a security policy is made possible by the underlying model with which it is associated. The access-matrix model is the most known of all security models. It is generic enough that it can represent almost any policy whether discretionary or mandatory. Its modeling of DAC, however, is more useful.

An access-control mechanism refers to a particular method, tool, or procedure for implementing an access control policy. Mechanisms are not necessarily always automated. They can be provided through offline processes—for example, through the manual intervention of an administrator. A policy sometimes is implemented by a well-known mechanism and thus becomes equated with that mechanism. An example of that is the access control list (ACL) implementing a discretionary-access policy.

Access-Control Paradigms

Three main categories of access control paradigms have emerged:

- ☐ Discretionary,
- ☐ Mandatory, and
- ☐ Role based.

Discretionary-access control centers around the concept of users having control over system resources. Users as such can transfer access rights to resources under their controls to other system users in a discretionary fashion. Control over a resource can be implicit by way of owning the resource or can be explicitly granted through a chain of commands, all of which involve discretion as well as the necessary access permissions that permit the dissemination of access rights. Users therefore gain access to a resource if they create it, if they are an administrator of the system, or if some other entity has conferred access to them. The essence of DAC is the propagation of access rights at the discretion of resource owners and authoritative entities. Depending on the type of permissions being propagated, the cumulative effect from incremental changes in the protection state of a system can be unbounded.

In contrast to DAC, a mandatory-access control is used when the protection decisions are not made by the owner of an object. RBAC is the paradigm that closely mimics real-world processes. We devote an entire chapter to RBAC, but a brief description of it follows in the next section.

Role-Based Access Control

Role-based-access control (RBAC) has emerged as an alternative to discretionary- and mandatory-access policies. RBAC regulates access to resources, systems, and business processes based on the role of the acting subject. Similar to the real-world definition, a role is an abstraction that encapsulates a set of responsibilities along with corresponding allowable operations. Unlike discretionary- or mandatory-access paradigms, in RBAC privileges are assigned to roles instead. RBAC appears to move access-control abstractions a level higher that allows it to be policy neutral. Researchers have demonstrated this fact by simulating both discretionary and mandatory policies using role-based access. Further details of RBAC are the subject of Chapter 8.

Delegation and Masquerading

Delegation and *masquerading* are similar in that both induce the same effect. In either case, one entity performs functions on behalf of another entity. Recall that acting on behalf of an entity implies the use of that entity's security context and hence its identity and entitlements. Masquerading under someone's identity, however, is a security violation. The key distinction between delegation and masquerading is that delegation implies the presence of two entities both of which are aware of one another and one is consenting that the other assumes its identity. Masquerading, on the other hand, happens when an entity assumes the identity of another entity without explicit or implicit consent. It represents a case of identity theft.

The Axiom of Attenuation of Privileges

Attenuation of privileges forms the basis under which access rights may propagate across the entities of a protection system [DENN76b]. It states that an entity may not grant rights to objects for which it does not have those same rights. Subject Alice, for instance, cannot give subject Elyes *read* access to a file "schedule" that she, in turn, cannot read. Evidently when Alice is the owner of the file, she is able to grant the read access to others even when she does not explicitly hold read access to the file. The principle of attenuation of privileges, therefore, is not applicable to the resource owner. The fundamental concept of resource ownership comes with the authoritative power of users over objects they own, including granting themselves as well as others access to any operations supported by an object. Without the principle of privilege attenuation, there can be no basic control over the propagation of access rights. Each system user will hold the maximal set of rights available in a protection system to every object, a situation that is equivalent to having no protection at all.

Trust and Assurance

Trusting an entity means having prior knowledge of that entity's expected behavior. In a trusted computing system, the expected behavior is that users and all programming entities remain in line with the security properties and policies adopted by the system. This implies that all protection states maintain consistency with the underlying security policy with respect to any computations taking place.

Trust is founded on the notion of confining expected behavior. The level of confidence in confining behavior to within a prescribed security policy defines the level of assurance. Trust, therefore, is coupled with an assurance measurement. Confidence is built on presenting evidence that entities meet the security requirements set in a computing environment, whether a single host system or a collection of hosts and computing resources joined by a network. Trust must be satisfied along any communications path established between the entities of a protection system. Trust paths must guard against spoofing, where users are tricked into thinking they are communicating with the security-enforcement portion of the underlying system.

Evidence of assurance includes the use of sound development methodologies, formalism in the design, and thorough testing of the security mechanisms under various deployment conditions.

Realizing Assurance

Establishing some level of assurance in a security system is a desirable goal. Naturally, the question arises as to how one arrives at determining a measure of that assurance. Three methods can be used:

- ❑ *Trust the vendor* In this case, an organization purchasing a security product relies on its relationship with the entity that is responsible for the development of the product. Trust leading to assurance in this case is discretionary and hence may not be verifiable through a neutral entity. Verification may in the end be the responsibility of the entity purchasing the product. Naturally, the list of vendors one might deal with is susceptible to growing over time, thus requiring trust in many vendors. This approach is not reliable.
- ❑ *Perform own testing* In this case, the entity using the product determines the level of assurance in the product based on its own testing effort. This method adds up the cost to the purchasing entity and comes with a degree of uncertainty as the test is performed after the product is purchased. Albeit better than trusting the vendor, this method can be costly and is somewhat of an after the fact process.
- ❑ *Rely on a third party* An experienced and perhaps well-recognized third party is responsible for establishing the assurance level of a product. This case alleviates the burden of assurance on the purchasing entity and lends itself to trust as the third party may have no special interest with any party. In the next section, we present an overview of the best-known assurance program, the *common criteria* currently adopted in North America and in Europe.

The Common Criteria: A Background

The *common criteria* (CC) are the outcome of a series of efforts to develop assurance methods for the security of systems and networks broadly encompassed under information technology. Trusted computer-system-evaluation criteria (TCSEC) were developed by the United States Department of Defense in the early 1980s. This effort is mainly known through the development of the *Orange Book,* summarizing the requirements for assurance in IT security [USDOD85]. In 1991, the Information Technology Security Evaluation Criteria (ITSEC) was published by the European Commission, a culmination of the work that had already been started by a number of European countries, including France, Germany, the Netherlands, and the United Kingdom [BDTI91]. Meanwhile, the Canadian government developed the Canadian Trusted Computer Product Evaluation Criteria (CTCPEC) which was published in 1993 [CANA93]. During that same year the draft Federal Criteria for Information Technology Security, known as the Federal Criteria (FC), was also published in the United States [NIST92]. FC was an effort to combine European and North American requirements and concepts for assurance evaluation.

In the early 1990s the International Organization for Standardization (ISO) began developing IT security-evaluation-criteria within the scope of the global IT market. In 1996 Version 1.0 of what has come to be known as the Common Criteria was published by ISO followed by Versions 2.0 and 2.1 in 1998 and 1999, respectively [NIST99]. In 1999 the Common Criteria officially became ISO standard 15408, merging both TCSEC and ITSEC. Adopting a global standard marks a milestone in the area of IT security-assurance criteria. It removes the need for multiple evaluations of the same product and thus presents a cost saving to the vendor as well as to the purchasing entities. Adopting a set of common international criteria is also expected to enhance IT security assurance as it is exposed to global scrutiny and contributions. A single reference for assurance of information security is useful as a guide for the development of computing products encompassing security functionality. Similarly, a single assurance authority is expected to facilitate the procurement of IT products with security functions.

Overview of Assurance in the Common Criteria

The philosophy that underpins assurance in the Common Criteria is based on the evaluation of IT security products, referred to as the *target of evaluation* (TOE), against a well-defined set of requirements called *protection profiles* (PPs). The PP describes the required security functionality referred to as the *security target* (ST), which is used as the basis for evaluation. Examples of TOEs include operating systems, computer networks, distributed systems, and applications implemented in hardware, firmware, or software. The core elements of the CC address information protection from security threats, such as unauthorized disclosure, modification, or loss of use (unavailability). These threats, as we have discussed, are countered through the mechanisms of information confidentiality, integrity, and availability.

A collection of assurance requirements relating to a specific area (such as configuration management, for instance) is referred to as an *assurance class*. Each assurance class contains a set of assurance families, such as installation, generation, and startup (ensuring that the TOE has been installed, generated, and started up in a secure manner as intended by the developer). An assurance family contains assurance components, which in turn contain assurance elements. Classes and families are used to provide a taxonomy for classifying assurance requirements, while components are used to specify assurance requirement in a protection profile or for a security target.

The scale for measuring assurance in the Common Criteria is called the *evaluation-assurance level* (EAL). EALs are hierarchically ordered such that higher EALs represent increasing assurance. The increase of assurance from EAL to EAL is accomplished by using a hierarchically higher-assurance component within the same assurance family. Currently, there are seven assurance levels defined in increasing order of assurance: EAL1, EAL2, EAL3, EAL4, EAL5, EAL6, and EAL7:

- *EAL1* This basic assurance level is applicable in situations where some confidence in correct operation of the product is required, but the threats to security are not viewed as serious. Nonetheless, this level provides a meaningful level of assurance over a product that is not evaluated altogether.
- *EAL2* This level is applicable to the situations in which a low to moderate level of assurance is required in the security functions of a product that has no readily available development records such as the case of a legacy application for instance. The increase in assurance over EAL1 is evidenced by requiring developer testing, a vulnerability analysis, and independent testing of the security functions.
- *EAL3* This assurance level requires making decisions on the security functionality at product-design time but without making significant changes to existing development practices or having to substantially reengineer the product. It is applicable to circumstances where a moderate level of assurance is required.
- *EAL4* This is the highest level at which it is feasible to retrofit a product so that it satisfies the security requirements without completely reengineering it. It is applicable in situations where a moderate to high level of assurance is needed.
- *EAL5* This level mandates rigorous security engineering based on sound development practices. The evaluated product is developed with the intent of achieving the EAL5 assurance level. EAL5 is applicable to situations requiring a high level of assurance and in which security is engineered in the product at early design stages and rigorous development techniques are used. Nonetheless, the cost attributable to security engineering should not be so high that it outweighs the development of the product's main functions.

- ❏ *EAL6* This level is applicable in situations associated with high risk and where the value of protected resources justifies the potentially high cost of security engineering and development. Semiformal methods for design verification are used.
- ❏ *EAL7* This level is applicable for the development of products guarding against extremely high-risk situations and where the value of the protected resources justifies the high cost of security engineering and development. Extensive formal analysis is required at this level.

The Common Criteria encompass seven assurance classes. Each is associated with a number of assurance families, as summarized below.

Configuration Management

Configuration management represents a critical element of product assurance. It requires discipline and control in the processes leading to the development and modification of the evaluated product. It mandates the use of rigorous methods for tracking the changes applied to the product in its development cycle as well as ensuring that those changes are authorized. This assurance class requires the following assurance families:

- ❏ *Automation* Automation of the tools supporting configuration management prevents errors and maintains execution order.
- ❏ *Capabilities* This assurance family measures the strength and effectiveness of a configuration-management system. It ensures the integrity of the evaluated product throughout its development life cycle.
- ❏ *Scope* This ensures that all necessary configuration items related to the product to be evaluated are considered by the configuration-management system. For example it includes tracking the level of software tools used in development such, as compiler levels and necessary switches.

Delivery and Operation

Delivery and operation set the requirement for correct delivery, installation, generation, and startup of the evaluated product. It encompasses the following assurance families:

- ❏ *Delivery* Provides assurance that the recipient (e.g., entity purchasing the product) receives the TOE without any modifications;
- ❏ *Installation, generation, and startup* Consists of the procedures ensuring that the TOE has been installed, generated, and startedup in a secure fashion and as designated by the developer. This requirement mandates a secure transition of the product from development to the deployment environment.

Development

Development encompasses all of the assurance requirements relating to the functionality of the TOE throughout the development life cycle. It includes the following assurance families:

- ❑ *Functional specification* Describes the user and programmatic interface characterizing the functional behavior of the TOE. The security functionality should be clearly addressed by the functional specification.
- ❑ *High-level design* Describes the product in terms of its major components and how they relate to one another in delivering the security functionality intended by the product.
- ❑ *Implementation representation* Describes the implementation of the TOE in terms of source code, firmware, or hardware components. It captures the internal workings of the security functions of the product.
- ❑ *Internals of the TOE security functions* Address the internal structure of the product's security functions. Requirements are expressed for the modularity and minimization of the complexity of various mechanisms enforcing the security functions for the TOE to be simple enough for analysis.
- ❑ *Low-level design* Describes the internals of the security functions in terms of subcomponents and modules as well as their interrelationships and dependencies.
- ❑ *Representation correspondence* Addresses the correct correspondence between various abstraction levels of the TOE to the least abstracted security functionality. A logical correspondence should be established across adjacent abstraction levels and should address complete instantiation of the requirements.
- ❑ *Security policy modeling* This family provides additional assurance that the security functions enforce the security policies as intended. This is accomplished by first developing a model of the security policy enforced and establishing a correspondence between that policy and the policy enforced by the security functions as provided by the TOE.

Guidance Documents

Guidance documents satisfy the requirement for user and administrator guidance through product documentation. All relevant aspects for the security functions of the TOE are described. It encompasses the following assurance families:

- ❑ *Administrator guidance* Refers to the product documentation intended to guide an administrator through various functions such as product configuration, maintenance, and administrative controls;
- ❑ *User guidance* Refers to the product documentation needed by users exploiting the product for nonadministrative functions such as programmers.

Life-Cycle Support

Life-cycle support is concerned with all aspects of establishing discipline and control in the processes of development as well as improvements of the TOE during its maintenance. It is supported by the following assurance families:

- ❏ *Development security* Provides assurance as to the security of the entire development environment, including physical, procedural, and personnel security measures;
- ❏ *Flaw remediation* Requires that discovered security flaws be tracked and corrected by the developer;
- ❏ *Life-cycle definition* Mandates the adoption of a systematic model for the development and maintenance of the TOE early in the development stage and prevents implementation flaws;
- ❏ *Tools and techniques* Refers to the seleciton of the various tools required by the development, analysis, and implementation of the TOE (for example, the programming languages used).

Tests

The *tests* specify all the elements that pertain to testing the evaluated product. Testing is a key aspect of the assurance provide by the TOE. The following assurance families are used:

- ❏ *Coverage* Addresses the completeness aspect of testing and measures the extent to which the TOE is tested against the functionality claimed in the specification of the product;
- ❏ *Depth* Deals with the level of details used in testing the security functionality of the TOE, and is based on increasing information about the internals of implementation derived from concise and thorough analysis of the TOE security functionality;
- ❏ *Functional test* Provides assurance that the functional security requirements of the TOE are satisfied and may also include verifying the absence of undesired security behavior;
- ❏ *Implementation testing* Demonstrates that the security functions of the TOE perform as specified (to some extent corresponds to the unit testing of various components of the TOE security functions).

Vulnerability Assessment

Vulnerability assessment is concerned with the existence of covert channels, the possibility of misuse or incorrect configuration of the TOE security functions, as well as any elements that may contribute to the TOE becoming vulnerable to security flaws and attacks. It encompasses the following assurance families:

- ❏ *Covert channel analysis* Addresses the potential for illicit information flows which can be exploited to breach the security defenses implemented by the TOE;

- ❏ *Misuse* Investigates the existence of TOE configurations that may lead to insecure operations when users and administrators reasonably believe the TOE is operating in a secure manner;
- ❏ *Strength of TOE security functions* Provides a measurement as to the strength of the mechanisms implementing the security functions of the TOE;
- ❏ *Vulnerability analysis* An assessment to determine whether any identified vulnerabilities of the TOE can be exploitable to cause the violation of the security policy intended to be enforced by the TOE.

Table 1.2 is a summary of the requirements needed to satisfy the various EALs defined by the Common Criteria [NIST99]. Rows of the table represent assurance classes along with corresponding assurance families, and the columns represent the EALs.

TABLE 1.2 Summary of the requirements for the Common Criteria.

Assurance Class	Assurance Family	Evaluation-Assurance Levels						
		EAL1	EAL2	EAL3	EAL4	EAL5	EAL6	EAL7
Configuration	ACM_AUT				X	X	X	X
management	ACM_CAP	X	X	X	X	X-	X	X
(ACM)	ACM_SCP			X	X	X	X	X
Delivery and	ADO_DEL		X	X	X	X	X	X
operation (ADO)	ADO_IGS	X	X	X	X	X	X	X
Development	ADV_FSP	X	X	X	X	X	X	X
(ADV)	ADV_HLD		X	X	X	X	X	X
	ADV_IMP				X	X	X	X
	ADV_INT					X	X	X
	ADV_LLD				X	X	X	X
	ADV_RCR	X	X	X	X	X	X	X
	ADV_SPM				X	X	X	X
Guidance	AGD_ADM	X	X	X	X	X	X	X
documents (AGD)	AGD_USR	X	X	X	X	X	X	X
Life-cycle	ALC_DVS			X	X	X	X	X
support	ALC_FLR							
(ALC)	ALC_LCD				X	X	X	X
	ALC_TAT				X	X	X	X
Tests (ATE)	ATE_COV		X	X	X	X	X	X
	ATE_DPT			X	X	X	X	X
	ATE_FUN		X	X	X	X	X	X
	ATE_IND	X	X	X	X	X	X	X
Vulnerability	AVA_CCA					X	X	X
assessment	AVA_MSU			X	X	X	X	X
(AVA)	AVA_SOF		X	X	X	X	X	X
	AVA_VLA		X	X	X	X	X	X

About the Confinement Problem

The *confinement problem* was first identified in 1973 by Butler Lampson [LAMP73]. It can be thought of as the way access control is viewed from the perspective of end users rather than the traditional definition of controls associated with the resources in the confines of a server. Stated explicitly, confinement is about controlling a service program from leaking confidential or any other information supplied to it by the client (the invoker) to other system processes or any other entity, such as a human. When enforced, confinement must be maintained throughout a chain of program calls. The transitivity of the confinement property maintains confinement along all threads and processes of an execution chain that takes place locally or remotely.

Clearly, the problem of confinement is much more difficult to solve than that of controlling access to system resources. When a service leaks user confidential information, there is generally no indication of compromise in the security of the system. Human-based trust becomes the only assurance one can have against a potential violation of confinement. A classical example of the need for process confinement is that of a user making a purchase order over the Internet. The user in that case will want to ensure that the server cannot pass his or her billing information, such as a credit-card number, to other entities.

Assurance of confinement provides confidence that a program remains unable to leak data throughout its execution. Any attempt to escape such a confinement by a misbehaving program is detected, and thus the program is trapped, as Lampson describes it. One simple scenario in which a server is programmed to leak user data is to have the service write the data to a file so that it can be passed to an administrator or to an entity taking part in a security breach. Similarly, the service may use any interprocess communication mechanisms available to pass data about the caller to other entities.

The paths by which a program may leak information can be known or unknown at program development and deployment time. Not all of the paths are obvious or can be determined through traditional means of code reviews and inspections. Some leakage paths are subtle and obscure and may include other cooperating elements, referred to as *channels*, which can be external to the program's executed instructions. Lampson classifies these channels into three categories:

- ❐ *Storage* The service leaks information by writing it to any available storage device, such as runtime execution memory or some volatile secondary storage.
- ❐ *Legitimate* The service may use any output that is part of its legitimate computation, such as a billing form, to leak the caller's information. This is also referred to as the use of *overt channels*, which in contrast to covert channels, uses the system's protected resources (such as data objects) to transfer information.

❏ *Covert Channels* These are any shared resources that are associated with hidden channels of transferring information and that are not deliberately designed for use as communication means.

Covert Channels

While storage and legitimate channels can be guarded against effectively, covert channels contribute a tremendous deal to the complexity of the confinement problem and can be very hard to uncover and remove. Covert channels are broadly classified into two categories:

❏ *Storage channels* Information is communicated between two entities sharing a storage medium by way of having one entity write a data object, so that the other entity reads and interprets the data based on a conspiring protocol between the two entities.

❏ *Timing channels* The sending entity modulates the amount of time needed for the receiving entity to detect a change in some attribute of the system known to both entities. The receiver interprets the temporal update of the attribute as a covert transfer of information between the two entities.

It is worth noting that both of these types of covert channels are about sharing resources. While storage channels are about sharing space, timing channels are about sharing time and modulating temporal events.

Examples

Due to the necessity for sharing system resources, covert storage channels are the easiest to develop and therefore many such channels are known to have been exploited for leaking information. A classical storage channel is one in which two entities A and B share a file system and have access to a common directory (write permission for A and read for B). A, being the entity leaking information, creates a file called either zero or one based on the information intended to be transferred. The receiving entity B detects the existence of file named 0 or 1, interprets the event in a certain way, and deletes the file to signal that it consumed the leaked information. The series of files with the names 0 and 1 could represent a stream of bits that are intended to be leaked. Entity B reconstructs the stream based on the order in which the files are created and realizes the intended leak.

A second example is the use of resource-access synchronization (e.g., locking a file before using it). In this case, entity A locks the file to signal that it is sending a 1. It releases the lock to signal that it is sending a 0. The receiving entity B detects this locking and unlocking events and interprets the leaked information accordingly.

Security-Design Principles

Security is pervasive throughout the entire cycle of information processing. Indeed, the safety of protection systems remains elusive, particularly in the absence of formally proven mechanisms in secure-system implementations. One, therefore, can rely only on the best practices of design methodologies that can help reduce risks and aid in the detection of security flaws at early stages of development without the burden of costly overheads. In the landmark paper authored by Saltzer and Schroeder [SALT75] in 1975, nine design principles were described. Remarkably, these principles remain valid and complete even after such a relatively long time in the history of secure computing. We discuss and shed light on these principles in the sections that follow.

Economy of Mechanism

Keep the design of a security mechanism as simple and small as can be possible. Be to the point in the design of a security function. Limit the design to solve a well-defined problem. Do not attempt to generalize the design to solving derivative or nonrelated problems. Overdesigning is costly, introduces complexities, and can be susceptible to errors. Large software systems are more error prone than smaller modular components. Code reviews are easier and more effective when smaller and simply designed components are used. Modular components lead to more efficient testing processes and expose a lesser number of information-flow paths to be concerned about.

Complete Mediation

No exceptions can be made in mediating access. Every access to every protected object must be checked for entitlement. This principle should apply to every protected or nonprotected system resource. In the case of unprotected objects, the mediating component simply allows access without the need for checking entitlements. Applying this principle yields a consistent systemwide view of controlling access and raises assurance and confidence. This principle imposes the constraint of identifying every subject attempting to access an object (i.e., having to determine the context of access).

Open Design

The design for a security mechanism should not rely on secrecy or (as it is known) providing security by obscurity. Maintaining secrecy of a mechanism shields it from public scrutiny and criticism and simply delays uncovering its weaknesses. Hiding the weaknesses of a security mechanism cannot go on for an indefinite period of time. With the wide distribution of a product, sooner or later someone will arrive at reverse-engineering the processing logic embedded in a software or hardware security module that is part of that product. The outcome may indeed signal the end of the product's protection mechanisms. It is better to have errors in a particular security mechanism uncovered in an open atmosphere of constructive criticism than to be taken advantage of by an attacker causing irreparable and costly damage.

Least-Common Mechanism

Minimize the amount of mechanism that is common to more than one user and depended on by all users [POPE74]. Shared mechanisms (such as secondary storage areas) or runtime memory blocks and structures (such as globally visible programming variables) all lead to potential information-exposure paths. This principle contributes to establishing the confinement property and reduces the risks associated with leaking information. Shared program libraries are examples of potential information flow along covert channels and should be subject to extensive scrutiny.

Fail-Safe Defaults

This principle was first introduced by Glaser in 1965 [GLAS67]. It means that the default access permission to any object by any subject is lack of access. It is the protection policy being enforced that may explicitly grant access. Adopting a conservative design in which arguments on why objects should be accessible, rather than why they should not, increases the safety of the system. Systems that are deployed with default accesses granted are prone to breaches, particularly in environments where security is not the top concern of users. Refusing access by default is safe and easily detectable. In the event a legitimate access is denied, an administrator can quickly correct the problem. On the contrary, a permitted access that is in violation of the security policy can go undetected for a long period of time, perhaps until damage has taken place. One prominent example to cite in this regard is the default policy of accepting user passwords that have a minimum length requirement of zero. This enables the creation of accounts on a system without having to set passwords. Ironically, this is the behavior on some of the *Windows* systems from Microsoft.

Separation of Privilege

Access to objects including systems and network resources should depend on more than one condition being satisfied. This principle is more in line with adopting multiple defenses. It stems from the observation that was pointed out in 1973 by Roger Needham as noted in [SIMO97] and that states that where feasible, a protection mechanism that requires two keys to unlock is more robust and flexible than one that allows access based on a single key. Coupling multiple defenses with the multiplicity of responsible entities yields the separation of duty principle. Examples of uses of this principle include separation of duties in role-based access control and the multiple lines of defense firewalls protecting network perimeters.

Least Privileges

Every system user or program acting on behalf of a user should operate using the least set of privileges necessary to complete a designated task. Every privilege assigned to a subject should be relevant only to the processing being performed. Extra privileges open the door for misuse and exploitation through human errors or malicious intents. This principle should be coupled with the fail-safe defaults principle denying access by default.

Privacy Considerations

Implementations should regard information of all protected entities as private. As such, this information should be presented to other entities only when necessary. Minimize the amount of an entity's attributes that are exposed at all times. For instance, instead of presenting an entire user profile to a programming module, one should only expose specific user attributes as needed by that application. Other considerations that may not be directly related to user privacy (such as exposing system configuration, operating system level, or host names) should be done only as necessary. The cumulative effect of such simple considerations may contribute a great deal to system security.

Psychological Acceptability

User interfaces to the security mechanisms used, whether through programming or graphic means, must be easy to comprehend and exhibit the inviting characteristics for their use. Otherwise, users, particularly application developers, will shy away from including security in their designs. Although not functionally important, it is essential that human interfaces be designed for ease of use, making it routine for users to consider security processes.

Chapter 2

Introduction to Identity-Management Models

Introduction

The elements of security in computing begin with an identity. An *identity* is a computer representation of an active entity that can be physical (such as a human, a host system, or a network device) or can be a programming agent. Such an agent can be assigned a well-known system function (such as a running daemon) or a program delivering a business function on behalf of some entity. Modern systems adopt a fine level of identification sustainable even at the basic computing tasks and execution threads of an address space and may cross the boundaries of single computing systems with the advent of network and distributed computing.

The evolution of computing to automate more and more of the aspects of human interactions such as in business transactions led to the need of identity representation in computing that reflects that of real-life entities such as human beings. An identity therefore evolved from being simply an assigned identifier to an identifier that points to various attributes and entitlements, collectively referred to as a *profile*. *Identity management* has therefore emerged to address the issues surrounding the proliferation of identity profiles among various computing platforms within the boundaries of an enterprise and cross-enterprises and organizations to even the Internet. Foremost of these issues is the cross-referencing among profiles that represent the same identity as well as the synchronization of attributes among these profiles.

We begin by providing a taxonomy of identity models that is based on the scope of an identity, the naming space in which it is uniquely known and used. We discuss the local identity scope, followed by the network and then the global scope. For each we present the benefits as well as the limitations. The global identity model is exemplified by the XNS approach, a novel method that holds the promise of an elegant Web identity-management model. Lastly, we discuss the emerging model of enterprise-level identity management as exemplified by the latest technologies. Without some level of assurance, an identity cannot stand by its own. After all, it is merely a representation of some active entity. In Chapter 3 we cover the foundations of identity trust and discuss various mechanisms that are currently available.

Identity-management paradigms in computing have taken a natural course that is analogous to real-life practices to a great extent. An individual person initially has direct knowledge of some people that he or she can identify with. That individual further builds knowledge of other persons by directly coming in contact with them or by way of introductions performed by existing acquaintances. The scope of individual identities varies from one person to another. An individual may be known only to his or her family, immediate neighbors, or a workplace; another person can be known throughout his or her locality or a much bigger geography; while some are known all over the globe. The scope of an identity in computing follows in a similar fashion. An identity can be known locally, known over a network of computing devices, or perhaps universally known. Knowledge of some entities can be direct, by way of a registration, or can be indirect, through some other brokering entity.

An individual person can be associated with multiple digital identities in the same manner he or she can be known to other people through multiple nicknames. Regardless of the number of identities one might be associated with, there is an increasing need in computing that all should unambiguously point to the same individual. Each such individual is uniquely identified by a set of attributes, commonly referred to as a *profile* and more recently a *wallet*. We divide the space of identity management along the scope in which an identity is known. We distinguish four classes of identity management that we list in the order of increasing scope as follows:

- ❏ Local identity,
- ❏ Network identity,
- ❏ Federated identity, and
- ❏ Global Web identity.

Local Identity

This paradigm evolved with centralized computing. A host system maintains and manages a local registry of identities (users). Computational units are all identifiable with identities locally known to the system. An external entity that wishes to use the system is required to acquire an identity for use with that system. The adopted namespace of identities is flat and is in reference to the local system. A newly added identity is expected to be unique with respect to the names already in the registry. Addition and revocation or removal of identities are discrete operations that do not side-effect other identities. Managed entitlements are associated with the privileges one might have over the local system resources. This model offers the advantage of simplicity. *Capacity scaling* and the *flat name space* are issues that it faces. Figure 2.1 represents a high-level view of the local identity model. In A each system

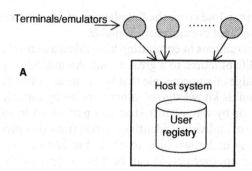

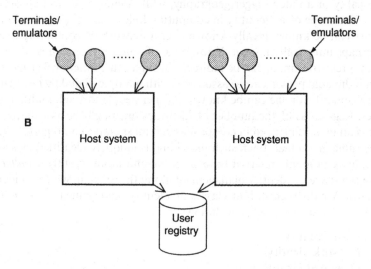

FIGURE 2.1 The local identity model

maintains a separate user registry, while in B the registry is shared across multiple systems. Sharing of user registries is an attempt by the local identity model to alleviate the overhead of the host-centric identity management by registering users only once and allowing them to have access to multiple systems.

Advantages of the Local-Identity Model

Simplicity

The simplicity of this model is mainly the result of the local scope of managed identities and the flat naming space that is generally adopted. Establishing an identity is a simple local process that compares the credential presented by an entity to that stored in the host registry for the same entity.

The flat naming model lends itself to the adoption of flat data constructs with relatively simple structures. Identities are managed as discrete entities except for when they interleave through group memberships. The centralized identity attributes are easy to administer but remain meaningful only within the scope of the host system.

Scalability

Scalability has two dimensions: one is capacity and the other is performance. In the local identity model, the issue of capacity becomes apparent as the population of users and subsystems using or running on the system grows. The system has to store and manage identity information for every such entity. The paradigm is that of directly "knowing everyone." This pushes the limits and capability of the user registry and may result in a performance downgrade. User groups are not considered a remedy to the issue of capacity scaling as identities need to be discretely defined and managed irrespective of group memberships.

Flat Name Space

The flat name space generally adopted in the local identity-management model sets a limitation on the scope of an identity and results in name collisions. The scope of an identity is confined to the host system in which it is defined. Name collisions will occur sooner or later as users select names that already represent other users in the system. The resolution to that usually comes in the form of names that are suggested by the system and that may not reflect the nature of a friendly name chosen by the user. Because an identity is known in reference to the system where it is defined, an identity can be used on multiple hosts without having to be associated with the same entity.

Management Issues in the Local-Identity Model

Each system is associated with its own local identity registry. Users, applications, and subsystem components need to maintain the credentials required for them to establish identity on each of the operating systems used. Passwords, the most prevalent method by which identities are established, are inherently associated with a number of issues. These issues are more apparent and prevalent in the local-identity model. We discuss some of them below.

Password and Attribute Synchronization

The proliferation of passwords on various systems and applications naturally makes it difficult to keep track of them. *Password synchronization* is an alternative solution that mitigates this problem by having each user adopt a single password for all systems. A synchronization mechanism automatically communicates a password change or reset to the participating systems. Unlike single-sign-on (SSO) solutions, however, the user still has to explicitly use the password for each system or application that requires it. Password synchronization is a much easier approach than single sign-on and does not require drastic changes to an organization's existing infrastructure as might be the case with SSO mechanisms. Similarly keeping various user attributes synchronized is a challenge in the local-identity model. Ultimately, synchronizing user attributes in this case tends to be a manual process which increases overhead and can be error prone. A communications means across registries of different systems is required to automatically synchronize passwords and user attributes across multiple systems in this case.

One solution to this problem is for multiple systems to share a single user registry. This method dispels concerns over synchronizing user passwords and attributes. It may, however, lead to a performance problem due to the registry becoming a bottleneck. To alleviate this, the single registry can be replicated locally across the participating systems.

Single Sign-On

SSO further advances the state of art as represented by password synchronization in that it lets a user establish his or her identity once. Thereafter, access to other applications and systems networked together becomes seamless as it alleviates the use from the burden of reauthenticating. Various SSO implementations have been developed. In homogeneous environments where a single authentication technology is used such as the case with Kerberos, SSO is automatically achieved. In the local-identity model with a stand-alone user registry, SSO is meaningful only across subsystems and applications deployed on the system such as database and transactional systems. The user authenticates once to the system; thereafter a security context is established and passed to different systems by the system runtime functions.

Identity Provisioning

This relates to the processes and procedures in use for the creation, revocation, and deletion as well as the maintenance of user accounts. This is an aspect common to all identity-management schemes, but it presents more overhead in the case of the local-identity model. This is because the effort of provisioning identities is proportionate to the number of systems used by an organization. Furthermore, related issues such as password reset and update tend to increase the cost of identity management. Centralized enterprisewide identity-provisioning tools are becoming the solution of choice to these issues. We discuss these later in the chapter.

Example: IBM Resource Access-Control Facility

The IBM Resource Access-Control Facility (RACF) providing security for the IBM MVS operating system family (recently evolved into z/OS) defines a user by way of creating a profile in its registry [IBMC02]. Information stored

TABLE 2.1 The main elements of the base segment in a RACF user profile.

Attribute	Description
USERID	Identifies the user
NAME	User's name
OWNER	Identity of the owner of this profile
DFLTGRP	User's default group
AUTHORITY	User's authority in the default group
PASSWORD	User's password information (one-way encrypted)
REVOKE	Date on which RACF prevents the user from accessing the system
RESUME	Date on which RACF lets the user regain access to the system
WHEN	Days of the week and hours of the day in which the user is allowed into the system
SECLEVEL	Security level of the user (used for mandatory access policy)
SECLABEL	Default security label associated with the user (used with for mandatory security policy)
SPECIAL	Gives the user the systemwide SPECIAL attribute
AUDITOR	Gives the user the systemwide AUDITOR attribute
OPERATIONS	Gives the user the systemwide OPERATIONS attribute
CERTNAME	Names of the profiles containing this user's certificates
CERTLABL	The labels for the certificate associated with this user
CERTPUBKY	The encoded public key of this user
CERTSJDN	User's distinguished name

in each RACF user profile is organized in two blocks. The first is called the base segment, present in all such profiles, and contains the key security definitions for the user such as its identity, its credential (e.g., a password), as well as the level of the RACF authority assigned to the user in his or her default group. Table 2.1 illustrates the base segment in the RACF user profile.

The second class of RACF user-profile information is optional and consists of a set of segments, each containing fields that define various attributes that can be associated with the user. These attributes have mostly evolved with the need of other subsystem components to maintain their own attributes about the user. This feature has allowed RACF to evolve over the years and adapt to the security requirements of newly developed subsystems and applications. Table 2.2 shows the segment of a user profile intended for use by the IBM's Customer Information Control System (CICS) terminal operators.

TABLE 2.2 Elements of the RACF CICS segment in a user profile.

Attribute	Description
OPCLASS	Classes assigned to this operator to which basic mapping support (BMS) messages are to be routed
OPIDENT	Identification of the operator for use by BMS
OPPRTY	Priority of the operator
TIMEOUT	Time that the operator is allowed to be idle before being signed off
XRFSOFF	Indicates whether the operator is to be signed off by CICS when XRF takeover occurs

A new user profile is defined by using the ADDUSER command. Thereafter attributes are added, removed, or updated using the ALTUSER command.

Network Identity

The advent of distributed computing has led to the emergence of the network-identity concept. The idea is simple but has far-reaching implications. An identity is authenticated to a network of computing nodes rather than to a single hosting system. Once an identity is established in this fashion, it navigates through the participating network nodes requesting services and accessing resources without having to explicitly engage in further identity establishment. The scope of an identity is no longer confined to a single system; instead, it is bounded by the network in which it is defined. To achieve this extended scope, identity services have evolved into network components.

The extent of the network in which an identity is defined generally remains limited to a single enterprise. Advances in network identity, however, have led to the ability of establishing cross-enterprise network identities. In some cases, this has resulted in tightly coupled interenterprise links (such as with cross-domain Kerberos implementations), while in other cases, interdomain identities are established via loosely connected enterprises (such as with cross-certification provided by public key infrastructures). We discuss these topics in further detail later in this chapter. The characterizing factor of network identity remains its confinement in scope regardless of the number of participating domains. Figure 2.2 represents a high-level view of a network identity. In A the identity is confined to a single domain, while in B an identity is used throughout two domains.

Federated Identity

Foundations of Federated Identity

The term *federation* has been used in the literature with varying semantics. Indeed, it conveys a generic sense of flexibility and perhaps speaks of the activities of a loosely coupled set of cooperating entities. In the Internet domain name services (DNS), for instance, the federation reflects the delegation of authorities among a hierarchical tree of name servers. The effect of such delegation is the decentralization of name-to-address resolution, the core function of DNS. In the electronic business, a federation can represent a relationship between two or more organizations where each has its own computing infrastructure. The federation manifests itself at the identity level by the mechanisms used to allow one participant organization to directly provide services to entities registered at another organization member of the

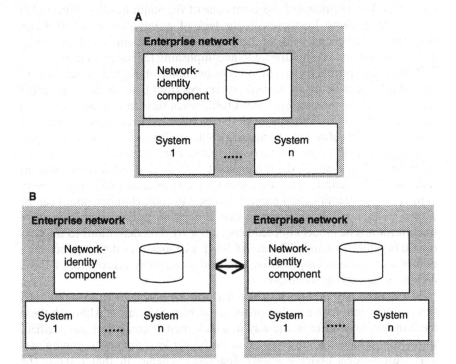

FIGURE 2.2 A High level view of network identity

underlying federation. The result is that each of the participants in a federation will have achieved an extension of the space of identities operating under its premises without having to manage the entirety of this space of identities.

Cross-organizational trust is the foundation of federated identity. The federation is accomplished by the means through which an organization is capable of acquiring the necessary information about a foreign entity that wishes to access one of its services. Furthermore, identity information about a foreign user is acquired from the home organization in a secure and trusted fashion. This process is achieved with full transparency to the users and applications crossing organizational boundaries. The end user remains unaware of such cross-domain activities taking place.

An end user does not need to register with foreign organizations, nor does he or she need to directly engage in an authentication process with an entity other than the home organization. Under the covers of the federation, attributes of an entity that is established at its home organization are communicated to foreign organizations. User attributes exchanged over a federation may ultimately be required to adhere to a common representation syntax and semantics. This requirement represents one of the major hurdles addressed in forming federations. Furthermore, the lack of a universal set of attributes that can be associated with an identity and be consistently interpreted by every organization is a hindrance to accomplishing federated identity.

While a user profile registered to his or her home organization may be contain all attributes necessary to request services from that organization, other attributes may be missing from that profile when services are requested from another organization. One approach that can be used to address this problem is to confine the definition of various profile attributes to third-party organizations that are the source of those attributes. For instance, the definition for credit information can be the responsibility of banking and financial institutions, while the definition for attributes that are universally common to every entity (such as identification name, address, and contact information) can be agreed on by a much wider forum that is open to participation from every organization. The model adopted here is to leave data definitions to the concerned organizations only. The use of XML as a means of defining such data elements can ease interoperability and lead to a speedy acceptance of those definitions across organizations.

The security mechanisms by which trust can be established and maintained across organizations are at the core of an identity federation. Although these mechanisms may differ in the way in which trust is computed and verified, standard mechanisms implemented at the higher level are key to joining various trust models under a unified federated scheme. In that respect, the advent XML-based component technologies such as the security-assertion markup language (SAML) is expected to raise identity federation to an unprecedented level.

A pure identity federation allows an entity to be profiled and registered only once, generally at its home organization. The scope of that identity, however, ends up spanning multiple domains participating in the federation. A generalized and a more practical federation approach allows a user to register at multiple organizations, yet accomplishes a single logical view of all such registrations if so desired by that user, the owner of the identity. Such is the case with the XNS infrastructure that we discuss below. With XNS identity, *federation* is defined as the distributed resolution of names and IDs across a decentralized network of identity servers and clients. The novel concept of addressable identities in XNS forms the foundation on which federation is based. Identity cross-referencing and linking in XNS enables users to participate in a logical federated web that is defined and controlled at the identity level. Synchronization of attributes in this federation is transparent and automatic. Control in XNS federations is brought to the level of an entity rather than the traditional confinement of such controls to participating organizations.

Figure 2.3 illustrates the high-level concept of identity federation. The different shapes representing organizations illustrate the fact that each participant organization manages its own model of identity that may or may not be

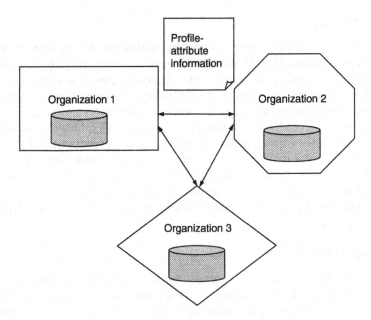

FIGURE 2.3 A high-level illustration of the concept of federated identity

the same model used in other members of the federation. The links between each two organizations represent an established trust that is securely verifiable.

Federation Topologies

Federated identity can be accomplished through various ways. Recall that the characterizing aspect of a federation is the fact that end entities undergo a single registration process. In the event that such registration is performed more than once (i.e., at different participating organizations), complete redundancy of profile attributes for the underlying entity should be avoided. Otherwise, the semantics of the federation become questionable. The differences among various federation topologies can be related to many factors. Most important is the way trust among the federation members is established and the model used to store, maintain, and manage profile attributes. One other differentiating factor is the level of scalability that the topology affords. After all, there is an implicit thinking that any federated identity scheme automatically implies the requirement for a reasonable level of scale.

In the following, we discuss a few possible federation topologies that we categorize based on the method of by which entity profiles are registered and managed. In all these cases, the concept of the home organization of an entity is maintained.

Local Profiling

In this scheme, each end entity is registered within the identity infrastructure of its home organization. Profile attributes of an entity are fully maintained and managed by the local organization. Attributes can expand and contract based on the privileges, roles, and entitlements of the end entity. All other member organizations are unaware of such registration except for when a service request crosses organization boundaries, at which time the underlying identity attributes are exchanged underneath the trust relationship defined by the federation. As we already have mentioned, this model becomes better suited for implementation when data elements for profile attributes are well defined and understood by the member organizations. Parties that are most concerned with the underlying attributes are the best candidates for defining standard attributes.

Distributed Profiling

In this topology, an end entity begins with a registration within its home organization. As the need arises, the entity may further expand and hence acquires new profiles at other member organizations. One reason for having additional registrations is the need for new attributes that are specific to a particular organization. In a sense, the definitions for an entity's profile become distributed across multiple organizations. As a consequence, definitions for the same profile attributes may be duplicated, and thus attribute synchronization may become an issue. This scheme offers the advantage of flexibility and somewhat leads to separation of concerns when it comes to managing user attributes among organizations.

Profiling by a Third Party

In this scheme, a designated third party within the established federation is tasked with brokering the management of end entity profiles. Member organizations are thus entirely alleviated from this task. The third party may distinguish among profile information that is common to all or to a subset of the member organizations as well as those that are pertinent to specific ones. This scheme offers the advantage of having to manage trust establishment with the third party only. Attribute synchronization problem will be limited to the confines of the single third party where specific organizational information may be duplicated for two or more target organizations. One disadvantage can be the issue of scalability as more and more member organizations may contend over the single third party for the retrieval and update of profile information. The replication of the third party may be needed to relieve such a problem. When that happens, the replicas are required to be kept synchronized.

Global Web Identity

The need for a global identity seems to be driven in large part by the emergence and the viability of the World Wide Web as a computing platform. A *Web identity* is one that is uniquely known throughout the Internet Web. Like an Internet resource that is identifiable via its universal resource identifier (URI) [BERN98], a Web identity exists in the global context of the Internet. Every Web identity stands alone to represent the entity that owns it in the same way a Web URI represents the physical resource behind it. Unlike Internet identifiable resources that represent objects that remain locally managed by an enterprise's computing domain, Web identity information is capable of being uniquely resolved to one entity and being recognized and used locally as well as by other Web nodes.

Identity Mapping and Synchronization

The ushering of the Web computing era is increasingly accepted due in large part to the fact that it builds on existing computing infrastructures. The advent of global Web identity mechanisms should not represent an exception. It needs to exploit the identity-management services that have been in deployment and existed for so long. These services are generally based either on local or network identity registries. For that to happen, a unified Web identity requires a mapping to various identity registries in which it exists. The single Web identity would allow navigating the myriad of Web services that ultimately may be deployed over the World Wide Web in a seamless fashion and a great deal of transparency to end users. A number of identity-management technologies that provide this seamless navigation experience exist today. Among them are metadirectories and affiliate networks.

MetaDirectories

The metadirectory approach bridges disparate domains by exposing the user's identity to a higher level while retaining its relationship to various participating enterprise networks in which the identity is known. The relationships of the global identity to the corresponding enterprise-level identities are formed by the links binding metadirectory information to the directories of the participating organizations. Common user attributes are maintained by the metadirectory. Updating these attributes is centrally done, and synchronization is performed automatically. For example, a large organization that maintains information about its users in multiple directories (each is perhaps being used by a different application) can join them via a single metadirectory, thus enabling seamless sharing and maintenance of identity information. Figure 2.4 represents the operation of joining multiple directories using a single metadirectory. The metadirectory on the left joins multiple directories of the same

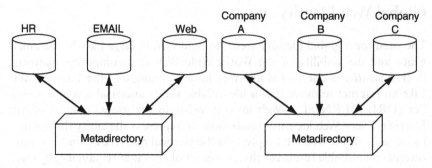

FIGURE 2.4 Joining multiple directories via a metadirectory

organization, while the one on the right joins multiple directories across different organizations.

The key drawback of this approach is that it cannot scale to the extent to which it can accommodate a potentially large number of worldwide identity domains. Figure 2.5 illustrates the concept of identity mapping from global to local using the metadirectory approach.

Affiliate Networks (Virtual Directories)

Affiliate networks, also called *virtual directories*, participate in a tightly coupled structure by directly mapping an identity defined in one directory onto

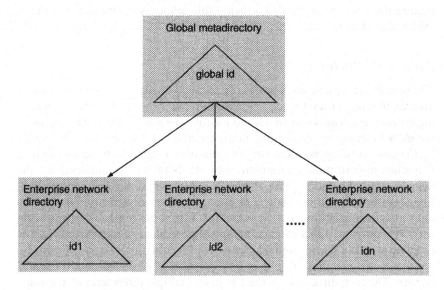

FIGURE 2.5 Mapping entities via a metadirectory

a corresponding identity in another enterprise directory. The main difference between this mapping approach and that enabled by metadirectories is that here the mapping is achieved without actually having to create an additional "join" in directory. This approach has a better scalability property over metadirectories in that the mappings are discretely distributed over the participating directories. Mapping users across all directories, however, creates management complexities associated with the *n*-wise mapping problem. Updating user-identity information requires updating *n* directories. Figure 2.6 depicts the three-way identity-mapping problem presented by the affiliate networks architecture.

Mapping an identity is not simply about associating names from one name space to another. Most important, the mapping applies to the attributes associated with an identity. Updates to such attributes in one directory may require synchronization across multiple directories. Synchronization, if not completely automated, increases administrative complexity, requires establishing cryptographically secure channels, and can be prone to errors. Directory-attribute synchronization is supported through extensions to the lightweight directory-access protocol (LDAP) [HOWE03] as well as the

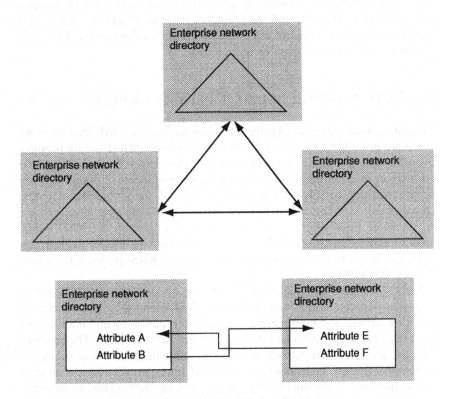

FIGURE 2.6 Joining multiple directories via affiliate networks

XML-based directory-interchange standards, such as the directory-services markup language (DSML).

Dynamic Scoping of a Security Context

A global identity that is navigating the Web should be encapsulated behind a security context that is reliably established and verified and cannot be forged. The security context carries with it attributes of the identity it represents, generally containing a subset of the user's profile. Exposing a user's attributes over the Web requires stringent security measures. A host of issues are relevant here, at the top of which are privacy concerns such as the Web transactional pattern or the medical attributes of an individual, identity impersonation, and theft of sensitive attributes such as a credit-card number or bank accounts. The user should be provided with the power to disseminate his or her digital profile information on a discretionary basis. This allows the user to maintain control over the propagation of his or her attributes to visited Web services. The Web security context, therefore, should allow for dynamic changes under the controls of the user and should be capable of expanding and contracting. Confinement or simply preventing information leakage of the user's attributes at the serving Web sites remains a major security concern that is compounded by the nature of the Web and the unlimited number of services that can all seamlessly cooperate in delivering a single end-user service request. The paths involved in such a request can be unbounded.

The XNS Approach to the Global Web Identity

Current technologies used to solve the issues surrounding Web identity as we noted are not addressing the problem from the basic infrastructure perspective. They are, instead, component solutions that do not form an integrated infrastructure. Existing identity-management components in many ways are being retrofitted to solve a new problem—that of the global Web identity. Development in Web-identity infrastructure is considered yet at its infancy. A promising novel approach is one being undertaken by the XNS Public Trust Organization (XNSORG), which is developing an infrastructure specification referred to as the extensible name service (XNS) protocol for a Web identity [XNSO02].

XNS is an XML-based protocol for identifying and linking together identities that participate in a Web transaction. It is intended by its designers to provide a flexible and interoperable method for establishing and maintaining persistent digital identities and the relationships between them. The protocol provides services for registering and resolving identities in a way similar to resolving addresses. It defines the elements of managing identity documents, conducting and protecting identity transactions, and linking and synchronizing identity attributes. XNS adopts XML-based technologies such as the

XML schema [W3CO01a, W3CO01b, W3CO99] and the Web services [W3CO02a] in defining its constructs and services. As such, it is designed to be platform-independent and extensible. XNS also builds on emerging XML security standards such as XML signatures [W3CO02b], XML encryption [W3CO02c] and the security assertion markup language (SAML) to protect identity documents and assert credentials and entitlements exchanged during Web transactions [OASI02].

The approach followed in the architecture of XNS is based on abstracting the user identity to a new logical level, that of the Web identity with a global scope. The architecture of XNS is inspired to a great extent from the Web architecture itself and in particular the design of the Internet domain-name service (DNS). The novel aspect of the World Wide Web as we know it is its elevation of enterprise data to a logical representation layer that can be accessed via a universal client tool (the Browser), using a ubiquitous proto-col (HTTP), and formatted in a standard markup language (HTML). Most important, this logical layer forms a global Web that links related content with an unprecedented level of location transparency, ease of use, and seam-less navigation experience. The designers of XNS have developed a parallel to that with respect to identity. Figure 2.7 illustrates the analogy between the Web architecture and the approach undertaken by XNS.

Two elements are key contributors to the level reached by the Internet Web today:

❑ The domain name service (DNS) that weaves interconnected systems together and enables the seamless navigation of Internet hosts and computing devices, and
❑ The mechanisms by which documents are linked through references to a universal addressing scheme.

Indeed, the XNS design appears to be entirely inspired from these two aspects of the Internet. We begin by first taking a quick tour of DNS which in itself provides an unprecedented global naming scheme that is hierarchical in structure.

Elements of DNS

DNS, defined in RFC 1034 [MOCK87a] and RFC 1035 [MOCK87b], has grown to become one of the most successful distributed systems for naming Internet hosts and resources and performing name resolution to correspon-ding Internet protocol (IP) addresses. DNS components define a hierarchy of services structured in an inverted tree. Each node in the tree is concerned with a particular naming subspace also referred to as a domain name. The latter consists of an ordered set of labels (symbolic names); each is associated with a subordinate node. This ordered set begins at a leaf node and follows up through a path leading to the root node (one with a null label). Labels are delimited using the dot character (.). By convention, the labels that compose

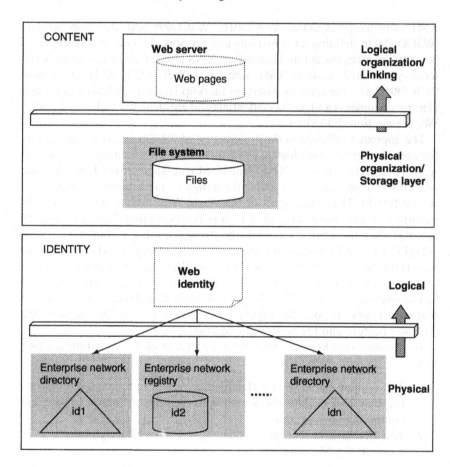

FIGURE 2.7 The XNS approach to Web identity (analogy to the World Wide Web infrastructure)

a *domain name* are printed or read left to right, from the most specific (far-thest from the root) to the least specific (closest to the root). In the example shown in Figure 2.8, the root domain has three subdomains—EDU, MIL, and ORG. The RPI.EDU domain has one immediate subdomain called CS.RPI.EDU.

DNS makes use of two key components:

❑ *Name servers* Maintain the mapping information about an entire domain tree or a particular subtree representing a subset of a domain naming space. In the latter case, a name server also maintains pointers to other name servers that can lead to resolving domain mapping information from any part of the domain tree. A name server is said to be the authority over the subspace it maintains. Authoritative information

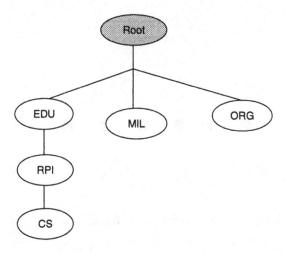

FIGURE 2.8 An instance of the DNS naming space

is organized into units called *zones*.

❑ *Resolvers* These are agents residing at the edges of the network and are directly invoked by application programs. They represent the client side of DNS. The purpose is to initiate the process of resolving a symbolic domain name into its IP address. Resolvers are configured to access at least one name server and use that name server's information to answer a mapping query directly or further pursue the query using referrals to other federated name servers authoritative over the entire name or a portion of it until the name is finally resolved.

Figure 2.9 depicts the layered structure represented by DNS. For an end user, a name resolution consists of an interaction with the local resolver, while to a resolver the interaction may lead to one or more remote name servers. Each name server is an authority over its own particular zone. The database of names operated by each server is basically a flat-file data store in which the primary key is the domain name and the main values maintained are the IP addresses forming the mapping from Internet domain and host names to corresponding IP addresses. The power of DNS stems from the federation formed by the participating name servers worldwide, each operating on its own local data store. As we know, the sum of these basic elements gave rise to one of the most reliable computing infrastructures known to date. We take it for granted every time we navigate the Internet, send an email, or browse the Web.

Three concepts are worth pointing out at this juncture: First, the uniqueness of an absolute IP address in representing a physical host or a network device at some location; second, the presence of a hosted resource, such as a

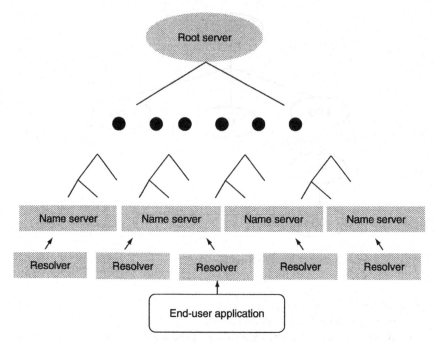

FIGURE 2.9 A view of the DNS federation

file or a service that can be reference relative to its globally addressable hosting system; and third, the user level addressing of hosts and network resources with semantic names in the form of domain and host names. XNS draws from these elements of DNS and the globally addressable Web resources (URIs) to bring identities to an unprecedented level of globally addressable entities.

The invention of the TCP/IP protocol suite as we know it led to the abstraction of disparate networks into a logically single global network, the Internet. DNS, although not an absolute necessity for the Internet to function, presents an immense value to the Internet-based protocols such as Telnet, SMTP, and HTTP. It enabled programmers to use human-friendly names to identify Internet endpoints, rather than the physical addresses as represented by the IP numbers. Figure 2.10 shows a higher level of abstracting IP addresses when DNS is present between the TCP/IP layer and applications. DNS provides the following benefits:

❑ Network endpoints are abstracted into location-transparent names. Addressing network entities in distributed applications therefore remains unaffected by changes in the physical address of an endpoint.
❑ Multiple names can be used to identify the same network endpoint if

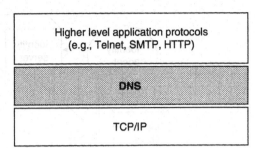

| Higher level application protocols (e.g., Telnet, SMTP, HTTP) |
| DNS |
| TCP/IP |

FIGURE 2.10 DNS brokering of network endpoints addresses

so desired. Such names ultimately will all resolve to the same target endpoint without ambiguity.

❑ Semantic names represented as domain or host names appear to be locally scoped, yet become global when translated through DNS.

Elements of XNS

From a higher-level perspective, the network architecture of XNS appears to be similar to DNS. Like DNS, XNS data-store is distributed across globally federated identity servers. Unlike DNS, however, the paradigm of interactions among XNS entities is peer-to-peer. In DNS the flow of execution is unidirectional in that at the lowest level an application invokes a resolver, which invokes its authoritative name server. The name servers are, in turn, federated in a way that requests are initiated by lower authoritative servers to higher ones. The separation between clients and servers is clearly defined in DNS. The peer-to-peer nature of XNS draws no distinction in the interaction between identity clients referred to as identity agents and identity servers. In XNS all requests are answered by identity agents that run on either a client or a server machine. The peer-to-peer aspect of XNS is a key defining characteristic of its Web identity architecture. Figure 2.11 illustrates the peer-to-peer relationships among XNS entities. The architecture of XNS is characterized by the following elements:

❑ Identity is the addressable unit or resource. This may be considered the key contribution from the XNS designers. The innovative aspect of XNS evolves around the view of an identity as an addressable entity like any other network resource. Identities are profiled and represented by *identity documents*, which are XML documents containing instances of XNS defined data types describing attributes associated with an identity.

❑ Peer-to-peer relationships exist across identity agents and servers. The liberating nature of peer-to-peer computing is brought to the Web identity, thereby increasing the level of flexibility, independence and reliability. Identity agents are the entities operating on identity docu-

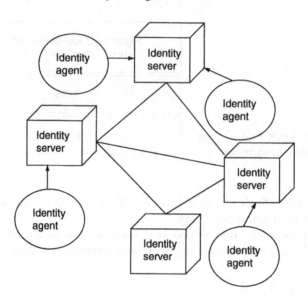

FIGURE 2.11 The peer-to-peer aspect of XNS

ments via a set of Web services defined by the XNS infrastructure. Each identity document is associated with an identity agent responsible for it.

❏ The presence of a discovery service allows agents to dynamically discover and invoke the services available from each other. By way of adopting XML as a mechanism for describing its constructs, XNS is self-defining. XNS service specifications are published as XNS identity documents capable of being discovered, versioned, published, subscribed to, and linked in the same way identity documents are.

The advent of TCP/IP followed by the high-level common application protocols such as SMTP and FTP is analogous to the newly emerging layer of the Internet infrastructure as represented by the exchange of XML-structured data objects via the simple-object access protocol (SOAP) [W3CO00]. This new abstraction layer promises to bring the composition of service elements to the same level reached by composing functional elements as we came to be familiar with in modern programming languages. The depth of such compositions can be unbounded and involving a large number of logical endpoints referred to as *actors*. Concern over the security of seamless combinations and compositions of actors involved in SOAP interactions has resulted in an ever greater need for the secure attachments of identities to various service elements. We refer to this as the Web global security context. With a striking resemblance to DNS, XNS is presented by its designers as the global identity layer of the

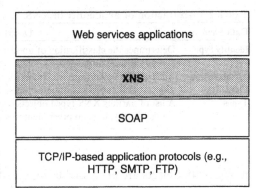

FIGURE 2.12 The XNS layer for the enablement of the XML/SOAP computing model

emerging Web services computing model. Figure 2.12 illustrates the positioning of the XNS layer with respect to Web services.

XNS Identity Types

XNS recognizes three types of physical entities that can be associated with identities. These entities are referred to as *identity controllers* in XNS; sometimes they are also called *identity owners*.

- ❏ *Persons* Identities assigned to individuals (*personal identity*).
- ❏ *Organizations* Also called *business identities*.
- ❏ *The general public* This extends the space of entities in XNS beyond just persons and organizations. Objects such as planets and various Web resources can also be assigned XNS identities. *General identities* are controlled not by persons or organizations, but rather by linguistic, cultural, or scientific conventions and remain under the auspices of XNSORG. This is somewhat a departure from the traditional meaning of an identity in computing. XNS identities extend beyond the realm of active entities such as end users and programmable agents.

Each of these three entities can be represented by one or more XNS identities. An XNS identity is not one-to-one with its controller or in general terms the entity with which it is associated. Nevertheless, XNS is capable of maintaining the relationships across multiple identities of the same principal in a way that results in a single logical identity. We discuss this in further detail below.

The XNS Identity Document

Identity information traditionally referred to as a *user account* is encapsulated by an *identity document* that maintains various elements profiling an entity including a set of associated attributes. These attributes or, in generic

TABLE 2.3 Abstraction of an identity in XNS.

Data Element	Description
IdentityType	Determines the classification of an identity which can be a person, organization, or general.
Memberships	A list of XNS groups to which this identity belongs.
PublicKey	The certified public key bound to this identity.
Types	A list of various XNS-typed objects containing attributes associated with this identity, links to other identities, contracts and so forth.

terms, XNS objects are expressed using data types that are defined in XML. XNS as such operates on a distributed database of identity documents. Each document is a highly structured object that contains the abstracted XNS data types described in Table 2.3, a generic instance of which is illustrated in Figure 2.13.

IDs and Names in XNS

An *XNS identity* (ID) is a logical abstraction of a semantic identity referred to as an XNS name and also called a *named URI*. An ID is invariant as opposed to the attributes of XNS names with which it may be associated. Once an ID is generated, it remains unchanged, persists, and is globally unique, while a name generally has a fixed lifetime, a fixed scope, and

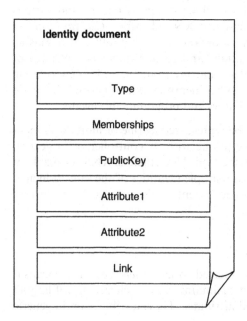

FIGURE 2.13 Abstract view of an identity document

context. XNS names are mutable semantic identifiers that are unique only within a particular name space. IDs are assigned once and never reissued. When a named entity is terminated, its ID is retired. The requirement for an XNS ID to persist is satisfied by the ID service generating and handling a globally addressable construct in the form of a uniform resource name (URN) [MOAT97].

Links across identities are based on XNS IDs and not named URIs. XNS supports moving identities to new hosting environments without breaking the links. Figure 2.14 illustrates the concept of identity abstraction in XNS. Names are handled by the name server, while IDs are handled by the ID server of XNS. A name is linked to an existing ID when it is first registered with the name server. Releasing a name results in removing the link to the corresponding ID.

XNS Resolvers

As we have noted the association between XNS IDs and names is one-to-many. The ID service and the name service of XNS are capable of resolving an ID to a name and a name to its identity address, respectively. An ID is resolved to the named URIs with which it is associated. These URIs are used to channel communication to the identity hosted at a network endpoint. It is worth noting that the addressability of an XNS identity is what brings identity management in XNS to a logical layer analogous to content in the World Wide Web. A hosting endpoint provides XNS hosting service to other identities defined at the same network endpoint. A hosting endpoint is associated with a host identity document that specifies among other things a list of transport protocols over which the host accepts XNS communications. The host forms the backbone of the community that it serves. Identity URIs are scoped by the identity of the system in which they are hosted. Figure 2.15 depicts the layering of XNS components involved in resolving identities.

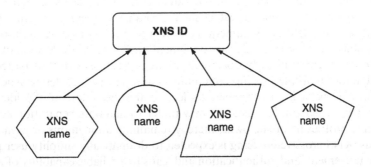

FIGURE 2.14 Abstracting semantic identities in XNS

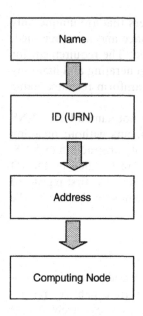

FIGURE 2.15 Resolving identities in XNS

Cross-Referencing XNS Identities

An entity such as a person may be associated with multiple XNS identities; each identifies the person to a particular domain of operations such as an organization, a community or a particular business. The proliferation of multiple identities per physical entity such as an individual person, although comes with all the complexities of identity management, it has become a common practice in computing. XNS builds on such existing identity paradigms and practices only to further enhance them. Multiple-identity documents owned by the same entity logically represent a single entity and thus generally contain common profiling information such as a person's name, home address, telephone number, and physical attributes. XNS allows identity documents controlled by an individual entity to be cross-referenced so that a logical equivalence is established across such documents. Any XNS object in an identity document can be cross-referenced with another XNS object in a different identity document anywhere in the XNS network, including an entire identity document. Shared attributes can thus be recognized across multiple hosting communities and can be seamlessly synchronized. This behavior is provided subject to the discretion of the identity controller. A person, for instance, may prefer to maintain separation across multiple profiles he or she owns, thereby remaining anonymous or pseudonymous. XNS cross-referencing is expected to dramatically simplify user profile management, and authentication and leads to a reliable capability of SSO in particular. Figure 2.16 illustrates identity cross-referencing in XNS.

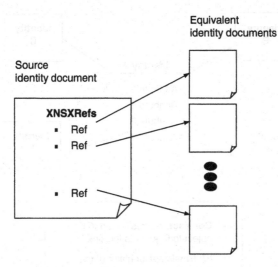

FIGURE 2.16 Cross-referencing XNS identities

Forming Trust Relationships in XNS

Access to identity attributes can be exposed to the public in general or can be constrained based on a policy adopted by the holder of the identity. The flow of identity attributes is a key enabling aspect of electronic commerce and transactions over the Web. Concern over privacy is a major issue that arises with the dissemination of user profile information. XNS takes a novel step in exposing identities over the Web. Support for privacy and protection of identity attributes transacted over the Web is fundamental to XNS. Transacting over such attributes is performed under the mutual consent and agreement of the parties involved using a *negotiation* service that is currently being specified in the XNS protocol.

XNS defines the trust relationships among its managed identities via contract links that can be embedded within identity documents. A contract is a uniquely identified construct that governs the exchange of attributes with some other addressable identity on the XNS Web. It specifies what data is to be exchanged, the protection mechanisms to be used for the exchange, and any policies that govern the automatic propagation of those attributes for synchronization purposes.

Although confinement of data to the trusted entities remains an issue that in the end simply falls in real-world trust among entities. Trust relationships that can be defined in an XNS Web are unbounded. The ability for expanding such relationships and their peer-to-peer aspect is a powerful concept underlying XNS. Figure 2.17 is a representation of the discrete dissemination of identity attributes in XNS.

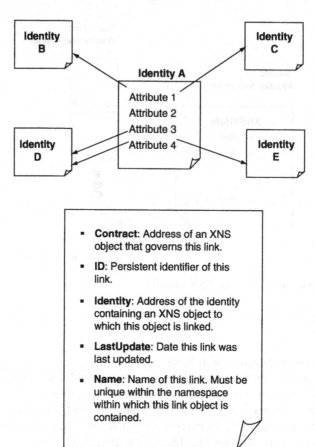

FIGURE 2.17 Identity linking and attribute dissemination in XNS networks

XNS Services

The XNS 1.0 infrastructure specifies a set of component services designed according to the paradigm of self-describing Web services. These services are organized along four major functions:

❑ *URN services* The URN services are at the core of XNS. They represent the novel concept of addressable identities and weave the identity web comprised of network actors in the same way DNS weaves network end-points together. The major aspect here is the separation of semantic identifiers, (names) from persistent abstract constructs (IDs) [MOAT97].

❑ *Attribute-management services* This service manages entity profiles as represented by collections of attributes expressed in terms of various XNS basic data types.

❑ *Exchange and linking services* These services allow the secure dissemination of attributes across identity controllers. Currently a negotiation service is specified for XNS entities to establish identity transaction contracts. An *introduction* service is expected to be developed also. This service permits an identity linked to two other identities to introduce those two entities to one another and thus result in a new direct linking relationship.

❑ *Credential management services* These services allow identity establishment, secure communication of credentials, and the management of secure associations (sessions).

Centralized Enterprise-Level Identity Management

Administration of identity-management processes is an important factor in controlling the cost of computing in large enterprises. Typically, the computing infrastructure of such an enterprise is composed of various resources distributed over a local or a wide-area network. These resources may include nodes of different operating-system platforms, a large number of application subsystems such as data-base systems and human resources repositories, Web application servers, directories, and possibly business applications that require managing user subscriptions. Such might be the case in a utility computing infrastructure providing services on demand. Each of these subsystems typically has its own identity registry. Managing each such registry separately inhibits scalability as it can easily introduce errors, and inconsistencies and may become very costly. Over a period of time, the growth of the computing resources will undoubtedly increase the complexity of managing the enterprise identity systems and may lead to loss of control when a large user population and a myriad of systems are in use.

Centralized identity management is an appealing solution to large enterprises. It is likely to reduce management costs and most important will enforce an element of control within the enterprise. It enables a single view of the multitude of systems in the enterprise, provides a consistent interface to all these systems, and unifies identity-management processes. The emerging model of centralized identity management defines a centralized layer that sits on top of existing systems, thereby enabling a common perspective to all managed systems. Figure 2.18 shows a high-level illustration of the centralized identity-management model. The different shapes showing managed systems represent the heterogeneity of systems that can be managed. The organizational structure of an enterprise is defined in the identity manager and managed objects such as suborganizations and end users are all defined at this layer. User access to a target managed service is represented by an account for that service. An end entity such as a person is in a one-to-many relationship with the set of available accounts. Attribute synchronization across various accounts of a single entity may be performed automatically if so desired.

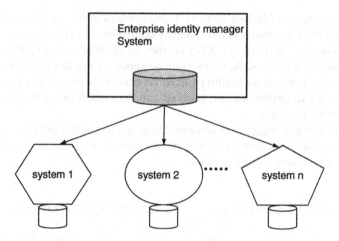

FIGURE 2.18 A high-level view of centralized identity management in the enterprise

Based on the data model adopted, we distinguish among two schemes of centralized identity management systems. We refer to the first one as the unified representation of identity and the second one as the decoupled identity representation scheme. But first we elaborate on two major benefits of a centralized identity-management system.

Synchronizing Identity Attributes

The side effect from updating attributes of a given entity at the level of the central identity manager may result in propagating the change to all or a subset of accounts associated with that identity on the managed systems. An example would be the synchronization of a security credential such as a password or a public key certificate on all systems and services in which the entity possesses an account. Attribute synchronization can be subject to various policies that may govern the underlying attribute. A password policy, for instance, may have different variations on each of the managed systems. In the event an attribute obeys different rules, it is treated differently on each of the managed systems, even when semantically it represents the same construct.

While a centralized identity manager may be mostly concerned with attributes being updated centrally and then pushed down to the managed services, updates that are initiated at the target services need to be accommodated as well. For instance, an individual that performs a password change while directly interacting with a managed UNIX system may result in the update propagated to other managed systems, including the central identity manager.

Policy-Based Identity Provisioning

Automation of account provisioning on the managed services and systems is an important element of reducing cost in enterprisewide identity management. Once an entity such as a user is defined to the central identity manager, it is likely that the same entity will require creation of accounts on one or more of the managed services and systems. Policy-based account provisioning refers to setting up provisioning policies to perform this automation process. Such policies can be based on various conditions such as role, position within the organization, or possession of a particular attribute. They should be easy to develop, be flexible enough, and allow for coarse and fine granularity. For example, a coarse policy may state that all users in a particular organization will automatically have accounts on a designated managed service. A finer policy may state that such accounts be created only to individuals with a particular job function.

Unified Identity-Representation Scheme

In this scheme, the centralized identity manager defines and maintains a superset of attributes that can be assigned to a managed entity such as an end user (Figure 2.19). Managed target services contribute to this overall superset of attributes by introducing attributes of their own. A managed service therefore may be aware of only a subset of the overall attributes. A record with the full set of attributes is maintained for each managed entity by the central identity manager. Some attributes in this record may not necessarily have values assigned to them. For example, a user that does not have an account on a particular service will not require values for any of the attributes that are specific to that service. A mapping may be needed to relate an attribute defined by the central identity manager to the corresponding attribute on

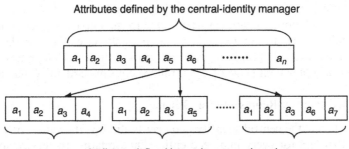

Attributes defined by the central-identity manager

Attributes defined by each managed service

FIGURE 2.19 Attribute relationships between the central identity manager and the managed services in the case of the unified identity-representation scheme

a managed service. This definition would take place during the process of defining the managed service to the identity manager. Multivalued attributes are used to maintain the fact that the same attribute is assigned different values depending on the target service in which the entity has an account. For example, due to conflicting identity policies, a user identifier (uid) may be required to have different values on each target service where an entity maintains an account.

This scheme offers the benefit of maintaining all identity data in one central repository in addition to the fact that data is replicated piecewise across the managed services. Attribute retrieval operations therefore can be processed at the identity manger layer and do not require involving the managed services.

The drawback of the unified-identity-representation scheme is that it does not easily allow for dynamic changes to the schema representing the unified identity. Such changes can be easily introduced when a managed service defines attributes of its own and they are not already known to the identity manager layer. The change in the identity schema as such may require reconfiguring the identity-management system. Furthermore, one cannot expect to indefinitely keep defining new attributes that are sparsely common to the managed services.

Dynamic Definition of Identity Attributes

If we think of a representation of an identity as being a set of attributes and associated values, the first of the issues addressed in such a unified identity-representation model is the size of attributes that can possibly be assigned to an identity. Each of the target-managed services may contribute its own set of attributes that may or may not be common with other services. The unified identity that is visible at the centralized identity-manager level may require dynamic redefinition and potentially will be associated with more and more attributes. These dynamic changes may require periodic redefinitions in the data model used by the central-identity manager. Implementation examples include a change in the schema used by an underlying LDAP repository or that of a relational database system. Due to the impact of redefining the set of unified attributes that an entity may possibly have at any of the managed systems, careful thought needs to be given to the set of attributes to use early in the deployment stage of a centralized enterprise-identity manager.

Decoupled Identity-Representation Scheme

In this scheme, the central-identity manager maintains the values of a fixed set of attributes for every managed entity. Data relating to service specific attributes is kept at the target service. The identity manager remains aware of the schema for the attributes of the managed service, however. The key benefit here is the flexibility by which a service can be added to the identity-manager pool of managed services without impacting the overall data schema of the identity manager. Any operations that apply to attributes that are service specific will require the interaction with the underlying managed services. Availability of these services, therefore, is necessary, whereas in the unified-identity-representation scheme such operations can take place in the identity manager and be scheduled to side-effect the managed service later when the services are available. Figure 2.20 illustrates the attributes relationship for this scheme. Attributes b_i are specific to the managed services.

Example: IBM Identity Manager

The IBM-Tivoli identity-manager (TIM) product adopts the unified identity-representation scheme that we previously defined and represents the latest in enterprise identity-management technologies. TIM maintains identity information about the entities that it manages in a central LDAP repository where an organization is modeled as a hierarchical structure that is horizontally scalable. A large number of related or independent organizations can coexist below a single root organization. TIM is a Web-based application that executes within a Web application-server (WAS) environment. Its design is highly modular and is composed of various independently developed components, each of which addresses a separate concern. Examples include workflow management, policy management, identity and password policy management, as well as reporting. But most important perhaps is the remote-services component that enables distributed systems and application subsystems that may exist in an enterprise to become TIM-managed resources. As a demonstration of its modularity, a special such managed resource is the TIM service in itself. Managed services and systems can be incrementally added as needed. The interaction of TIM with a managed service is accomplished through the deployment of a service agent, also referred to as an *adaptor* or a *connector*. A service agent acts as the intermediary to the managed service, and thus from one side it adheres to the protocol interactions with TIM that are common to

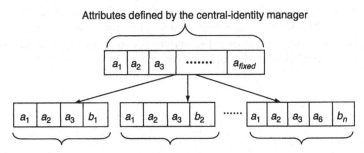

FIGURE 2.20 Attribute relationships between the central-identity manager and the managed services in the case of the decoupled attributes representation scheme

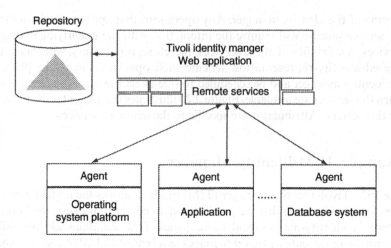

FIGURE 2.21 A high level view of the IBM-Tivoli identity manager structure

all agents, while on the other side it interacts with the target service using the service's native protocol interface.

The modeling of an enterprise in TIM begins with the definition of the hierarchical organizational structure. Each user of the enterprise is represented as a person entity. Such entity becomes an active user of any of the managed services, including TIM, by way of acquiring an account for that service. In which case, the user is said to be provisioned on the target service. Each service may contribute its own subset of identity attributes. Various policy-based rules can be used to automate identity provisioning within an organization structure. Synchronization of identity attributes across multiple managed services can also be achieved. Furthermore, reconciliation of existing identity registries with the TIM central repository can be performed.

TIM access-control mechanism enables flexible controls over the managed entities and objects residing in its repository, which is further enhanced through delegated administration support. Controls can apply at a coarse level (such as an organization) or at a much finer level (such as an identity attribute). TIM adopts a role-based model in its provisioning policies as well as in the controls it asserts over the managed constructs. Figure 2.21 represents a high-level view of the logical structure of TIM.

Chapter 3

Elements of Trust Paradigms in Computing

Introduction

Assurance in an identity is established by way of authenticating it. The entity claiming to hold a particular identity asserts its claim by providing verifiable information to the authenticating entity. Trust in identity authentication is founded on computing the following assertion: *The entity performing authentication is presented with information that only the entity being authenticated is able to provide.* This information is referred to as *proof of possession* (POP) of identity. The authenticating entity establishes trust in this process through a secure verification of the presented proof.

While in Chapter 1 we discussed various authentication factors, the POP of an identity has traditionally been based on shared secrets or derivatives thereof, something the holder and the verifier of the identity know. The advent of public key cryptography has led to establishing identities without having to disseminate shared secrets, provided assurance in the binding between a public key and the identity being authenticated can be reliably established. Advances in network-distributed computing have pushed the scope of an established identity beyond the boundaries of hosting systems and local networks to larger networks as wide as the Internet. An established identity yields a verifiable security context, the strength of which depends on the processes involved in providing an identity POP. We refer to the components that establish and maintain the flow of secure contexts as *identity trust mechanisms*.

We survey the major paradigms and mechanisms of identity trust in computing. The objective is to highlight and classify the core techniques known to date. Although some specific ones are broadly discussed, we do not intend to enumerate all known techniques. Even when the elegance, strength, and soundness of one method or another can be apparent, we do not recommend a specific one. The intent is to expose the elements of trust that characterize each method.

Although other aspects such as policy management and enforcement as well as access-control subsystems are all relevant to trust [ABAD93, BLAZ96, BLAZ99, GRAN00, LAMS01, GRAN02], it is evident that trust in identity is the gate to all other factors of trust-management systems. As such, our definition of trust here is specific to the confidence and assurance in an identity. Trust in real-life practices is relative and can be rated along a continuum scale varying from weak to strong [SHAN02]. Trust forms an inverse relationship with the level of risk that can be associated with processes, programming agents, and individuals [KONR99]. Trust as it relates to identity is a reflexive relationship but not always transitive, symmetric, or associative. However, *transitive trust*, also referred to as *delegation*, can be a key requirement along a particular chain of computing tasks in the same way it can be relied on by individuals accomplishing manual processes.

Brokered trust or *trust through a third party* has emerged as one of the key trust paradigms. We classify third-party authentication schemes in two categories. We refer to the first one as the explicit model, while we call the other one implicit. We give examples of each, with detailed descriptions of the trust elements of Kerberos being the most elegant of third-party authentication protocols. The details of trust in the public key model including the Internet public key infrastructure are presented. We conclude by reviewing three mechanisms for expressing and conveying trust over the web. These are the emerging Web services security, the security assertion markup language, and Web cookies.

A Third-Party Approach to Identity Trust

The local paradigm of identity management, as we discussed in the previous chapter, implies that user-identity information be maintained in the user registry of every system used. Furthermore, a user's shared secret under which the element of trust is built (e.g., a password) is expected to be different for each system accessible by that user in order to minimize the scope of a potential compromise. The complexity of managing multiple passwords and secrets, therefore, increasingly becomes an inconvenience to end users as well as to programming agents that rely on them.

Local identity management recognizes each identity as a local construct that is defined within the scope of the system in which it is known. Identity- and trust-management relations in this case can be modeled as a bipartite graph in which n users and m computing systems are tied through the shared secret relationship. As Figure 3.1 illustrates, this requires managing $n \times m$ relations.

The complexity and lack of scalability inherent to the local identity- and trust-management model has led to the emergence of the third-party authentication scheme. Here a single host in a networked environment is designated as the sole entity trusted by all of the participants in the network, such as users, computing systems, and applications. The user registry maintained by this third-party service contains identity information for all network participants. Trust is founded on the secret shared between each entity and the

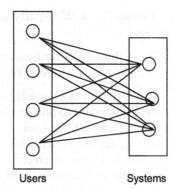

FIGURE 3.1 Managing secret sharing relationships in the local identity model

Users   Systems

third-party authentication service. No entity in the network has any direct trust relationship with any of the other entities. Two authentication paradigms that are based on third-party have emerged:

- ❏ Implicit authentication by secure introductions of entities to one another via a known and trusted third party-entity and
- ❏ Explicit authentication of an entity by invoking a third-party authentication service.

In the first scheme, authentication is cryptographically deduced from the secret shared by an entity and the third party, while in the second case, authentication is explicitly requested from a third party by the authenticating entity. Figure 3.2 illustrates the secret sharing relationships that are in place when an implicit third-party authentication scheme is in use. Providing authentication across n users and m computing services requires managing $n + m$ secrets, a considerable decrease from $n \times m$ required for direct identity relationships between users and destination systems and services.

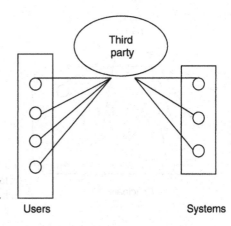

FIGURE 3.2 Reducing the complexity of managing cross-entity authentication relationships using a third party

Users   Systems

Essentially, a third-party authentication scheme recognizes two broad entities:

❏ A third-party authentication service and
❏ The rest of all other entities.

All of the entities participating in a third-party authentication realm form peer relationships to one another with respect to authentication. As shown in Figure 3.3, the differences between entities of a third-party authentication realm are inexistent. The third party has a consistent view across all entities regardless of whether an entity acts as a client or a server. Each of such entities is now abstracted under the term of a *principal*.

Below we discuss the Kerberos authentication protocol as being the most reliable and well-known third-party authentication system to date. Kerberos follows the implicit authentication paradigm, as we outlined above. We also discuss the mechanisms suited for the third-party authentication that fall along the explicit paradigm.

Kerberos: The Implicit Third-Party Authentication Paradigm

Kerberos is the name that became famously associated with the third-party authentication protocol developed at the Massachusetts Institute of Technology (MIT) in the 1980s. The ideas preceding Kerberos go back to the work published by Roger Needham and Michael Schroeder, in which the third-party authentication concept was introduced [NEED87]. Here a third-party key distribution center (KDC) is trusted by every entity participating in a distributed computing environment to maintain its secret key (i.e., every entity shares its secret key with the KDC). As a result, the trusted KDC

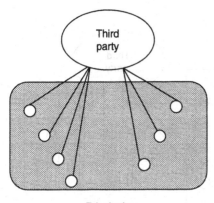

Principals

FIGURE 3.3 Peer-to-peer authentication relationships enabled by a third-party scheme

becomes responsible for the secure introduction of the participating network entities to one another. Trust is founded on the simple fact that two entities A and B that wish to communicate with one another are introduced to each other by the trusted KDC. Trust is not assumed. It is rather computed based on the following:

Entity A whose secret key is known to the key distribution center authenticates itself to the KDC by presenting its proof of possession. The KDC, also knowing the secret key of entity B (peer of A), communicates its authentication of entity A to entity B (indirectly via entity A). Trust in this communication is based on a channel encrypted with a key derived from the secret key shared between the KDC and entity B.

A High-Level View of the Kerberos Protocol

Three entities are engaged in the Kerberos protocol sequence:

- An initiating client,
- The third-party Kerberos server acting as the KDC, and
- The target entity, such as an application server.

A successful execution of the protocol steps results in the authentication of the client to the application server, via the third party, and establishes a message protection channel that is governed by a secret session key between the two entities. Kerberos v5 has evolved into an Internet standard that is widely implemented [KOHL93].

The underlying data construct used in Kerberos is called a *ticket*. A client c establishes its identity with a target server s by presenting a ticket denoted by $T_{c,s}$ issued by the Kerberos server and an authenticator denoted by A_c. The authenticator protects from replay attacks and indicates the freshness level of its accompanying ticket by carrying a timestamp.

In the first message of this protocol sequence, the client contacts the KDC, identifies itself and, presents a nonce such as a timestamp or some nonrepeating value identifying the request. On receipt of the message, the KDC generates a random encryption key $K_{c,tgs}$, called a *session key*, and constructs a special ticket, the ticket-granting ticket (TGT), intended for use with the ticket-granting service (TGS), a component of the Kerberos server. The TGT identifies the client, contains a session key, and indicates the lifetime of the ticket (start and expiration times). The ticket is then encrypted using the secret key K_{tgs} of the TGS that it shares with the KDC and is sent in the response to the client. In addition to the ticket for the TGS, the response includes the session key and a nonce, both of which are encrypted in the client's secret key K_c (a derivative from the client's password). The client receives the response, decrypts the portion that is encrypted using its secret key, and thus unravels the session key $K_{c,tgs}$, used to establish an encrypted channel with the TGS.

The acquisition of the ticket first for the TGS instead of a target application server is introduced to reduce the risk of exposure of the client's secret key K_c. Once a TGT for the TGS is acquired, the client has no need to keep a copy of its secret key in the runtime environment. With respect to clients, the TGS represents no distinction from any server, such as one representing a business application. The TGS represents a logical distinction from the KDC but is physically colocated on the same host and has access to the same registry of keys, as does the KDC. Furthermore, both the KDC and the TGS can be implemented as separate components that run in the same address space.

A client that has successfully acquired a TGT for the TGS becomes ready to request tickets for participating target-application servers. On each such request, the client presents its TGT to the TGS and identifies the target application. The TGS verifies the ticket, along with the authenticator and the associated request information. It then replies with a ticket for the target application. The reply is protected using the session key with the TGS (as determined from the TGT). The client uses its session key with the TGS to extract its new session key with the target service. It forms a fresh authenticator, encrypts it with the session key, and sends it along with the ticket to the target application. If the client requests mutual authentication from the server, the server responds with a fresh message encrypted using the session key. This establishes the fact that the server used its own secret key to decrypt the ticket and determine the session key. Figure 3.4 illustrates the steps of the Kerberos V5 protocol.

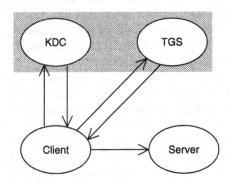

(1)   Client → KDC: c, tgs, $nonce$

(2)   KDC → Client: $\{K_{c\ tgs},\ nonce\ \}\ K_c$, $\{T_{c\ tgs}\ \}\ K_{tgs}$

(3)   Client → TGS: $\{A_c\}\ K_{c\ tgs}$, $\{T_{c\ tgs}\ \}\ K_{tgs}$, s, $nonce$

(4)   TGS → Client: $\{\ K_{c\ s},\ nonce\ \}\ K_{c\ tgs}$, $\{T_{c\ s}\ \}\ K_s$

(5)   Client → Server: $\{A_c\}\ K_{c\ s}$, $\{T_{c\ s}\}\ K_s$

FIGURE 3.4 Kerberos V5 protocol steps

Federated Kerberos

Each Kerberos server is responsible for providing secure identity and trust management to a single realm. A realm has well-defined network boundaries and is made of a finite number of participating entities, such as hosts and applications. A large network may suffer from the bottleneck exhibited by a single Kerberos server managing identity trust for the entire network. Scalability of Kerberos can be an issue for large networks. Kerberos addresses this problem by dividing a large network into separate domains; each is supported by its own Kerberos server. Cross-domain relationships are provided by the inter-realm trust feature of Kerberos. This feature enables a client from one realm to obtain a ticket for a service that resides in another realm, referred to as a *foreign realm*. The aggregation of all realms in this fashion makes it seem like a single large domain of trust.

Interrealm trust in Kerberos is based on sharing secret keys between ticket-granting services of cooperating Kerberos domains. Recall that each TGS is like any other entity with respect to its local KDC. A client obtains a ticket for a server in a foreign realm by first obtaining a TGT to the remote TGS from its own local KDC. Figure 3.5 illustrates the protocol steps used by Kerberos V5 in support of the cross-domain trust relationship. It is assumed that the client is already in possession of a TGT to its local TGS.

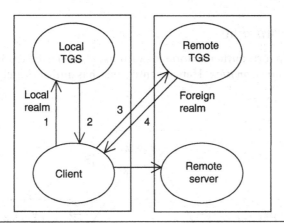

(1) Client $\rightarrow$ TGS$_{local}$: $\{A_c\}\ K_{c,\ tgs},\ \{T_{c,\ tgs}\}\ K_{tgs},\ tgs_{remote}$

(2) TGS$_{local}$ $\rightarrow$ Client: $\{K_{c,\ tgs\ remote}\}\ K_{c,tgs},\ \{T_{c,\ tgs\ remote}\}\ K_{tgs\ remote}$

(3) Client $\rightarrow$ TGS$_{remote}$: $\{A_c\}\ K_{c,\ tgs\ remote},\ \{T_{c,\ tgs\ remote}\}\ K_{tgs\ remote},\ s_{remote}$

(4) TGS$_{remote}$ $\rightarrow$ Client: $\{K_{c,\ s},\ remote\}\ K_{c,\ tgs\ remote},\ \{T_{c,\ s\ remote}\}\ K_{s\ remote}$

(5) Client $\rightarrow$ Server$_{remote}$: $\{A_c\}\ K_{c,\ s\ remote},\ \{T_{c,\ s\ remote}\}\ K_{s\ remote}$

FIGURE 3.5 Kerberos protocol steps for cross-realm establishment of trust

A Topology of Kerberos Federations

Bidirectional interrealm trust in Kerberos requires a pairwise of key exchanges. Applying this arbitrarily to a set of n realms yields $O(n^2)$ key exchanges. This topology can be modeled by a directed-complete graph in which the nodes represent the realms and the edges represent key exchanges, as shown in Figure 3.6 for five realms.

To alleviate the problem of having to deal with a large number of key exchanges, a Kerberos Version 5 specification recommends organizing the realms in a hierarchical structure. Key exchanges across ticket-granting servers from various realms are performed only along this hierarchy structure. Specifically, key exchanges take place across realms that are directly descending or ascending from one another. Exceptions to this rule are referred to as *shortcuts* where two realms unrelated by the hierarchy relationship are directly joined via a key exchange to optimize heavily used paths. A hierarchy defined along domain names of the participating realms is a natural fit. The number of key exchanges required by this topology is $O(\log(n))$. Figure 3.7 illustrates the hierarchical interrealm trust in Kerberos. The dotted edge represents a shortcut.

When an application needs to send requests to a server in a foreign realm, it traverses the tree upward, downward, or through shortcuts until the destination realm is reached. In each step of this traversal, a TGT is acquired for the next foreign TGS.

Ticket Forwarding

Kerberos supports authentication forwarding, also referred to as *delegation in the form of impersonation*. Here an entity that has authenticated to the KDC

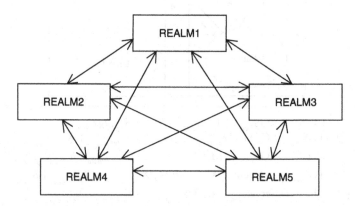

FIGURE 3.6 A pairwise key exchange across five realms modeled using a complete graph

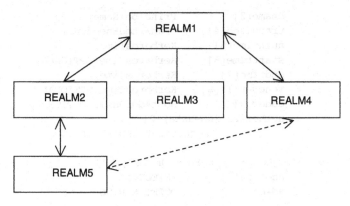

FIGURE 3.7 Cross-realm hierarchical key exchange

(i.e., holds a valid TGT) delegates its authenticated context to another entity on a local or remote host. Thereafter, the delegated entity impersonates the original entity and may acquire tickets to downstream servers on its behalf. An example where delegating credentials is useful is the case of a server that needs to access a file stored on a network file system that is accessible by the client only. Such may be the case of a print server, for instance.

Delegation in Kerberos is enabled by way of the client forwarding its TGT to a server. During the initial TGT acquisition, the client requests that the ticket be marked forwardable. The session key established between the client and the TGS is also forwarded to the target server so that it can form a fresh authenticator as it attempts to acquire a service ticket from the TGS.

Entitlement Attributes in Kerberos

In addition to serving the purpose of authenticating clients to target services, a Kerberos ticket may contain a set of authorization privileges that are associated with the holder of the ticket. The following definition expressed in Abstract Syntax Notation 1 (ASN.1) illustrates the structure of authorization information contained in a Kerberos ticket.

```
Ticket :: = [APPLICATION 1] SEQUENCE {
                        tkt-vno[0]        INTEGER,
                        realm[1]          Realm,
                        sname[2]          PrincipalName,
                        enc-part[3]       EncryptedData
}
EncTicketPart :: =  [APPLICATION 3] SEQUENCE {
                flags[0]          TicketFlags,
                key[1]            EncryptionKey,
                crealm[2]         Realm,
```

```
                cname[3]              PrincipalName,
                transited[4]          TransitedEncoding,
                authtime[5]           KerberosTime,
                starttime[6]          KerberosTime OPTIONAL,
                endtime[7]            KerberosTime,
                renew-till[8]         KerberosTime OPTIONAL,
                caddr[9]              HostAddresses OPTIONAL,
                authorization-data[10]
                            AuthorizationData OPTIONAL
}
AuthorizationData ::= SEQUENCE OF SEQUENCE {
                ad-type[0]            INTEGER,
                ad-data[1]            OCTET STRING
}
```

Authorization information is marshaled in a Kerberos ticket as a sequence of (*ad-type, ad-data*) value pairs with ad-type representing the parameterization factor. This parameter is an integer that classifies the value of the authorization attribute with which it is associated. Negative values are reserved for local use. Nonnegative values are reserved for registered use (i.e., one that is known to the Kerberos community at large). The fact that the data type of an authorization attribute is a stream of octets allows it to be extensible and dynamic.

Cross-realm support in Kerberos enables the federated management of user entitlements over widely distributed computing resources. Principal entitlements are maintained by the Kerberos service associated with the realm in which the target service resides. This is expressed by the fact that a principal obtains a service ticket directly from the TGS of the target service's realm. Authorization privileges and user-profile attributes fit well with the local management paradigm in which access control is performed by the local resource managers. In this approach, the semantics of entitlement attributes are locally scoped, and thus ambiguity and collision among attribute names are prevented. The security model enabled by Kerberos therefore follows the paradigm of global authentication and local management of authorization. The latter encompasses the semantics of access privileges and provides resource-access control. Adherence to this paradigm is an important aspect of identity and trust management in highly distributed computing models.

A Kerberos service ticket carries information about the home realm of its holder in the crealm field. This field indicates the name of the realm in which the client is registered (i.e., with which the client explicitly authenticates). Resource managers that receive service tickets from principals in foreign realms can further qualify the semantics of the access privileges and entitlements by the foreign realm. This adds another parameterization factor that can be used to scope or distinguish among entitlements for local versus foreign principals. For instance, attribute A from a foreign user's profile may require more stringent trust-verification procedures than when that same attribute is associated with a principal that is local to the realm of a service.

A Kerberos identity is always qualified with the name of the realm in which it is defined. Even when two principal names from different realms are identical, they differ when qualified by the respective realms. Principal name collisions across realms are therefore eliminated. The partitioning of Kerberos naming space along realms plays an important role in the federated trust of Kerberos. This information is reliably and securely carried in the encrypted portion of a Kerberos ticket.

Explicit Third-Party Authentication Paradigm

The third-party authentication method via entity introductions is a novel approach that advanced the state of art in the field of authentication, particularly with the development of Kerberos. A number of aspects, however, characterize this model with some level of rigidity. For one thing, it requires all participating entities to adhere to a predefined authentication protocol. Programmers need to abide by a relatively advanced programming model, and the protocol has a degree of infrastructure complexity built into it. The predominant alternate approach is a much simpler one, easy to use but of lesser strength and eloquence. This approach uses an explicit authentication scheme in which the authenticating entity does not manage its own user registry; instead, it calls out to a third-party service or subsystem.

The explicit paradigm of third-party authentication is based on the principle of outsourcing the authentication process within a distributed environment to a third party that manages an identity repository, performs authentication, and dispenses entity entitlements. Typically, an application server directly receives an authentication credential such as an identity and a password from a requesting client. The credentials are then forwarded to the third party for authentication as well as the retrieval of entitlements. Various forms of third-party entities have been used for this purpose. An example is a database system against which a user credential is validated (e.g., by attempting to connect to a database using the user's credential). A widely used third-party registry is the hierarchical X.500 directory service exposed through the LDAP protocol [HOWE03, WAHL97, HOWE95]. Here an identity is established by way of a successful bind operation to the directory using the credential supplied by the client.

This trust model is characterized by being loosely coupled in that the interacting entities are not required to participate in a well-defined protocol sequence. The client communicates with the target service using application-level interfaces. Similarly, the server engages the third-party entity using interfaces specific to that third party. The target-application service, in particular, needs to secure the communication channel used for the transmission of credentials between the client and the application, on one hand, and the application and the third party, on the other hand. Typically, a secure socket-layer (SSL) [FREI96] channel is used for that purpose. This model offers the advantages of simplicity and extensibility. Connectors to various third-party identity services can be incrementally built and used.

Plugging an application server with a third-party identity and trust manager in this fashion is exploited by a number of evolving Web application servers (WAS) such as IBM's Websphere [IBMC03]. Websphere further generalizes this approach by abstracting the third-party authentication services and repositories in what is referred to as a *pluggable authentication mechanism*. This can be represented by an LDAP service or some native operating system repository such as IBM's RACF or one that is customized. Figure 3.8 illustrates the third-party explicit authentication paradigm.

The Public-Key Infrastructure Approach to Trust Establishment

Public-key cryptography was developed with a revolutionary concept—that of establishing trust without having to share secrets. The premise of freely disseminating a public key, however, remains a proposition that nevertheless comes with cost, as well, perhaps only less than that of distributing secret keys. Security services, particularly origin authenticity, rely on the single foundation that a particular public-key material is indeed bound to its legitimate user. The public-key establishment problem relates to trust in the binding that exists between a subject and a public key. The novel paradigm brought about by public-key encryption relies on the fact that public keys are intended to be universally accessible. As long as the binding of a public key can be securely established, the key material can be distributed over secure and nonsecure channels and stored in public repositories. An established public key is one that exhibits the property of being securely and unambiguously associated

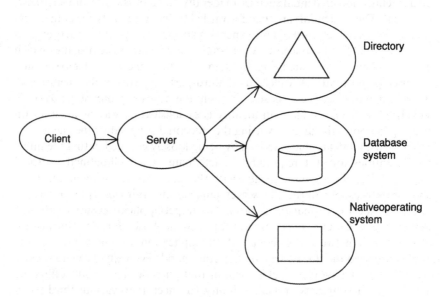

FIGURE 3.8 Layout of an explicit third-party authentication scheme

with its legitimate owner. This association should remain invariable no matter the transport over which the key is being communicated or the storage medium in which it resides or an execution runtime where it is processed.

In the Internet world, public-key establishment is defined through the X.509 digital certification performed by a trusted third party known as the *certificate authority* (CA) [BENA02]. The result of this certification process is a data construct in the form of an X.509 certificate representing a cryptographic binding between the public key material and its holding entity referred to as a *subject*. The foundation of such certification rests on the digital signature of the authoritative CA vouching for the trustworthiness of the certified public key and hence the associated private key. We begin by taking a brief overview of public-key cryptography, pointing out its underlying strength in representing trust. An instance of that is expressed by the capability of public-key cryptography in realizing digital signatures. We subsequently elaborate on the trust elements that form the foundation for the Internet public-key trust.

Foundations of Public Key-Cryptography

Public-key cryptography emerged in the mid-1970s with the work published by Whitfield Diffie and Martin Hellman [DIFF76a, DIFF76b] as well as by Ralph Merkle [MERK78]. The concept is simple and eloquent yet it has had far-reaching impacts on the science of cryptography and its applications as a whole. Public-key cryptography is based on the notion that encryption keys come in related pairs—private and public. The private key remains concealed by the key owner, while the public key is freely disseminated. Data encrypted using the public key can be decrypted only using the associated private key and vice versa.

In the following, we consider a simple example that illustrates the dual key concept of public-key cryptographic systems. We restrict our plaintext to 27 characters drawn from the 26-letter English alphabet plus the blank character. We then assign numerical equivalents to our plaintext alphabet sequentially from the integral domain of [0...26] with the blank assigned the numerical 26. We consider our encryption function E to be the affine transformation that takes in a plaintext character P and maps it into a ciphertext C as follows:

$$E(P) = (a * P + b) \bmod 27 = C,$$

with a and b being fixed integers. Solving for P in terms of C in the prior equation yields the inverse transformation, decryption D:

$$D(C) = (a'* C + b') \bmod 27 = C, \text{ where}$$

$$a' = a^{-1} \bmod 27, \text{ and}$$

$$b' = -a^{-1} * b.$$

For a to be invertible while computing in $Z/27Z$, it is necessary and sufficient to have a and 27 relatively prime. That is to say, there is no number that divides both a and 27 but for the trivial divisor of 1. Note that this condition guarantees a one-to-one mapping between P and C. $Z/27Z$ is the set of equivalence classes (residue classes) with respect to the relationship of congruence *modulo 27*.

The parameterized affine transformation in the example, and its inverse can be used for a basic public-key cryptosystem with the private and public keys being *(a, b)* and (a', b'), respectively. An example would be to have $a = 2$ and $b = 1$, resulting in $(a', b') = (14, -14)$. The premise here is for an entity to maintain secrecy of the private key while freely distributing the public key. An encryption performed using the public key can be decrypted only using the corresponding private key. Since the owner of a public-key pair is presumed to be the sole entity with knowledge of the private key, encrypting information using the private key leads to establishing data-origin authenticity. Furthermore, with tamper-proof storage and manipulation of private keys, nonrepudiation can be established as well. Besides the provision for data integrity and confidentiality, public-key encryption is about establishing authenticity without having to disseminate or manage secrets.

In practice, however, the public-key cryptographic system in our example is easily defeated, even with its generalization to longer blocks instead of single characters. A block of size s yields a ciphering transformation that maps each block to a value in the range $[0...N^s - 1]$, where N is the size of the alphabet. The weakness of this algorithm rests in the ease by which a decryption key can be deduced from an encryption key in a deterministic fashion, using very simple operations (multiplication and additions *modulo* $(N^s - 1)$). But first and foremost is the fact that the encryption function admits a deterministic inverse function.

The premise behind public-key cryptography is that it should be computationally infeasible to compute the private key by simply knowing the public key. Along this key premise, we discuss some of the mathematical foundations of the processes by which modern public-key cryptosystems derive their strength and reliability when it comes to the generation of public and private key pairs. Figure 3.9 is an illustration of the duality between corresponding public and private keys.

Modern public-key cryptography derives from eloquent mathematical foundations that are based on the one-way trapdoor functions existing in the abstractions of number theory. Encryption is the easy one-way trapdoor. Decryption is the hard direction. Only with knowledge of the trapdoor (the private key) can decryption be as easy as encryption. Three of these currently known trapdoor one-way functions form the basis of modern public-key cryptography, and we discuss them in the next sections.

The Problem of Factoring Large Numbers

The first of the well-known trapdoor one-way functions is based on the ease of multiplying two large prime numbers, while the reverse, factoring a very

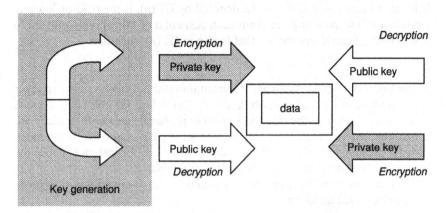

FIGURE 3.9 The duality between public and private keys in public key cryptosystems

large number is a far more complex task. Factoring an integer n is the process of finding a series of prime factors, such that their products together yields n. A prime number, by definition, is one that has no divisors other than 1 and itself; otherwise, a number is called *composite*. Factoring large numbers (over 1,024 bits) is known to be computationally infeasible with today's computers and technology. Modular arithmetic renders the multiplication of such numbers a far easier task. Consequently, the one-way trapdoor problem here is to make a very large number a public knowledge and secretly maintain its prime factors. Note that the trapdoor function discussed here in essence requires deciding on whether a randomly picked very large number is prime. Primality testing is a much easier task than the actual factorization [GORD85].

A number of methods have been devised to determine the primality of an odd number N. The most trivial of which is to run through the odd numbers starting with 3 and determine if any of such numbers divides N. The process should terminate when we reach $\sqrt{N}$. Due to the time complexity that this method requires, in practice it is stopped much earlier before reaching $\sqrt{N}$ and is used as a first step in a series of more complicated primality test methods.

The best example of this class of public-key cryptosystems is the Rivest-Shamir-Adleman public-key algorithm, known by its acronyms of RSA [RIVE78].

Computing Discrete Logarithms in a Large Finite Field

The second well-known trapdoor one-way function that exists in number theory is the ease of computing a function f that consists of raising a number to a power in a large finite field, while the inverse function f^{-1} of computing discrete logarithms in such a field is known to be a much harder problem. A finite field, also known as a *Galois field*, denoted by GF(p), is the field of integers modulo a prime number p, and thus each element a of GF(p) is guaranteed to have a multiplicative inverse a^{-1} that is also in GF(p), such that

$$a * a^{-1} = 1 \bmod p.$$

The time complexity required for the computation of $f(x) = a^x = y$ in Z/pZ is polynomial in log x. Computing $x = f^{-1}(y) = \log_b(y)$ given y is a much harder task known as the *discrete logarithm problem*. Here both x and y are constrained to be elements of the discrete set Z/pZ as opposed to the much easier continuous problem in the set of real numbers, for instance (hence the use of the term discrete in qualifying this problem).

The one-way trapdoor function as defined by the discrete logarithm problem can be stated as follows:

Knowing a and x, it is an easy operation to compute a^x in Z/pZ (using the repeated-squaring method). On the other hand, if we keep x secret and hand someone the value y that we know is of the form a^x and ask to determine the power of a that gives y, they can use up all the computing resources that they have available but will indefinitely fail to hand back a response.

A number of modern public-key cryptographic algorithms are based on the discrete logarithm one-way trapdoor function. Most notable is the Diffie-Hellman key exchange algorithm [DIFF76b] and the El Gamal cryptographic system [ELGA95].

Elliptic Curves over Finite Fields

Elliptic curves over finite fields have been proposed for use with existing public-key cryptographic systems [KOBL87, MILL86]. Given a point P from an elliptic curve E, defined over a finite field, and an integer a, the one-way function here consists of the ease of computing the product a^*P, while the inverse of finding a such that a^*P results in a point over E is intractable. Elliptic curves as such form a reliable and secure source for computing public keys. The elliptic-curve analogs of existing algorithms that are based on the discrete log problem, such as Diffie-Hellman and ElGamal, can be deduced in a straightforward manner. The discrete log problem on elliptic curves is likely to be harder to tract than its counterpart on finite fields. This property has led to the adoption of elliptic cryptosystems in many situations requiring stringent security measures.

Digital Signatures

The advent of public-key cryptography combined with the strength and reliability of intractable one-way hash functions gave rise to the digital signing of a document. This process inherently enables data-origin authenticity and can be strengthened to further withstand repudiation. Using the private key of a public-key pair to encrypt a data stream automatically binds the subject with whom the key is associated to the data. The cost of encrypting an entire document to simply establish this binding can be prohibitive, particularly in light of the compute-intensive public-key cryptosystems. Fortunately, the alternative is eloquent and is computationally affordable as it does not require encrypting an entire document. Two of the well-known digital signature algorithms are the RSA and the DSA [NIST94]. We briefly outline the RSA algorithm below.

RSA Signature

The RSA digital signature algorithm proceeds along two main steps:

□ Using one of the common hashing algorithms such as MD5 or SHA-1 [RIVE92, [NIST95], a document is first digested into a much smaller representation, a hash value.

□ Encryption is applied to the hash instead of an entire document

Provided there is no need for a confidentiality service, the signed document is then transmitted in its cleartext form, and the signature is provided to the recipient for verification. Figure 3.10 illustrates the RSA signature computation and verification procedures.

Trusting a Public Key

From the outset, public-key cryptography seems to eloquently solve the key distribution and management problem introduced by secret key cryptography.

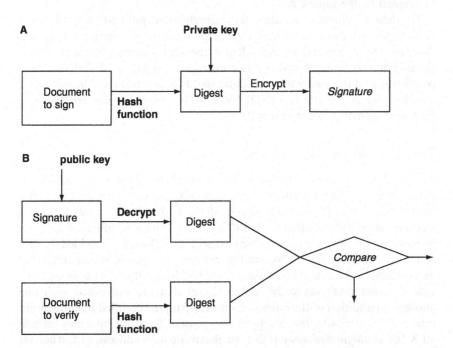

FIGURE 3.10 A Generating a RSA signature and B verifying the signature

Anyone can use the public key to encrypt data, but only the owner of the private key can decrypt it. A community of users that wishes to communicate in confidentiality can adopt a public-key cryptosystems, publish the public keys of its community members in a directory, and completely dispel any concerns that may otherwise arise when distributing secret keys. Unfortunately, the secure binding of a public key to its legitimate holder remains a critical problem on which trust is completely dependent. In a sense, the authenticity of a public key with respect to its holder is at issue.

One promising answer to the question of assurance in a public key lies in the certification process that a *public key infrastructure* (PKI) can provide. At the heart of a PKI is the digital signature technology that we outlined earlier. Parties relying on public keys confine their trust in a single entity, known as the *certifying authority* (CA). Before a user's public key is disseminated, the underlying high-assurance CA uses its own private key to digitally sign the user's key, which is then distributed to a public repository. The concept of a verifiable public-key certification can be traced back to the work published in [KOHN78].

A relying party securely installs the public key of the trusted CA and uses it to verify the signature of each user's public key that might thereafter be used. Only on a successful verification does the reliant party initiate a communications channel. This simple method of certification thwarts against an attacker who does not have a public key signed by the same CA as that of the two communicating parties but fails when the attacker is in possession of a key signed by the same CA.

To yield a reliable assurance, a comprehensive public-key certification process necessitates more security elements than simply signing an encryption key. These elements are embodied in the data construct that is to be certified. For the Internet realm this construct is called an *X.509 Version 3* certificate, and the secure infrastructure that makes it is the public-key infrastructure for X.509 (PKIX) [HOUS99a, HOUS99b]. We discuss the main PKI trust elements in the next section.

Foundations of Trust in PKI

An Internet public-key certificate (PKC) provides a high degree of assurance in the public key that it certifies. At the core of this assurance is a trusted issuing authority that is either the signer of the PKC or one situated along a chain of certificates leading to that PKC. Such a chain is called a *trust path*; its meaning will become clear in the next sections. The trust provided by PKI is demonstrated by a provable binding between the public-key material and its associated subject and hence the private key. Recall that the public and private keys are mathematically related values that are associated with one another. In addition to the public-private key pair, the certified binding implicates a set of attributes that a subject may possess. Such attribute may include an X.500 *distinguished name* (DN), an electronic mail address, or further yet

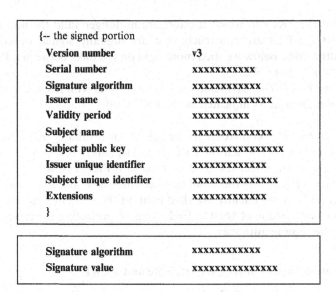

{-- the signed portion	
Version number	**v3**
Serial number	**xxxxxxxxxxx**
Signature algorithm	**xxxxxxxxxxxxx**
Issuer name	**xxxxxxxxxxxxxx**
Validity period	**xxxxxxxxxx**
Subject name	**xxxxxxxxxxxxxx**
Subject public key	**xxxxxxxxxxxxxxxx**
Issuer unique identifier	**xxxxxxxxxxxxx**
Subject unique identifier	**xxxxxxxxxxxxxxx**
Extensions	**xxxxxxxxxxxxx**
}	

Signature algorithm	**xxxxxxxxxxxx**
Signature value	**xxxxxxxxxxxxxxx**

FIGURE 3.11 Data elements of the X.509 v3 certificate

a customized personal attribute profiling the certificate holder. Figure 3.11 illustrates the major elements that are implicated in a certified public key using X.509 V3 certificates.

The trust model in PKI is anchored through the degree of assurance in the public-key certificate of the issuing CA. The public key of the issuing CA as determined from its own PKC is, in turn, used to verify the digital signature of that CA in the user's PKC. That signature is computed over the data elements of the certificate as illustrated in the bottom part of Figure 3.11 including, of course, the public key material. Given the assurance in the PKC of the issuing CA, a successful verification of this signature establishes trust in the binding of the public key being verified and hence the corresponding private key to the end entity that holds the PKC.

The need for the secure verification of an end entity's public key is likely due to the involvement of that entity in a public-key-based security protocol or simply in data signing or encryption. Besides the signature verification step, establishing trust in a PKC is foremost based on the certificate itself being valid. Two key factors are decisive in determining the validity of a certificate:

❑ *Revocation of the certificate* First the certificate is checked for membership in a *certificate revocation list* (CRL). A revoked certificate is invalid regardless of its signature being valid. A PKC may be revoked before at any time before expiry arrives. Various revocation policies may be instituted based on circumstances. A CRL is the second major data construct that is available for PKI consuming entities. It attests that the PKCs to which it refers are no longer valid for use. Like for PKCs, CRLs are constructs that are digitally signed by certificate authorities. Below we shed more light on the links between a PKC and its entry in a CRL.

❏ *Time of use* The certificate use has to be valid with respect to its designated lifetime as indicated in the PKC itself.

The elements that contribute to the validity or invalidity of a PKC are all included in data over which the PKC digital signature is computed. A number of aspects can affect the level of trust in a PKI. Below we discuss two such aspects. The first is the serial number embedded in a PKC and its relation to a CRL. Subsequently, we shed light on the element that is without a doubt the cornerstone of trust in PKI—that of protecting the private key of a certificate signing authority.

Identification Links Between a Certificate and a CRL

As it is shown in Figure 3.12, the certificate serial number is about the only field that identifies a certificate membership in the list of revoked certificates contained by a particular CRL. A collision in certificate serial numbers therefore may lead to erroneous decisions by validating entities. Since it is only within the confines of a particular certificate authority that the serial-number-generation process can be controlled, it becomes an implicit requirement that a certificate be revoked by the same authority that had issued it. Furthermore, assuming that the serial numbers are generated in some incremental fashion, the serial-number-generation functions need to maintain a persistent representation of the current number over the lifespan of the authority. Due to the importance of using a unique number for each certificate, the persistent form of the current serial number may need to be encrypted while it is saved in auxiliary storage.

Certificate membership in a CRL needs to be decided by the identification parameters as represented by both the serial number as well as the issuer name.

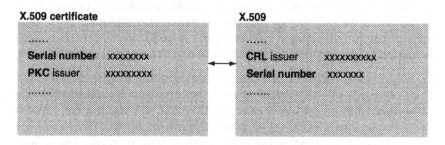

FIGURE 3.12 Identification links between a certificate and a CRL

Protecting the CA Signing Key

The CA private key deserves being the object in need of most protection possible within a public-key infrastructure. After all, the verification of assurance in the certification process is entirely dependent on the security of this key. Indeed, once a CA signing key is compromised, the whole infrastructure and any relying entities and applications are breached. A compromised CA key can lead to all sorts of attacks. Issued and published certificates can be modified. Others can be illegitimately revoked. Most dangerous is that certificates can be issued under the auspices of the compromised CA to subjects that are not entitled to certificates. It is prudent measure to treat the CA signing key with particular care. Software solutions can provide an increasing degree of security to the signing key through encryption. However, because the key must be exposed to generate signatures, it may become vulnerable to interception and capture.

One approach that affords the CA key a high level of security is the use of tamper-resistant hardware in the form of PCI-based cards to store cryptographic keys and perform encryption and signing operation without exposing the key. One reliable product in this category is the IBM 4758 coprocessor card that is delivered with a high level of assurance and manufacturing certification. This cryptographic coprocessor provides a simple access interface using the IBM Common Cryptographic Architecture (CCA) APIs as well as the RSA Laboratories PKCS #11 interfaces (cryptoki) [RSA99]. It relies on a key-encrypting key, the master key, stored in a tamper-resistant circuitry that withstands physical attacks.

The IBM 4758 provides a whole set of cryptographic operations such as random number and key generation, hashing, encryption, generating message-authentication codes (MACs) as well as signing and verifying signatures. These operations are based on common cryptographic algorithms such as SHA-1, MD5, DES, Triple-DES (DES3), RSA, and DSA. In addition to the cryptographic hardware engine, the card includes a small general-purpose processor. The access-control module serves as an authentication mechanism used to log on users to the coprocessor as well as performing access-authorization checks based on the different roles a user might assume. Enforcing access policies as such is achieved by the hardware and protected software. The coprocessor manages DES and public-key algorithm (PKA) keys separately.

PKI Trust Topologies

Trust verification in PKI may involve more than one CA certificate. Depending on the trust topology in use, the validation process can become a recursive process involving a chain of CA certificates. We outline the trust topologies commonly found in PKI in the sections below.

Hierarchical Trust

A hierarchical topology is one that maps the trust layout of an organization top down into a tree structure [HOUS99a]. At the top of the tree is the root certificate authority. Extending branches may lead to leaf nodes that represent end entities in the organization or may lead to other subauthorities. The rational for the partitioning may stem from the need to manage a large organization as a set of smaller entities, each with its own authoritative CA. Figure 3.13 shows an example of a hierarchy structure. Generally, there is no requirement that one CA certify end entities only or other CAs only. A particular CA may issue certificates to end entities as well as to other certificate authorities. But for all practical purposes, however, the role of each CA may be best managed by requiring that it certify subordinate CAs only or end entities only. Such a separation enforces the authoritative hierarchy structure of an enterprise and points out the controlling elements of trust.

The hierarchical trust topology enables the delegation of trust down to subordinate authorities. The root, high-trust authority becomes concerned with the trust-delegation task down to a smaller number of subordinate authorities. The fact that the top CA is concerned with the dissemination of trust to a small number of entities allows for managing the strict controls and policies that need to apply at this highest level. One such policy may require the offline distribution of the root CA certificate in a highly secured fashion to the immediate subordinate CAs that it manages. There is a fundamental reason behind the secure distribution of the top certificate; the process of building a trust chain begins at the root CA.

Building a trust chain consists of backtracking the path from an end entity certificate all the way to the root-trusted CA. This backtracking process

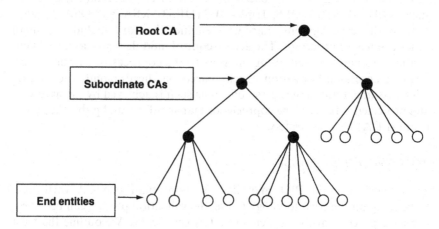

FIGURE 3.13 A hierarchical trust topology with one root governing a two- and a three-level hierarchy

entails a number of validation steps, two of which are fundamental. The first is the determination of the chain by starting at the leaf end-entity certificate, associating an issuer name at this level with a subject name in a certificate of an authority at the immediate upper level until the root is reached. Figure 3.14 depicts this process of computing a trust path. For each subject name determined as such, the corresponding CA certificate is retrieved, perhaps from a repository such as a directory service or one referred to through some URI.

The second step consists of validating the series of cryptographic signatures in the previously computed trust chain. This process begins with the certificate of the root trusted CA and proceeds until it reaches the leaf end-entity certificate.

As illustrated in Figure 3.14, the determination of the path via the back-tracking of issuer and subject names is computed in a bottom-up fashion starting with the end-entity certificate. By contrast, the signature-validation process is performed in a top-down fashion beginning with the certificate of the trusted authority.

Signature validation is the process during which the fundamental trust of a certificate is built. It is all based on the basic assumption that the public key of the root CA is trusted. Recall that assurance in this assumption is based on the secure distribution of the root CA certificate. This distribution process defines what can be termed as the "boot-strap" of trust.

The high-assurance public key of the root is used to validate the signature value in the CA certificate immediately below it in the hierarchy as determined by the path. Once this is validated, the immediate subordinate CA

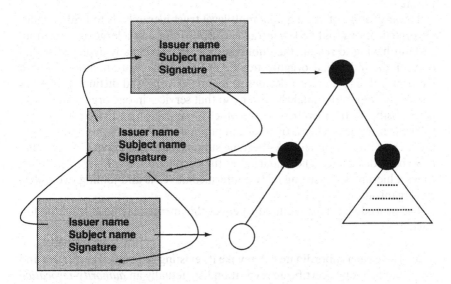

FIGURE 3.14 Computing a trust path in a hierarchical trust model

implicitly inherits the highly assured trust property and becomes the trust root. This procedure continues recursively until the signatures in the leaf end-entity certificate is validated. A special case of this path-validation scheme is one in which there is only one level of hierarchy, and thus the self-signed root CA certificate is used to directly validate the signature in the end-entity PKC.

The fundamental element of trust in a certificate chain rests in the secure distribution of the root CA certificate to all of the entities below it in the hierarchy. The dissemination of the root CA certificate may involve an offline distribution method to increase security. For instance, the certificate can be mailed to the respective human entities in a nonvolatile medium such as a diskette or a compact disk. On receipt, each entity computes a digest of the certificate using, for example, SHA-1 or MD5 and then calls the human trusted with the administration of the CA to confirm the digest value and hence this distribution process.

The notion of a single point of trust does not necessarily concern the root CA only. Rather, it can be applied down the tree hierarchy in a delegated fashion. The property that makes this delegation stand is that the recursive signature-validation scheme, as described, can also be started at some highly trusted intermediate CA. Any compromise in the signing keys above this intermediate CA will ultimately be detected once validation reaches the trusted intermediate CA. The trust path therefore requires the existence of at least one high-assurance authority along the path irrespective of its position in the tree hierarchy. A delegation scheme of this kind lends itself well to situations in which end users of some global enterprise need only to be aware of "regional" certificate authorities that directly manage their part of the business but need to be concerned with the corporate CA.

The advantage of setting up a multilevel trust hierarchy is to bridge multiple organizations (public-key infrastructures within, say, a large organization) without having to reissue the public-key credentials already deployed within each of the individual organizations. Let us assume that an enterprise that has grown due to a merger decides to join its existing and distinct public-key infrastructures into a single hierarchy so that services in one organization can be accessible to the members of the other organization and vice versa.

The hierarchical scheme of trust can provide a solution in this case by having each of the disjointed CAs become subordinate to the root CA, one that is perhaps designated and managed at the corporate level. Figure 3.15 illustrates a hierarchy consisting of two intermediate CAs and joining two different organizations.

The procedural steps required to effect this merge may consist of the following:

❑   Have each subordinate CA revoke its existing self-signed certificate and publish it in a certificate revocation list, actually an *authority-revocation list* (ARL). This will ensure that a trust path should always lead to the new root CA.

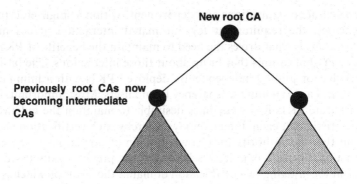

New root CA

Previously root CAs now
becoming intermediate
CAs

FIGURE 3.15 Joining two organizations using the hierarchical trust model

❑ Have each subordinate CA acquire a new certificate from the new root CA. To avoid a CA key-update process, each CA may use its current public key when requesting the new certificate.

❑ Distribute the new root CA certificate in a secure fashion to all of the end entities in the merged organizations including the two subordinate Cas, and have each entity replace this certificate for the old trusted root.

The net effect of this join operation is the dissemination of trust across the two previously disparate organizations via the new root CA that represents the trust anchor for the larger organization. Note that if so desired one can split the two organizations by reversing each of the steps in the join operation as described. To accomplish this, first, each CA requests revocation of its own certificate from the root CA. Each subordinate CA then uses its current public key to issue a self-signed certificate for itself and push it down to each of the entities it certifies through a highly assured channel.

Joining existing public-key infrastructures by building a single multilevel hierarchy results in a unified trust model. In this model, a single authority represents trust in the entire organization. Similarly, the affected trust join operation enables the organization to continue delegating to each subordinate CA the PKI management tasks for its own domain of operation.

The use of multilevel hierarchies, however, extends a certificate trust path and thus may affect performance of the certificate validation process. To mitigate the extent of this problem, a PKI deployment as such may resort to computing and then pushing the trust paths to each end entity's local environment ahead of any validation processing.

Cross-Certification

The proliferation of PKIs, particularly in the Internet space, ultimately leads to the need for extending the benefits provided by public-key certification across the boundaries of certification domains. Such domains may span disparate organizations and departments within a single enterprise. In many cases, the requirement for automated interaction across multiple organizations is what drives the need to maintain the benefits of PKI-based security in applications that bring about those interactions. The basic issue here is that of joining independently deployed PKIs with a minimum disruption and a maximum transparency to end users. Most important, in joining disparate PKIs it is sometimes desirable to maintain the independence characteristic that each domain enjoys whereby each certification authority remains the sole authority for its own domain of operations.

Functionally, the hierarchical scheme that we previously discussed can be sufficient for bridging two certification domains, the result of which is tightly linked organizations, virtually becoming a single domain. The drawback of the hierarchical merge is that end entities will not be completely shielded from the join operation. Cross-domain certification, on the other hand, achieves similar trust semantics in joining disparate PKIs, yet it maintains a complete transparency of the process with respect to end entities.

Cross-certification is a method of joining two disparate PKIs without incurring any effect on the end entities and without subordination of either infrastructure to a new authority. It is a peer-to-peer contract between two CAs to honor certificates exchanged, through security protocols, on service requests crossing each other's domain. Each end-entity member in the communities joined via a cross-certification process remains in possession of the certificate of its respective trusted root CA prior to the merge taking place. This is contrary to the hierarchical scheme in which end entities are to acquire the certificate for the new root CA. The trust model remains invariable in the cross-certification case while it takes a different form in the hierarchical scheme.

A CA A that issues a cross-certificate to authority B underscores the fact that end entity certificates issued by B to its own community members are now trusted for use within the domain certified by authority A. Similarly, authority B may issue a cross-certificate for authority A, and thus domains A and B are said to be mutually cross-certified, also referred to as a *two-way cross-certification*. In essence, a two-way cross-certification is equivalent to joining two domains under a single trusted root CA but without a direct impact on end users.

It is worth noting that structurally a cross-certificate is simply an X.509 v3 certificate with a base constraint extension indicating that it is a CA certificate and in which the subject and issuer names represent two different CAs. It certifies the public key of an already operating subject CA as a signing key used for issuing certificates.

Cross-Certification Grid

Given a network of CAs, the cross-certification process can be modeled as a direct graph whose nodes represent the participating CAs while the edges represent the direction of the certification. A directed edge from A to B indicates a one-way cross-certification of authority B by authority *A*. Figure 3.16 illustrates a cross-certification grid comprised of five CAs.

Note that because the cross-certification in one direction is a transitive relationship, CA2 becomes implicitly engaged in a two-way cross-certification with CA5. This is because CA2 is explicitly cross-certified by CA5. Meanwhile, CA2 cross-certifies CA1, which in turn cross-certifies CA3, and hence CA2 indirectly cross-certifies CA3. In turn, CA3 cross-certifies CA5 and thus CA2 implicitly cross-certifies CA5. In that sense, the respective communities of CA2, CA1, CA3, and CA5 are now entitled to interact across the domains represented by these CAs. For a purist, such communities are defined by the strongly connected component in the directed graph representing the cross-certification network of trust [DIES00].

Hub-Based Cross-Certification

Because of the transitivity property exhibited by the cross-certification operation in each direction, a common hublike CA can be used to bridge a network of CAs, thereby establishing a complete cross-certification grid (one in which each CA is cross-certified with each other CA in the network). In this trust topology, every CA is mutually cross-certified with the hub CA only. Trust is then disseminated by way of the transitivity property. Figure 3.17 depicts this topology. Note that the advantage here is that the number of cross-certifications performed in this case is linear in the order n of the number of CAs involved, while in the previous case it is in the order of n^2.

Hybrid Model

The hybrid model is a trust scheme that combines the hierarchical and the cross-certification methods. A multilevel hierarchy can be the result of merging of two organizations, while the cross-certification process might be driven

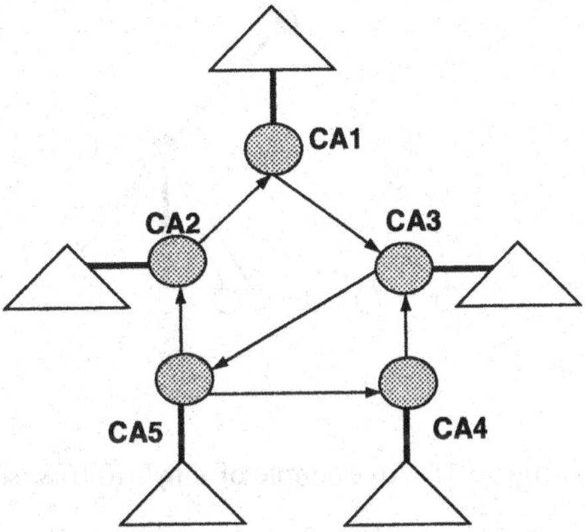

FIGURE 3.16 An example of a cross-certification network

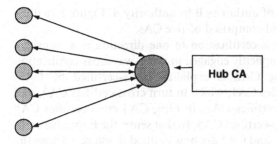

FIGURE 3.17 A network of CAs mutually cross-certified through a hub CA

by the need to extend the trust to a third-party business partner in one direction or another. The complexity of a federation formed by a hybrid configuration may directly affect the performance of constructing a trust path. Implementations may need to optimize path construction by caching constructed paths for subsequent uses. Figure 3.18 shows a trust path between two communicating entities. The path spans two domains in a hybrid scheme of trust.

Web-of-Trust Model

The web model evolved with the advent of the SSL as a security protocol between two HTTP endpoints, mainly the client browser and a target Web server. It uses a more relaxed trust model in which a user can pick and choose

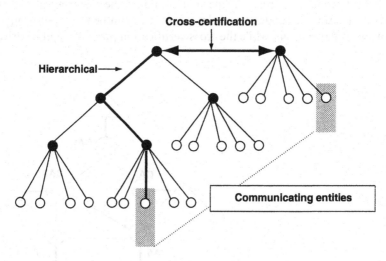

FIGURE 3.18 An example of a hybrid trust scheme bridging two entities

among the trust anchors that he or she deems worthy of being root CAs. An end entity in the web-trust model maintains one or more root CA certificates in its local environment (the browser's key store, for example). Validating a certificate as such consists of finding a trust path to one of the trusted CAs. Generally, these trust paths are shallow and in the most part consist of two certificates, the end entity's and that of the root CA from the local key store. The reason for this is to achieve high performance of the web-based applications. Figure 3.19 illustrates a web-trust model of completely disjointed CAs.

A variant of this trust model is defined by the pretty good privacy (PGP) web of trust. PGP, which evolved into a family of software, was initially developed by Philip Zimmermann as an email encryption program [CALL98]. It uses public key encryption for the distribution of strong secret encryption keys. The trust scheme in PGP known as the PGP web of trust is a simplistic model founded on the discretionary trust of individuals. There is no concept of an authoritative entity that certifies public keys in PGP. An individual user generates a public-private key pair that he or she binds to a unique identifier usually in the form of (name, emailaddress) and is responsible for its distribution to other individual entities or key distribution services. The simplistic information model of PGP certificates is intended for the main purpose of securing email exchanges. Each user maintains a set of public keys of other individuals deemed trustworthy. Furthermore, a key can be signed by a trusting entity and distributed to other individuals. The signing entity is referred as an *introducer*. Trust in the PGP model like in the Internet PKI is not transitive. The fact that A trusts B as an introducer and in turn B trusts C does not necessarily establish that A trusts C. This basic trust scheme has evolved from real-life behaviors. Because PGP has gained popularity mostly as an email encryption tool, its web-of-trust model has naturally

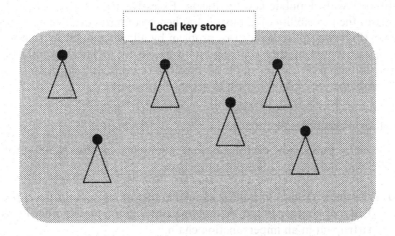

FIGURE 3.19 The web-trust model: Discretional trust of certificate authorities

evolved along a paradigm that mimics trust in human relationships. For this, it is sometimes referred to as a model of the grassroots in which authority is equally distributed across all participating entities.

The PGP web of trust can be modeled by a directed graph $G = (N, E)$ where the set of nodes N represents the collection of entities participating in a PGP web of trust, and edge $e \in E$ from entity A to entity B represents the fact that A trusts the public key of B.

Proxy Certificates: Delegated Impersonation in PKI

Impersonation, the simplest form of delegation, allows an entity A to grant to another entity B the right to establish itself as if it were A. In that process entity B generally inherits a subset of privileges of A. In computational terms entity A may represent an end user, while entity B can be a programming agent running on the user's behalf. Similarly, the initiating entity A can be an identifiable programming agent as well. The use of inherited privileges can be subject to various constraints that may result in what is referred to as restricted impersonation, a benefit of which may be to limit damage from a potential compromise. Impersonation can be recursively applied along a chain of requests, where, for example, a sequence of computing tasks are composed then executed in the course of servicing an end-user request.

Proxy certificates have recently been advanced by the IETF as the mechanism by which chained impersonation can be accomplished in a PKI using X.509 certificates. They were originally introduced by the Globus Project (www.globus.org) as a means for providing single sign-on and delegation in what has come to be known as the *grid security infrastructure* (GSI), a key element of grid computing.

The main motivation behind proxy certificates appears to be the strong requirement imposed in the public-key arena for safeguarding the private key associated with a public-key certificate. Excessive use of the private key increases the probability of exposure and hence compromise. The proxy certificate (PC) concept remedies this problem by allowing an entity that initiates a distributed multitasked request to access its private key only once during initiation. Processes and tasks involved thereafter all impersonate the same initiator yet without having to access its private key.

The Proxy-Certificate Approach

A PC is a public-key certificate that conforms to the X.509 profile [HOUS99a] and has the following properties:

- ❑ The signer (issuer) of a PC is either a holder of an *end-entity certificate* (EEC) or another PC. A PC-holding entity that issues another PC is a participant in an impersonation chain.
- ❑ It contains its own public- and private-key pair, distinct from any other certified key pair.

- ❏ It can be used to sign another PC but not an entity certificate (i.e., an EEC).
- ❏ A PC certificate chain must have a signing end-entity root certificate, which is a PKC. This underscores the fact that impersonation is controlled by a single delegating entity at the root of the chain.
- ❏ An EEC acting as a proxy issuer must have a nonempty subject name.
- ❏ A PC does not stand on its own in binding an identity to the certificate.
- ❏ A PC inherits its identity from the subject field of a signing end-entity certificate. This may possibly be inherited from the subject alternate name extension of the EEC.
- ❏ The subject field of a PC is used as a unique identifier in tracing back the chain of certificates leading up to the original signer. It does not define a new identity by its own.

Typically, a proxy certificate is generated along a delegation chain. An entity B that is authorized to impersonate A generates a public-private key pair, forms a PC and signs it using the private key corresponding to its own PKC. Similarly, a PC that is received by another entity C, during the authentication of a cascaded request, can be used by C to issue another PC, thus further extending the impersonation chain. The entity issuing a PC is called a *proxy issuer* (PI). A PI represents either an end entity or another PC. One key difference between a CA signing a certificate and a PI signing a PC is the fact that the CA performs a unique key to name binding, while the PI does not. Recall that the identity associated with a PC has to be traced back to an EEC. Figure 3.20 illustrates an example of an impersonation chain using proxy certificates.

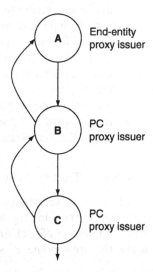

FIGURE 3.20 Proxy certificate chain

Elements of the X.509 Proxy Certificate

A proxy certificate conforms to the X.509 profile. Two elements make this profile dynamic and flexible. The first is the specification of optional fields that may or not be present in a certificate. The second and the most important one is the extensions field intended to be exploited by various PKI-based applications. Besides being simply an X.509 PKC, the characterizing elements of a PC are described below.

- ❏ *The PC extension* The PC profile describes a new X.509 certificate extension designated to identify a PC and to place constraints on its use. This extension, called the ProxyCertInfo, must be present and marked critical in every PC. Its pC field of a Boolean data type must be set to TRUE.
- ❏ *Naming requirements* Because a PC does not represent a name binding of its own, it must not contain the issuerAltName extension. The subject field of a PC must be a sequence of one or more proxy identifiers concatenated together. A proxy identifier is a common name (CN) attribute and should be unique among all PCs issued by one proxy issuer. This characteristic is an important element in tracing back a path of a PC chain when evaluating trust. For example, if the proxy issuer of a PC is an EEC, the subject field must be one single proxy identifier—say, id_1. When that same PC becomes a proxy issuer, the subject field is the concatenation of id_1 and id_2, where id_2 is the unique identifier of the PC (the entity that became a proxy issuer). The proxy identifier value can be the same as the PC serial number. Finally, the subject of PC should be used for path validation only and not for name binding or for use in authorization decision for instance.
- ❏ *Extended key usage* Because a PC inherits the attributes of its issuer, if the issuer certificate includes the extKeyUsage extension, then the PC must include that same extension. The key contained in the PC cannot be used for any purpose for which the issuer certificate is not designated for. Key usage in the PC must be a subset of the issuer's key usage. If the issuer certificate does not contain the extKeyUsage extension, then the PC may or may not include such extension. The criticality of this extension must be preserved top down along a chain of PCs.
- ❏ *Basic constraints* The basic constraints extension that is used to designate a CA certificate must not have the cA field set to TRUE.

Computing Trust in Proxy Certificates

A PC is a representative of some end-user entity with an actual EEC. Ultimately, the binding of a PC to an identity has to involve the root EEC. Validation of a chain of PCs needs to trace back a PC to an EEC. To make the appropriate PCs and the EEC available for path validation, an authentication protocol using a PC may pass the entire PC and EEC chain as part of that protocol.

Computing a PC trust path consists of tracing an issuer name in the PC being validated to a subject name in the issuer's certificate until an EEC is reached. The EEC, in turn, is subjected to the standard trust-path validation that we outlined before to arrive at a trusted root authority CA_r. After the EEC is validated, its subject name can then be used for authorization purposes. Figure 3.21 illustrates the construction of a PC trust path.

In computing a PC trust path, the issuerCertSignature part of the ProxyCertInfo extension found in a PC can be used to add accuracy to the computed path. The optional issuerCertSignature field, when present, can be used during path validation to ensure that each PC path starting with an EEC and ending at the PC is unique. If certificate $N+1$ in a certificate path is a PC, then issuerCertSignature is used to verify that certificate N is actually the PI that issued it and not some other certificate with the same name and public key. Without this field, if a PI were to issue two different proxy certificates (P_1 and P_2) with the same subject and public key but different proxy restrictions or validity time constraints, then the path-validation algorithm would accept a path in which P_2 appears as the issuer of a certificate that in reality was issued by P_1.

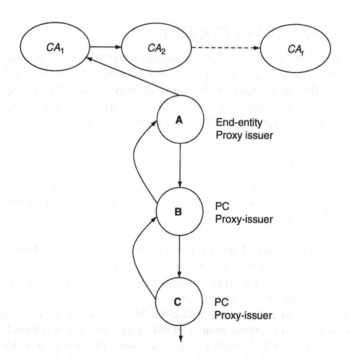

FIGURE 3.21 Constructing a PC trust path

Attribute Certificates: Entitlement Management in PKI

An X.509 PKC is signed and issued by a CA. It binds an identity with a public-private key pair. An *attribute certificate* (AC) is a data construct that is similar to a PKC; it is signed and issued by an attribute authority (AA). The main difference between a PKC and an AC is that an AC contains no public key. Instead, an AC carries with it a set of attributes associated with its holder. These attributes may specify privileges in the form of group membership, roles, a security clearance, or any information profiling its holding user. In essence, an AC binds a user with a set of authorization attributes, capabilities, or in general terms a profile.

Authorization attributes of an entity can be placed in the extensions field of its PKC. The key arguments against this proposition stem first from the fact that certificate extensions are intended for describing certificates and thus expressing user attributes in certificate extensions overloads the semantics of X.509 extensions. The second argument is due to the difference in lifetime between a PKC and an AC. Given that a PKC binds its holder with a public key, its validity period is likely to outlast the lifetime of an AC. User entitlements are much more of a dynamic nature and are constantly subject to change. In contrast, a PKC is likely to remain unchanged and valid for a long period of time. Extending a PKC to include user privileges therefore may increase the cost and complexity of managing the underlying PKI.

Elements of Attribute Certificates

Among pieces of key information contained in an AC is a set of user attributes, a validity period, and a signature certifying the integrity of the AC and establishing the authenticity of its issuing authority. Except for the signature information, all attributes are encapsulated in the AttributeCertificateInfo data type as expressed by the ASN.1 notation of Figure 3.22.

Binding Information

To enable an AC verifier to assert trust, AC binding information defines the association between an AC, its issuer, and its holder. The following data fields represent this binding:

- ❑ *Issuer* The issuer of an AC is represented by its X.500 distinguished name. All AC issuers must have nonempty distinguished names. It is up to the AC verifier to appropriately map the issuer name to a PKC for the issuer before asserting trust.
- ❑ *Holder* In an environment where the AC is passed in an authenticated message or a protocol session in which authentication is based on the use of X.509 PKCs, such as is the case with TLS/SSL, the holder field should contain the holder's PKC serial number and issuer (it asserts the

```
{ -- the signed portion
    AttributeCertificateInfo ::= SEQUENCE  {
    Version                        v2,
    Holder                         Holder,
    Issuer                         AttCertIssuer,
    Signature                      AlgorithmIdentifier,
    SerialNumber                   Certificate Serial Number,
    AttrCertValidityPeriod         AttCertValidityPeriod,
    Attributes                     SEQUENCE OF Attribute,
    IssuerUniqueID                 UniqueIdentifier OPTIONAL,
    Extensions                     Extensions OPTIONAL
}
```

```
Signature algorithm        xxxxxxxxxxx
Signature value            xxxxxxxxxxxxxx
```

FIGURE 3.22 Elements of the X.509 v2 attribute certificate

holder in way analogous to establishing its security context). The holder can also be expressed as the subject name or the subject alternate name from its corresponding PKC. This binding leads to establishing an authenticated security context in which the AC can be used to perform authorization checks.

❏ *Serial number* The serial number assigned to the AC. For any conforming AC, the (issuer, serial number) pair must be unique.

Attribute Information

This field contains a sequence of uniquely identifiable attributes. Each contains a set of key-value pairs. Privilege attributes that are designated for use in access control form the basis of an AC. At least one attribute must be present in an AC. Evidently the absence of attributes altogether defeats the basic purpose of an AC. To foster interoperability across various security domains, a number of AC attributes have been standardized. The following is a brief description of some of them:

❏ *Service authentication information* This attribute identifies the AC holder to a target service by name. It may also include optional service-specific authentication information. Typical application of this attribute is to communicate the holder's identity and password to a legacy application service. An encryption scheme is likely to be used to provide for the security of the password. The use of the target service's public key to encrypt such information lends itself well for the protection of authentication information. As shown in Figure 3.23, the verifier of an AC, a target service, first establishes the trust path to the holder's PKC. It then uses its private key to decrypt any authentication information. The latter can be passed to a legacy application that is based on such authentication information to establish the identity represented by this attribute.

❑ *Charging identity* This attribute identifies an identity that can be used by the AC holder for charging purposes. Such attribute can be exploited by a billing service for example.

❑ *Role* Used to specify a role that the AC holder is capable of assuming. Additionally, it may specify the name of the authority issuer of the role specification as a reference.

❑ *Clearance* It carries clearance information associated with the AC holder. This attribute can be exploited by systems enforcing multilevel security. The clearance is scoped within an associated policy identifier field in which the semantics of the clearance are defined.

A Note About AC Attributes

The data types used to describe an attribute are designed to provide a high degree of flexibility and extensibility through a parameterization that describes an attribute as a (type, value) pair expressed by the following ASN.1 syntax [BENA02]:

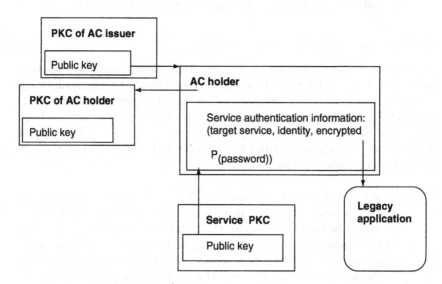

FIGURE 3.23 View of trust verification elements for an AC and its service attributes protected using the PKC of the service

```
Attribute :: = SEQUENCE {
               type      AttributeType,
               values    SET OF AttributeValue
               - at least one value is required
}
AttributeType :: = OBJECT IDENTIFIER
AttributeValue :: = ANY DEFINED BY AttributeType
```

The extensibility of AC attributes is due to the opacity of an attribute's value with respect to the structure of the AC itself. Entities can exploit an attribute embedded in an AC only when they are capable of interpreting both its type and value—of course, provided they are also able to verify any trust elements associated with that attribute. The syntactic and the semantics scope of AC attributes is unbounded and thus can be exploited by various applications.

Extensions

Although most PKC extensions provide information about the certificate itself instead of its holder, some extensions defined for ACs provide a way for associating additional information with holders. Below we enumerate some of the AC extensions relating to identity management and trust:

- *AC targeting* An AC may be designated for use by a specific target entity. The AC targeting extension is intended for that purpose. Target information may specify multiple services. Relying parties not explicitly named in this extension must reject the AC. This targeting information can be useful in the transactional web. The absence of this extension is an indication that the AC can be used by any relying party.
- *Audit identity* To satisfy cases where data privacy laws, for example, require that audit trails not reveal or even contain records that identify individuals, an audit identity extension can be added to an AC. This extension allows the logger of an audit trail to use an identity designated by the value of this extension. This value along with the AC issuer name or the AC serial number should be used for audit or logging purposes
- *Trust-related extensions* By this we mean not one specific extension but a set of AC extensions relating to the evaluation of trust in an AC. These are all defined by the X.509 v3 certificate profile [HOUS99a]. The first is the *authority-key identifier*, which can be used to assist the AC verifier in validating the signature of the AC. The second is the *Authority-information access*, and the third is the *CRL distribution points*. Both of these can be used by a relying party to verify the revocation status of the AC.

Generalized Web-of-Trust Model

The web-of-trust scheme that we discussed under the public-key models can be generalized as a mechanism by which heterogeneous cross-enterprise identity models are joined in a federated web. The building block of this federation is the trust relationship that can be established across heterogeneous identity and trust-management systems using secure network-authentication protocols, some of which we have previously discussed. The trust protocols used can be negotiable between each of two domains entering into a relationship as such. Trust can be one-way or mutual. The potential advantage of this comes from the incremental weaving of trust across domains that builds on existing heterogeneous trust and identity management schemes that may exist in each participating domain. The basic element of trust here relies on the principal of trust by introductions in which entity A that trusts entity B may also trust entities presented to it by B, provided A establishes a trust relationship with B in a secure and verifiable manner.

Federated domains that are based on the generalized web-of-trust model that we propose are characterized by the following:

❑ Cross-domain identity-management systems are joined through a negotiated trust mechanism in which an agreed on authentication and trust protocol is used. Authentication is performed between agents of two domains entering in a trust relationship. The direction of trust (one-way or mutual) is based on the policies of the participating domains.

❑ Subjects are registered to their, respective, generally local domains. Subject authentication and profile management is performed with its domain of registration only.

❑ Subjects authenticate to their respective domain of registration but can seamlessly access services and resources managed by other domains via the trust relationships established across these domains.

❑ Identity profile information can be used across domains that have established trust relationships, provided its syntax and semantics are similarly interpreted. Translation of profile information in any direction can be performed by gateways local to each domain.

❑ Identity information of a subject remains attached to its original domain of registration as it is passed across domains. The identity of the home domain is attached to this information as it is passed across domains with established trust relationships.

❑ Secure transports such as those based on strong cryptographic channels are required for exchanging profile and identity information. These channels depend on the trust scheme adopted between each two domains.

Figure 3.24 illustrates this concept of the generalized web of trust, which can be modeled by a directed graph where the edge directionality represents trust (i.e., edge (x, y) represents trust of y by x). The transfer of profile information for subject s is shown across three domains.

Transitive trust may be used at the discretion of the security policies implemented by each domain. Domain A that enters into a trust relationship with domains B and C may apply the transitive trust policy with domain B

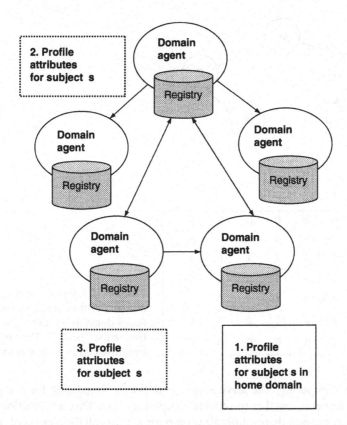

FIGURE 3.24 An example of the generalized web of trust model federating five domains

but not with domain C. Once a trust relationship between domains A and B is designated as transitive, all domains reachable through B for example can be trusted by A. Similarly, the depth of such transitive trust can be limited if so desired. Figure 3.25 illustrates an example of a generalized web-of-trust model in which trust relations are all transitive. Trust paths in this case correspond to the transitive closure of the graph representation.

Examples of Trust-Exchange Mechanisms over the Web

Web services are at the leading edge of deploying highly distributed software components that can be published, discovered, and invoked seamlessly. They build on two of existing technologies, HTTP and XML, which are widely accepted and expected to dominate computing at least in the foreseeable future. Due to the higher level of abstracting the programming components of

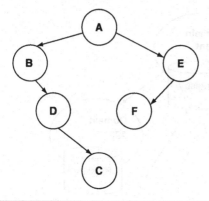

	A	B	C	D	E	F
A	1	1	1	1	1	1
B	0	1	1	1	0	0
C	0	0	1	0	0	0
D	0	0	1	1	0	0
E	0	0	0	0	1	1
F	0	0	0	0	0	1

FIGURE 3.25 Graph representation of a web of trust across six heterogeneous domains adopting the transitive trust policy. The resulting transitive closure matrix is shown

network computing, web services appear to lay the foundation for composing service elements together to provide complex services. This composition capability may potentially revolutionize computing. It has all the aspects of achieving seamless web navigation in a way analogous to what users have experienced with the advent of manual navigation of the Web through browsers. Such composite computations over the seemingly unbounded frontiers of the Web further highlight the need for strong and reliable computational trust.

We look at three emerging mechanisms for the exchange of security constructs to enable trusted and secure Web computing, all of which are complementing each other. The first is a method for exchanging trust enabling constructs on Web service calls, web services security (WS-Security). The second one is a standard method for how to express trust and identity constructs in the computing web, the security assertion markup language (SAML). The third one represents a way to establish security sessions between a client and a remote service, Web cookies. A programming model in which these three techniques are used together expresses trust elements using SAML; transports the SAML statements using WS-Security and then maintains a session using Web cookies that contain SAML constructs.

Web-Services Security

Recently IBM, Microsoft, and VeriSign, Inc. have cooperated on the development of a Web-services security (WS-Security) specification submitted to the Organization for the Advancement of Structured Information Standards (OASIS) [OASI03]. Web services are at the leading edge of deploying integrated Web software components that can be published, discovered, and invoked seamlessly. Furthermore and due to their higher level of abstraction, Web services appear to lay the foundation for composing service elements together to provide complex services. This composition capability may potentially revolutionize computing. It has all the elements of achieving seamless Web navigation in a way analogous to what users have experienced since the advent of manual Web navigation driven through the end-user browser. Such composite computations over the seemingly unbounded frontiers of the Web further highlight the need for computational trust that can be established with reliability.

WS-Security is an attempt to retrofit security in the design of the Web-services protocol referred to as the simple-object access protocol (SOAP). It builds on existing mechanisms to generate security tokens for use across SOAP interlocutors referred to as *actors*. Data transfer in SOAP is based on exchanging XML documents. From a high perspective, such documents all adhere to a well-defined XML schema [W3CO02a] that governs the structure of SOAP messages. This structure consists of an enclosing envelope within which are nested zero or more control headers, followed by one body containing the application-level message payload.

Because WS-Security is an attempt to fit security into an already specified Web-service document format, the header portion of the document seems like a natural fit. The header element <Security> provides a means for attaching security-related information that can be targeted for a specific receiving entity. The latter can be an intermediate node traversed by the Web service or some other endpoint target.

A SOAP message can have multiple <Security> elements embedded in its header. Each of such elements may be designated to target a particular receiver specified through the S:actor attribute. Security information targeted to different receivers is required to appear within different <Security> elements. The omission of a S:actor attribute from a security element indicates that it is intended for consumption by all intermediate hopes of the message including the endpoint. Only one <Security> header block can omit the S:actor attribute, and no two elements can have the same S:actor attribute. This enforces a consistent rule in which security information that is targeted to all recipients or that is intended for a specific target is all structured respectively in a single <Security> element.

Security elements can be dynamically added to a Web-service message as it navigates the Web. Figure 3.26 depicts two examples of embedding security information within the <Security> elements of a SOAP message. In A we illustrate an acceptable syntax in which two <Security> elements are inserted, one targeted to a specific SOAP actor, while the second one is intended for all recipients. In B we show an invalid insertion syntax caused by having two <Security> elements targeted for consumption by all recipients.

A

```
<S:Envelope>
    <S:Header>
        ...
        <SecurityS:actor="weburi"
            S:mustUnderstand="TRUE">
            ...
        </Security>
        <Security S:mustUndertsand="TRUE">
            ...
        </Security>
    </S:Header>
    ...
</S:Envelope>
```

B

```
<S:Envelope>
    <S:Header>
        ...
        <Security S:mustUndertsand="TRUE">
            ...
        </Security>
        <Security S:mustUndertsand="TRUE">
            ...
        </Security>
    </S:Header>
    ...
</S:Envelope>
```

FIGURE 3.26 Inserting security elements in a SOAP message

As subelements are incrementally added to the <Security> header block, they are prepended to existing ones. The header therefore is an ordered sequence of elements combining security tokens, XML signatures, as well as encryptions. The processing of the security elements by a recipient is likely to be performed in accordance to this sequencing rule where no forward dependency across security subelements is permitted. When a subelement refers to a key placed in another subelement, the security token containing the key should be prepended following the subelement using that key. An example of that is a key-bearing subelement that contains an X509 certificate used for a signature. The X509 token in this case should be prepended following the signature subelement.

The security mechanisms that can be used in WS-Security may span technologies ranging from simple user identifier and password to more sophisticated constructs such as X.509 certificates and Kerberos tickets. Security elements may also contain signatures and encryptions computed over particular elements of the exchanged SOAP document. They also provide a natural transport for SAML assertions that can be attached to Web-services requests. We discuss the details of SAML shortly.

Identity and Trust Tokens

WS-Security provides an extensibility mechanism that can be exploited to embed any type of identity token. Three specific types of tokens are currently defined. You may attach a simple user-identifier token that consists of a user name and password, an X.509 v3 certificate, or a Kerberos v5 ticket. The types of tokens that can be used are classified in two categories: simple user-name tokens and binary tokens.

Simple User Name Token   A user name token has the following XML structure:

```
<wsse:Security>
    <UsernameToken  Id ="...">
    <Username>
    ...
    </Username>
    <Password        Type ="...">
    ...
        </Password>
    </UsernameToken>
</wsse:Security>
```

The ID attribute can be optionally used to label the token. Username is a required element that specifies the identity of the token holder. The optional password element is intended to establish Username. Password information includes a type and a value. Protecting the password may require at least some level of transport security. Two formats for the password are currently defined by the optional Type attribute: a plaintext form and a bse64 encoding of the SHA-1 digest of the UTF8-encoded password.

Binary Tokens   Binary tokens provide a way to embed cryptographic identity and privilege tokens in the security header block of a soap message. The parameterization of these tokens is based on two factors. The first one defines the type of encoding used. This allows the token to be handled appropriately. Two encoding types are currently specified:

❑   Base 64 encoding (wsse:Base64Binary) and
❑   Hex encoding (wsse:HexBinary).

The second parameter defines the type of the token's value. Three such types have been defined:

❑   X509 v3 certificate (wsse:X509v3),
❑   Kerberos v5 TGT (wsse::Kerberosv5TGT), and
❑   Kerberos v5 service ticket (ST) (wsse:Kerberos5ST).

wsse is the name space defined specifically for WS-Security. An X.509 certificate and its data components such as the public key can also be embedded in a <ds:KeyInfo> element defined by the XML name space of the digital

signature standard [W3CO02b]. Below is an example illustrating the inclu-
sion of an X509 v3 certificate as a binary security token within a <Security>
element.

```
<wsse:Security>
    ...
<wsse:BinarySecurityToken
xmlns:wsse="http://schemas.xmlsoap.org/ws/2002/04/secext"
    Id="myX509Token"
    ValueType="wsse:X509v3"
    EncodingType="wsse:Base64Binary">
    MITEZzIQEmt9CgCCAJZ0cqr5ihk...
</wsse:BinarySecurityToken>
    ...
</wsse:Security>
```

Referencing Security Tokens   A token may be embedded in a security element by reference instead of value. Referencing a security token consists of
specifying a URI for its location. The token can then be pulled by a relying
party. This approach affords the advantage of having to marshal less data on
a Web-services request. The following XML snippet illustrates the syntax of
specifying tokens by reference:

```
<SecurityTokenReference
        Id="...">
    <Reference URI="...">
    </Reference>
</SecurityTokenReference>
```

SAML Approach: Unifying Trust and Identity Constructs

The security markup language (SAML) is an evolving standard that defines
the syntax and semantics for XML-encoded statements that represent security assertions about a user or some programming entity [OASI02].
Assertions can be constructed by an initiating entity or can be acquired from
a third party and presented to another entity where they are validated based
on a predefined trust model. The unifying approach undertaken in SAML
stems first from its generality and second from the fact that it represents a
higher level of abstraction above any underlying security mechanisms, trust
paradigms, transport, or the security protocols being used. Furthermore,
SAML can be applicable irrespective of the trust model adopted whether
it is a two-party or a third-party scheme. It lends itself to forming trust
federations as assertions may span a large web of network endpoints and
intermediaries.

   With SAML, security decisions are not computed based on the traditional
security context established by a controlling process in which an application

executes. With SAML, an application acts as a container and provides a conduit for the security context associated with the underlying entity. This context therefore becomes exposed to the transaction level as opposed to the traditional paradigm in which contexts are managed and kept by control programs. Being part of the transaction's constructs, a SAML context follows the network routes taken by a Web application. As such, the flow of SAML constructs over a network may follow an arbitrary topology dictated only by the chain of requests with which they are associated. The depth of such request chains can be unbounded.

The vision of the network as a computer has indeed arrived with the federated Web-based applications that can be limited only by the scope of the Internet. The seamlessly unbounded journey of a network service request requires single sign-on of the initiating endpoint and transparent forwarding of user trust elements, such as authentication and authorization credentials. Furthermore, an adaptive dissemination of the user's profile elements that can be enforced by a dynamic and adaptive security policy is a key requirement for privacy control.

The SAML approach defines three types of identity management and trust assertions:

- *Authentication* The subject specified by the assertion was authenticated by a particular mechanism at a particular time. Authentication assertions merely state acts of authentication that happened in the past.
- *Authorization* The specified subject is either allowed or denied access to a particular resource.
- *Attribute* The specified subject is associated with the list of attributes provided in the assertion. Attribute elements define what is commonly known as a *user profile*.

An assertion may optionally be accompanied by one or more conditions constraining its validity. Assertions have a nested structure in which an outer generic element provides information common to all assertions. A series of inner elements representing authentication statements, authorization decision statements, and attribute statements all describe the specifics of the assertion. Instead of duplicating the statements issued via other assertions, one assertion may simply refer to those assertions via their unique identifiers (e.g., by a URI). Entities consuming assertions with external references to other assertions are responsible for resolving and validating those references as well as the assertions that they contain.

To broaden the scope of SAML and make it independent of any particular trust model, the concept of a SAML authority is introduced. SAML assertions are issued by SAML authorities that are distinguished based on the type of assertions they can issue. A SAML authority can be an authentication authority, an authorization authority, or an attribute authority. This distinction is conceptual and logical but is not necessarily physical as all types of assertions can be issued by a single authoritative entity. SAML distinguishes

among three actors—a requester, a relying party, and an authority. The relying party is the entity that consumes and validates SAML assertions. The
requester is the entity responsible for initiating the acquisition of assertions.
A requester may also be considered a relying party, and thus one might
broadly distinguish two main entities: an asserting party (an authority) and a
relying party (consumer of SAML assertions). Figure 3.27 provides a conceptual view of the relationships across SAML entities. A dotted arrow linking an
assertion type with a SAML authority indicates that the authority makes use
of the assertion to issue new assertions. For instance, an authorization authority requires one or more authentication assertions to issue one or more
authorization-decision assertions.

SAML authorities rely on various information sources to issue assertions.
Most important, an external registry containing policy information may be
consulted by an authority before an assertion is formulated. Additionally,
SAML authorities may rely on previously issued and verified assertions to
compute new ones. Requesting entities send existing assertions to SAML
authorities when acquiring new assertions. Similarly, a SAML authority may
pull referenced assertions from specified network URIs. In that respect,
SAML authorities consume and produce assertions at the same time. On the
other hand, clients, requestors, or relying parties can only be consumers of
SAML assertions.

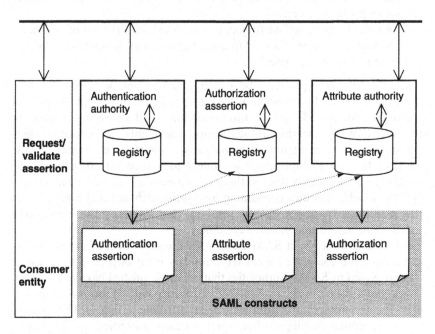

FIGURE 3.27 A conceptual view of the relationships across SAML entities

In addition to the syntactic and semantic definition of assertions, SAML defines a basic request and response protocol for the acquisitions of assertions.

SAML Constructs

Computations in SAML are performed over assertions. Each assertion is composed of a nonempty set of XML statements characterizing a particular subject with a temporal fact, such as an act of past authentication, an attribute, or a decision on whether access is allowed to a specific resource. The following is a discussion of major data elements of SAML.

Assertion   An assertion is described by *AssertionType*, which is an XML complex type. This type specifies the basic information that is common to every assertion including the following attributes:

- ❑ *MajorVersion* A required attribute designating the major version of this assertion,
- ❑ *MinorVersion* A required attribute indicating the minor version of this assertion,
- ❑ *AssertionID* A required attribute uniquely identifying this assertion (a URI, for instance, can be used for such identification)
- ❑ *Issuer* A required attribute that unambiguously identifies the SAML authority that issued this assertion (an issuer might be identified by a URI), and
- ❑ *IssuerInstant* A required attribute specifying the time of issue in UTC.

Conditions   This is an optional element that adds constraints to an assertion. The use of the assertion is subject to the constraints specified in this element. For example, a time constraint may set the validity of an assertion to some future time. Similarly, the validity of an assertion may be set to expire after a specified time.

Advice   An optional element containing additional information that aids in processing an assertion.

Signature   An optional element for marshalling XML signatures.

Statement   This defines an extension point allowing the derivation of other statement constructs by an assertion-based application.

Subject Statement   Defines an extension point from which other subject-related statements can be derived by various assertion-based applications. It contains a <Subject> element that defines a single entity associated with the statement. <Subject> encompasses two other elements: <NameIdentifier>, which identifies the subject by name and security domain, and an optional <SubjectConfirmation> element, which contains authentication information establishing <NameIdentifier>.

Authentication Statement This element is used by an issuing authority to indicate that the subject of the statement was authenticated by a particular authentication method and at a particular time in the past. An example of such assertion is shown below:

```
<saml:assertion     MajorVersion="1" MinorVersion="0"
    AssertionID="128.9.164.32.132547698"
    Issuer="Company.com"
    IssuerInstant="2003-04-26T11:03:00Z"
    <saml:Condition
            NotBefore="2003-04-26T11:03:00Z"
            NotAfter=""2003-04-26T11:10:00Z"
    <saml:AuthenticationStatement
            AuthenticationMethod="password"
            AuthenticationInstant=
            "2003-04-26T11:03:00Z"
            <saml:Subject>
                    SecurityDomain="Company.com"
                    Name="JohnDoe"
            </saml:Subject>
    </saml:AuthenticationStatement>
</saml:Assertion>
```

Authorization Decision Statement This element provides a statement by the issuer to the fact that the named subject is granted or denied access to a resource which is unambiguously specified by means of a URI. An example of an authorization decision assertion is shown below:

```
<saml:assertion     MajorVersion="1" MinorVersion="0"
    AssertionID="129.9.164.32.132547690"
    Issuer="Company.com"
    IssuerInstant="2003-04-26T11:03:00Z"
    <saml:Condition NotBefore="2003-04-26T11:03:00Z"
                    NotAfter="2003-04-26T12:10:00Z"
    <saml:AuthorizationDecisionStatement
        Decision="Permit"
        Resource="http://Travel.com/Servlet/reserve"
            <saml:Action
                Namespace="http://WellknownURI">
                Execute
            </saml:Action>
            <saml:Subject>
                    <saml:NameIdentifier
                        SecurityDomain="Company.com"
                        Name="JohnDoe"
                    </saml:NameIdentifier>
            </saml:Subject>
    </saml:AuthorizationDecisionStatement>
</saml:Assertion>
```

Attribute Statement   This element underscores a statement by the issuer that the specified subject is associated with the attributes indicated. The following is an example of an attribute assertion:

```
<saml:assertion    MajorVersion="1" MinorVersion="0"
    AssertionID="130.9.164.32.132547691"
    Issuer="Company.com"
    IssuerInstant="2003-04-26T11:03:00Z"
    <saml:Condition  NotBefore="2003-04-26T13:03:00Z"
                     NotAfter=""2003-04-26T13:10:00Z"
    <saml:AttributeStatement
        <saml:Subject>
                    SecurityDomain="Company.com"
                    Name="JohnDoe"
        </saml:Subject>
        <saml:Attribute>
                <saml:AttributeDesignator>
                AttributeName="Department"
                AttributeNamespace="http://Company.com"
                </saml:AttributeDesignator>
                <saml:AttributeValue>
                    Sales
                </saml:AttributeValue>
        </saml:Attribute>
    </saml:AttributeStatement>
</saml:Assertion>
```

Note how attributes are parameterized by names. This parameterization exemplifies the degree of flexibility in SAML. Furthermore, the name of an attribute is accompanied with a URI for the namespace in which the attribute is defined. Thus the semantics of an attribute is resolved to its defining source, which prevents ambiguity and collisions.

Trust Elements of SAML

SAML assertions are consumed by relying entities to establish subject identities and confine the use of resources to predefined policies. Affirming such assertions manifests itself through trust relationships that can be established between a relying party and the authority issuing the assertion. Trust establishment and verification in SAML is based on various constructs expressed through SAML assertions. In the following, we enumerate the major such elements that contribute to trust.

Digital Signatures   The XML element <ds:Signature> may optionally be part of an assertion. When present, it represents an XML digital signature computed over the statements carried by the assertion. An assertion signed by an asserting party (AP) such as a SAML authority provides support for the integrity of the assertion, its authenticity, and possibly allows for nonre-pudiation when a tamper-proof public-key mechanism is used. An assertion can also be part of a request message made to a SAML authority. Likewise, the signature over the assertion in this case supports data integrity, origin authenticity, and possibly nonrepudiation between the message originator and the destination authority.

User Confirmation   A <SubjectStatement> contains a <Subject> element used to describe an active entity. In turn, the <Subject> element consists of two nested elements: <NameIdentifier>, which specifies a subject by name in accordance with a particular naming scheme such as in X.509 [HOUS99a], or an email address based on IETF RFC2822 [RESN01]. The second element is <SubjectConfirmation>, used to provide data allowing the subject to be authenticated. This element may encapsulate any authentication token or credential that can lead to establishing the named identity.

Authority Binding Information   The <AuthorityBinding> element may optionally be part of an authentication statement. It can be used to indicate to a relying party that a SAML authority may be available to provide additional information about the subject of an assertion. This authority is specified by location and through its supported protocol binding.

Authorization Evidence   An authorization statement may optionally contain an <Evidence> element that carries an assertion used by the issuer in making the authorization decision. This assertion can be specified either by value or by reference. Authorization evidence may also be supplied by an entity requesting an authorization decision from a SAML authority.

Other Trust Elements of SAML

Other elements of trust in the SAML definition for an assertion include the name of the issuer <Issuer>. A name in the form of a URI allows a relying party to inquire further information about the subject of the attribute to verify a particular trust relationship. The time of issuance of the assertion <IssueInstant> as well as a validity interval as defined by the <Condition> element allow for the timely usage of an assertion. Additionally an <Advice> element may encompass further trust-related information about the assertion.

A Note on Federated Trust in SAML

Federated SAML authorities are expected to play a key role in the proliferation and success of the SAML constructs over the Internet. Forwarding SAML authentication and authorization assertions across security domains without re-authentication requires the existence of a well-defined trust across participating SAML authorities. SAML in itself has not introduced a new federated trust paradigm; rather, it relies on existing models of trust such as those based on PKI or Kerberos for instance. Trust verification in this case will ultimately involve the low-level mechanisms producing the SAML constructs.

Web Cookies

The HTTP protocol that made the World Wide Web a household name is stateless and simple. The statelessness of HTTP precludes the need for managing persistent sessions and all the complexities that may arise thereof. Users connect anew and identify themselves whenever needed, each time they navigate a Web link even with the same server. Although they face a number of reliability and security issues, cookies were invented as an ad-hoc mechanism to establish continuity and sate on the Web. Cookies are data constructs that are initially sent from a Web server to the client's browser environment, referred to as a *user agent* and subsequently exchanged between the browser and Web servers visited by the user. They can serve many purposes from the basic functions of keeping track of the display mode that a user selects (e.g., graphic frames or text only) to representing the current state of a shopping cart for a Web store buyer. The concept of cookies is an interesting one in that it simplifies managing HTTP states by involving the client yet in a seamless manner. An end user is generally unaware of cookies placed in his or her machine. The server maintains no state constructs in its runtime except for when they arrive through client cookies. The server is said to forget about the client until the latter reminds it of who he or she is.

Structure of Cookies

Cookies have a flat data structure that is simple and easy to manipulate. A cookie is a sequence of attribute name and value pairs as defined in the IETF RFC 2965 [KRIS00]. A few control attributes are introduced by the standard. The most important aspect, however, is the generality of attribute-value pairs that can be marshaled into a cookie. Application-level attributes can be arbitrarily defined as indicated by the following syntax:

```
av-pairs  =  av-pair(";" av-pair)*
av-pair   =  attr ["=" value];optional value
attr      =  token
value     =  token | quoted-string
```

Attribute names, instances of attr, are case-insensitive. While the above syntax shows value as optional, evidently most attributes will have values associated with them. Figure 3.28 illustrates the structure of a generic cookie.

Server Role

A server application that needs to establish a cookie-based session with a particular client returns cookie information in the HTTP response header preceded with the label of "Set-Cookie2" as shown by the syntax below.

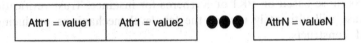

FIGURE 3.28 Generic structure of a Web cookie

```
set-cookie        =    "Set-Cookie2:" cookies
cookies           =    1#cookie
cookie            =    NAME "=" VALUE(";" set-cookie-av)*
NAME              =    attr
VALUE             =    value
set-cookie-av     =    "Comment" "=" value
                  |    "CommentURL" "=" <"> http_URL <">
                  |    "Discard"
                  |    "Domain" "=" value
                  |    "Max-Age" "=" value
                  |    "Path" "=" value
                  |    "Port"[ "=" <"> portlist <"> ]
                  |    "Secure"
                  |    "Version" "=" 1*DIGIT
portlist          =    1#portnum
portnum           =    1*DIGIT
```

The Set-Cookie2 response header comprises the token Set-Cookie2: followed by a list of one or more comma-separated cookies. In turn, each cookie begins with a required NAME=VALUE pair representing the cookie name, followed by zero or more semicolon-separated attribute-value pairs. Among the standard control attributes we point out the following list, which is to some degree relevant to the security and reliability of the cookie mechanism:

❑ The optional Path attribute specifies the server URLs for which the cookie is applicable.

❑ The optional Port attribute restricts the ports to which a cookie may be returned by a client in an HTTP request header.

❑ The optional Secure attribute (with no value) indicates that the cookie is secure. The security level or mechanism by which the cookie is protected is unspecified and remains application-specific. When the client sends a "secure" cookie back to the server, the level of security as indicated by the server should not be downgraded.

❑ The presence of the optional Domain attribute specifies the domain name for which the cookie is valid. Generally, the domain of the server is the one specified, although cookies can also be generated by one server and consumed by another server located in a separate domain. This attribute is a bit of information that can be used to further extend the generation and consumption of cookies across federated domains.

❑ The optional attribute Max-Age represents the lifetime of the cookie in seconds. A value of zero means the cookie should be discarded immediately. The absence of this attribute can be interpreted as representing an indefinitely valid cookie.

❑ The optional attribute of Discard is used to instruct the client program (the browser, for example) to discard the cookie unconditionally when it terminates.

❑ The optional attribute of CommentURL is used by the server to inform the client of any privacy-related information as well as the intended use of the cookie. The client agent should give opportunity to the user to inspect this information before he or she initiates a request.

Client Role

When a client wishes to continue interacting with a server, it returns cookie information in the HTTP request header based on the Set-Cookie2 data that it had received. The cookie header sent from the client to the server adheres to the following syntax.

```
cookie           =   "Cookie:" cookie-version 1

(("; " | ", ")* cookie-value)
cookie-value     =   NAME "=" VALUE [";" path] [";" domain]
                     [";" port]
cookie-version   =   "$Version" "=" value
NAME             =   attr
VALUE            =   value
path             =   "$Path" "=" value
domain           =   "$Domain" "=" value
port             =   "$Port" [ "=" <"> value <"> ]
```

Attributes values returned by the client reflect those sent by the server through Set-Cookie2.

Cookies already stored at the client side can be sent to the server based on the following:

❑ The host and port designated by the request,
❑ The URI of the request, and
❑ The age of the cookie.

Example: Cookies Exchanged Between a Client and a Web Server

The following steps illustrate cookies exchanged between a client and a web server presented through a fictitious URL of http://www.webstore.com. It is assumed that the client has no stored cookies for the server and he just visited the home of webstore.com that displays a login form. The client fills and then submits the form. The server receives client log on information and processes it. Subsequent interactions between the client and that same server result in the following exchange of cookies.

Server → User

```
Set-Cookie2:Customer="JohnDoe";Version="1"; Path="/webstore"
Cookie identifies the client.
```

User → Server User selects an item to order.

```
Cookie: $Version="1"; Customer="JohnDoe"; $Path="/webstore"
[form data]
```
Server → User Shopping basket contains an item.
```
Set-Cookie2: Part_Number="Diesel_Engine_101";
Version="1";Path="/webstore"
```

User → Server User selects shipping method from form.
```
Cookie: $Version="1";Customer="John Doe"; $Path="/webstore";
Part_Number="Diesel_Engine_101"; $Path="/webstore"
[form data]
```

Server → User New cookie contains shipping method.
```
Set-Cookie2: Shipping="UPS"; Version="1"; Path="/webstore"
```

User → Server User chooses to process order.
```
    Cookie:$Version="1"; Customer="JohnDoe;
Part_Number="Diesel_Engine_101";
$Path="/webstore";Shipping="UPS";
[form data]
```

Server → User
Transaction is complete.

Issues with Use of Cookies

The concept of cookies is controversial in a number of aspects. Foremost is the ability of a Web server to push data constructs into a user's machine. This process may in fact be taking place without the user's full awareness of potential consequences. Nonsavvy users in many cases are not cognizant of what a cookie is. Indeed, this paints an element of intrusion under the auspices of normalcy and thus users will tend to accept cookies. The user's Web navigation behavior can be easily tracked thereby raising concerns over privacy. Malicious servers may attempt to flood a user's machine with cookie files. The transparency of uploading cookies to Web servers, the fact that cookies issued for one host may be consumed by another one, and cookies stored in one machine can be copied and used on another machine all are factors that increase the risks associated with cookies.

The risk factor is further exacerbated with the misuse of nonsecure cookies for identity management, such as authentication, single sign-on, and for carrying entitlements. Although the IETF standard for the use and management of cookies emphasizes the adoption of informed consent where the end user is made aware of cookies, the potential for misuse can be abound, particularly when in fact the user is subsumed by his or her agent, the browser. The fact that a cookie generally tends to have a lifetime that is sufficient enough for an intruder or a malicious user to modify it or completely regenerate it with new information poses a considerable risk. Park and Sandhu [PARK00] classify threats of using cookies into three types: network threats, end-system threats, and cookie-harvesting threats. Network threats can be carried by intercepting HTTP requests and responses, extracting cookies, and implanting them for a malicious use. The use of secure connections such as SSL protects cookies during transport but leaves them in cleartext once they reach an endpoint. End-user threats stem from the fact that cookies can be easily altered and copied from one machine to another. Attackers can therefore forge cookies and perhaps impersonate other users in a scheme of identity theft. An attack for harvesting cookies can be mounted by a Trojan Web site that impersonates a site that accepts cookies from users. The harvested cookies can later be used to compromise all other sites accepting them.

Secure Cookies

The level of security required by cookies depends on the sensitivity of information carried in a cookie, the type of potential threats and risks, as well as the cost incurred in the event of a compromise. Usage of cookies may require data integrity, origin authenticity, and confidentiality. Despite the controversy surrounding it, the cookie paradigm can be securely and reliably exploited to the benefit of Web computing. Sometimes an encrypted transport channel such as one using SSL/TLS is established between a client and a server to encrypt the entirety of a data payload exchanged just because a few bytes of the payload require confidentiality. Instead, one might use cookies with only the sensitive information encrypted.

Any reasonable level of secure cookies will, in all likelihood, require encryption. We distinguish three scenarios in which encryption of cookies may take place.

Use of a Public Key on the Client Side   Cookie information can be signed, encrypted, or both signed and encrypted using the private key of the client. Decryption as well as signature verification is performed by the destination server. The public key of the client is established by the server according to a predefined PKI trust scheme. This approach is applicable in situations where the client is sending information that has no risk of exposure but requires integrity and origin authenticity. An example would be the signing of a shopping-cart cookie so that some level of nonrepudiation can be achieved.

Cookies secured in this fashion can be used across multiple servers provided the certified public key of the client is available.

Use of a Public Key on the Server Side   In this model, the server uses its private key to sign or encrypt cookies before they are pushed into a client machine. The client may elect to verify signed cookies to establish server authenticity. The server may choose to encrypt sensitive information from the user's profile or other session-related information using its public key. When such a cookie bounces back on the server side, the server uses its own private key to decrypt it and thus the cookie is guaranteed confidentiality, data integrity, and authenticity of the origin server. In this scenario, encrypting a cookie with the server's public key is relevant to sensitive data. Server signing of the cookie enables data integrity, and enforces authenticity of the origin server. Simply encrypting cookies using the server's public key, however, is not adequate since the server's public key can be available to other entities and thus eavesdropping and impersonation may take place. Such encryption should be performed over data that is signed by the server to ensure both confidentiality of cookie information and origin authenticity of the server.

Use of a Shared Secret Key   A symmetric encryption key shared between a client and a server may also be used to encrypt cookie information or apply a keyed MAC to cookies requiring data origin authenticity and integrity. When the client origin authenticity is required, however, a shared secret key needs to be distinct for each client-server pair. This does not lend itself to scalability and faces the key distribution issue. A session key established through key exchange protocols such as the encrypted key exchange (EKE) or Diffie-Hellman can also be used [DIFF76a, BELL92].

Chapter 4

Mandatory-Access-Control Model

Introduction

Mandatory-access control (MAC) stands as a well-established model in computing security. Despite the fact that it lends itself well to military environments, it represents clearly distinguishing aspects in controlling information flow. Such information flow is foremost characterized as being deterministic. We begin with an introductory to the foundations of information flow. We describe the mathematical elements underpinning MAC as a lattice-based information-flow model. Subsequently, we discuss the details of the Bell-LaPadula and the Biba models. The first one is based on the need to preserve confidentiality of information flow, while the second is concerned with maintaining integrity. We compare the two models and describe scenarios in which they can be combined. Finally, we introduce the Chinese-wall policy as an instance of the lattice-based information-flow policy applicable in commercial environments.

Mandatory-Access-Control Theory

In a system governed by the mandatory-access-control model, user privileges are not resource-owner centric. In fact, no concept of ownership does exist in MAC, which is rather based on a policy that is driven by the sensitivity of the protected information. To access a MAC-protected object, one must hold the proper security clearance required by that object. The security label of a resource is matched up against the clearance of an attempting accessor. MAC policies fall under what is known as *lattice-based access-control system*. Information flow in these systems is formally determined by the mathematical structure of the underlying lattice that reflects it. We begin by reviewing the foundations behind the MAC model.

Partial Orders

A set S is said to be *partially ordered* along a binary relationship R between S and itself if and only if the following conditions are satisfied:

- ❑ R is reflexive: $a\,R\,a$ for every element a in S.
- ❑ R is transitive: if $a\,R\,b$ and $b\,R\,c$, then $a\,R\,c$.
- ❑ R is antisymmetric: if $a\,R\,b$ and $b\,R\,a$, then $a = b$.

A partially ordered set is sometimes referred to in the literature as a *poset* for short. Note that it is not required that every pair of elements in a partially ordered set to be related, and hence the use of the term *partial ordering*. When every pair of elements x and y of a partially ordered set S can be compared with each other (i.e., $x\,R\,y$ or $y\,R\,x$) the set S becomes a *totally ordered* set also referred to as a *linearly ordered* set or simply an *ordered set*.

Example: Partial Orders

Consider the elements of set S to be the subsets of $\{a,b,c\}$ and R to be the containment relationship denoted by $\subseteq$. The set:

$S = \{\Phi,\{a\},\{b\},\{c\},\ \{a,b\},\{a,c\},\{b,\ c\},\{a,b,c\}\}$ forms a partial order along the relationship $\subseteq$ because

- ❑ $\subseteq$ is reflexive: for every element x in S, $x \subseteq x$.
- ❑ $\subseteq$ is transitive for every x, y, and z in S, $x \subseteq y$ and $y \subseteq z \Rightarrow x \subseteq z$.
- ❑ $\subseteq$ is antisymmetric: for every pair of elements x and y in S, $x \subseteq y$ and $y \subseteq x \Rightarrow x = y$.

Similarly, $(Z, \leq)$ is a total order, where Z is the set of negative and non-negative integers.

Lattices

A *lattice* is a partially ordered set in which all nonempty finite subsets have a *least upper bound* and a *greatest lower bound*. If $\leq$ denotes a partial order over S, then the *least upper bound* and the *greatest lower bound* of a subset V of S are, respectively, defined as follows:

- ❑ A least upper bound of V, denoted by *lub*, is an element u in S such that $x \leq u$ for all x in V, and
  For any y in S such that $x \leq y$ for all x in V, it holds that $u \leq y$
- ❑ A greatest lower bound of V, denoted by *gub*, is an element l in S such that
  $l \leq x$ for all x *in* V, and
  for any y in S such that $y \leq x$ for all x in V, it holds that $y \leq l$.

In particular, every two elements of a lattice have a least upper bound and a greatest lower bound. It can be easily shown that the least upper bound and greatest lower bound of any set are always unique: if x and y are both a least upper bound of V, then it follows that $x \leq y$ and $y \leq x$, and since $\leq$ is anti-symmetric, it follows that $x = y$.

Example: Lattices

The poset $(P(S), \subseteq)$, where $P(S)$ is the power set (all possible subsets of a three-element set S), forms a lattice. Every pair of elements x and y in $P(S)$ has a unique least upper bound given by $x \cup y$ and a unique greatest lower bound given by $x \cap y$. Both of these bounds are computed based on the $\subseteq$ relationship. By definition, for every x and y in $P(S)$, if $u = gub(x, y) = x \cup y$, then x and y are necessarily contained in u, and for every other subset of S (say, s) containing both x and y, it implies that u is contained in s. Similarly, if $l = lub(x, y) = x \cap y \Rightarrow l \subseteq x$ and $l \subseteq y$ and for every s in $P(S)$ if $s \subseteq x$ and $s \subseteq y \Rightarrow s \subseteq l = x \cap y$. Figure 4.1 depicts a poset constructed from $S = \{a,b,c\}$.

Lattice-Based Access-Control Models

Predicting the paths of information flow is central to maintaining confidentiality and integrity of data. When information access in a protected system is modeled along a lattice structure, any policies dealing with control of information flow are directly reflected by the lattice. Lattice-based access control is an essential aspect of computing security in environments requiring stringent information-flow controls.

In lattice-based protection systems, information-flow policies bind system objects and subjects to security classes. Flow of information from one object to another is thereafter governed by this binding. Denning [DENN76b] formally defines an information-flow model denoted by FM as

$$FM = < N, P, SC, \oplus, \rightarrow >,$$

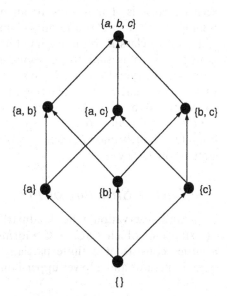

FIGURE 4.1 A depiction of the lattice corresponding to the poset $(P(\{a,b,c\}), \subseteq)$

where $N = \{a,b,...\}$ is a finite set of system resources (objects) that includes users that are, in effect, active objects of the system. $P = \{p,q,...\}$ is the set of system processes running on behalf of users. $SC = \{A,B,...\}$ is a finite set of *security classes* corresponding to disjoint classes of information containers. An example of SC corresponds to the classification:

$SC = \{TOPSECRET, SECRET, CONFIDENTIAL, UNCLASSIFIED\}$.

Each object $o \in N$ is statically or dynamically bound to a security class $O \in SC$. As a result, each process $p \in P$ is also bound to a security class from SC. We adopt the notation of using upper-case characters to indicate a security class while a corresponding lower-case character represents an object bound to that security class.

The class combining binary operator defined within $SC \times SC$ to SC, $\oplus$ is associative—that is,

$$A \oplus B \oplus C = A \oplus (B \oplus C) = (A \oplus B) \oplus C \text{ for all } A, B, C \in SC$$

and is commutative—that is,

$$A \oplus B = B \oplus A \text{ for all } A, B \in SC.$$

Applying the $\oplus$ operator to any pair of security classes A and B yields the security class to which information derived from security classes A and/or B belongs. The security class corresponding to any function that operates on objects from classes A and B is thus $A \oplus B$. By an intuitive extension, the class of a transformation by an n-ary function $f(a_1, ..., a_n)$ is $A_1 \oplus A_2 \oplus ...A_n$.

The flow relationship of $\rightarrow$ is defined over the elements of $SC \times SC$ and is essentially what defines an information-flow policy. The notation $A \rightarrow B$ is used to indicate the fact that information contained in an object whose security class is A may flow to an object that has security class of B. Simply stated $A \rightarrow B$ if and only if information from class A is permitted to flow into class B through some kind of transfer. The information-flow model as such is said to be secure if and only if any execution of a sequence of operations in the system yields a state of information flow that is consistent with a predefined flow policy expressed in terms of the $\rightarrow$ relationship. If a data value resulting from a series of operations denoted by function $f(a_1, ..., a_n)$ flows to an object b that is statically bound to security class B, then $A_1 \oplus A_2 \oplus ...A_n \rightarrow B$ must hold as part of the stated flow policy.

The Lattice Structure of the Information Flow Model

Denning's observation in her landmark paper [DENN76b] established a set of axioms for which $<SC, \rightarrow, \oplus>$ forms a universally bounded lattice. Such a lattice consists of a finite partially ordered set that has a least-upper bound operator and a lower upper-bound operator with respect to the flow relationship →. These axioms or rather assumptions are implied by the intuitive semantics of information flow and are stated as follows:

1. < SC, → > is a partially ordered set.
2. SC is a finite set.
3. SC has a lower bound L with respect to the → relationship.
4. The join operator ⊕ is a least upper bound that is totally defined over SC.

The rationale behind these intuitive assumptions is discussed in the following:

❑ *First axiom of Denning's information flow SC* along with the binary relationship → yields a partially ordered set. This result is evidenced by the nature of information flow.

1. The relationship → is reflexive (i.e., $A → A$ for every $A \in SC$). The source containing information and the receptacle destination of information are the same object. It is evident that information flow is permitted from object a to itself. Otherwise, an inconsistency in the definition of the → relationship arises.
2. The relationship → is transitive (i.e., $A → B$ and $B → C \Rightarrow A → C$). $A →$ B implies that information contained in object a of class A is permitted to flow to object b of class B. Similarly, $B → C$ implies that information contained in object b is permitted to flow to object c in class C. This basically means that one can transfer information from object a to object c through a two-step process and thus information might as well be permitted to directly flow from objects of class A to the objects in class C. Otherwise, an inconsistency arises in the semantics of →.
3. The relationship → is antisymmetric (i.e., $A → B$ and $B → A \Rightarrow A = B$). If information is allowed to flow from all objects of class A to objects in class B and similarly information is allowed to flow from all objects in class B to objects in class A then we are simply dealing with two redundant security classes. Thus, classes A and B are the same.

❑ *Second axiom of Denning's information flow* Assuming that SC is a finite set reflects a property of every practical system. One can always adopt finitely as many security classes as needed. Note that the number of objects associated with each security class can be unbounded.

❑ *Third axiom of Denning's information flow* This assumes the existence of a lower bound class $L \in SC$ which means $L → A$ for all $A \in SC$. First, this property can be assumed without loss of generality. Second, it allows the modeling of publicly available information, which is a useful property in many information systems. Theoretically, this class can be represented by an empty set as the availability of public information in a system does not necessarily hold all the time.

❑ *Fourth axiom of Denning's information flow* To show that the class-joining operator ⊕ combines two security classes into their least upper bound, Denning shows that the following two properties hold for all $A, B, C \in SC$:

1. $A \rightarrow A \oplus B$ and $A \oplus B$.
2. $A \rightarrow C$ and $B \rightarrow C \Rightarrow A \oplus B \rightarrow C$.

Property 1 is intuitively arrived at. If $A \oplus B$ is the security class resulting from information obtained collectively from objects in classes A and B, then information from objects in class A as well as from objects in class B is permitted to directly flow into objects from class $C = A \oplus B$.

Property 2 states that if information can flow individually from classes A and B to class C, then information combined from A and B should also be permitted to flow to C. For clarity, we refer to the example given by Denning [DENN76b]. Consider five objects containing numeric values a, b, c, c_1, and c_2, and corresponding to security classes A, B, C, C_1, and C_2, respectively. Assume that we have $A \rightarrow C$, $B \rightarrow C$, and $C = C_1 = C_2$. Now consider the following transformation affecting values a, b, c, c_1, and c_2:

$$c_1 := a;$$
$$c_2 := b;$$
$$c := c_1 {}^* c_2.$$

Execution of this sequence of instructions assigns to c information derived from a and b, and thus $A \oplus B \rightarrow C$. Generalizing this fact for all types of transformations combining values from objects in classes A, B, and C, it follows that $A \oplus B$ yields the least upper bound of A and B.

The four axioms of Denning's information flow imply the existence of a greatest lower-bound operator over SC, denoted by $\otimes$. This, in turn, implies the existence of a unique upper bound for SC, denoted by H, therefore leading to the structure $<SC, \rightarrow, \oplus, \otimes>$ being a lattice. The greatest lower-bound operator, $\otimes$, is shown by Denning to be defined as

$$A \otimes B = \oplus L(A, B), \text{ where } L(A, B) = \{C \mid C \rightarrow A \text{ and } C \rightarrow B\}.$$

Applying the $\oplus$ operator to $L(A,B)$ yields the greatest lower bound of A and B. As with the least upper-bound operator $\oplus$, the greatest lower-bound operator $\otimes$ is also operable on subsets of SC. It follows that for a subset $S = \{S_1, ..., S_n\} \subseteq SC$, $\otimes S = S_1 \otimes ... \otimes S_n$. Information contained in object a with a security class A can flow into an object whose security class is a member of the subset S if and only if $A \rightarrow S_1 \otimes ... \otimes S_n$.

The totality of the operator $\oplus$ means that it should be defined for every pair of security classes (i.e., $A \oplus B \in SC$ for every $A, B \in SC$). An information-flow policy in which the class-combining operator is not initially totally defined can incrementally add security classes as dictated by the $\oplus$ operator until it is totally defined. In fulfilling this theoretical aspect one might end up defining security classes that are not bound to any system resources.

Implications of the Lattice-Based Flow Model on Access Control

Access-control systems that are based on policies drawn from a lattice structure as in Denning's flow model are automatically *safe*. The safety property of such systems is due to the fact that an information flow taking place from, say, object a to object b cannot occur without the policy stating that $A \rightarrow B$ directly or indirectly through the transitivity of the $\rightarrow$ relationship. Considering that a lattice structure maps directly to a directed graph, the safety property of lattice-based access-control models reduces to deciding whether a directed path exists between any two nodes in the graph. Although both end nodes of this path would generally represent two passive objects, it can also be illustrated using active entities. In this case the origin node of the path represents the security class associated with an active entity such as an end user, a host system, or some programming agent. The end node represents the security class of an object in the system. This determination is a straightforward process. Furthermore, the transitive closure of the graph can be computed, and hence all access decisions become known a-priori. A process p is capable of transferring information from object a to object b if and only if $A \rightarrow P \rightarrow B$.

This flow property is further generalized to $A_1 \oplus \ldots \oplus A_n \rightarrow P \rightarrow B_1 \oplus \ldots \oplus B_m$ to indicate that process p can transfer information from objects $a_1,\ldots,a_n$ to any of the objects $b_1,\ldots,b_m$.

Examples of Lattice-Based Information-Flow Models

A basic lattice information-flow policy is one in which there are only two security classes one is system low denoted by L and the other is system high denoted by H. For instance, all resources with nonconfidential information are bound to L, while those containing confidential information are assigned to class H. In this case, $SC = \{L, H\}$. Besides reflexivity, the policy mainly consists of a single rule $L \rightarrow H$ as shown in Figure 4.2A, where the lattice is derived from a linear ordering of the security classes L and H. A generalization of this policy to a set of n linearly ordered classes is depicted in Figure 4.2B. A richer policy based on partial ordering is illustrated in Figure 4.2C. Figure 4.3 shows a policy derived from a poset of $\{A, B\}$.

Since the Cartesian product $\times$ of two lattices is a lattice, a richer lattice structure of an information-flow policy can be generated from the product of two lattices. An example of such structures is to combine one lattice from a linearly ordered set and one from a partially ordered set. In practice, the linear ordering is drawn from a set of authority levels referred to as *security levels*. An instance of such a linear ordering consists of

$SC = \{unclassified, confidential, secret, TopSecret\}$. The partial ordering is derived from the poset of a *set* of properties known as *categories*.

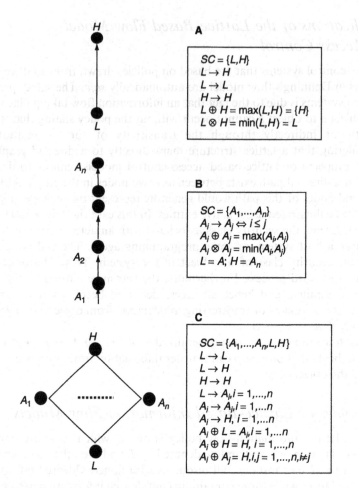

A

$SC = \{L,H\}$
$L \rightarrow H$
$L \rightarrow L$
$H \rightarrow H$
$L \oplus H = \max(L,H) = \{H\}$
$L \otimes H = \min(L,H) = L$

B

$SC = \{A_1,...,A_n\}$
$A_i \rightarrow A_j \Leftrightarrow i \leq j$
$A_i \oplus A_j = \max(A_i,A_j)$
$A_i \otimes A_j = \min(A_i,A_j)$
$L = A; H = A_n$

C

$SC = \{A_1,...,A_n,L,H\}$
$L \rightarrow L$
$L \rightarrow H$
$H \rightarrow H$
$L \rightarrow A_i, i = 1,...,n$
$A_i \rightarrow A_i, i = 1,...n$
$A_i \rightarrow H, i = 1,...n$
$A_i \oplus L = A_i, i = 1,...n$
$A_i \oplus H = H, i = 1,...,n$
$A_i \oplus A_j = H, i,j = 1,...,n, i \neq j$

FIGURE 4.2 Basic examples of lattice-based information flow policies

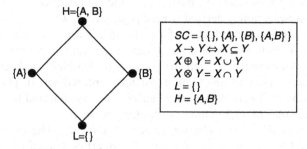

$SC = \{\{\}, \{A\}, \{B\}, \{A,B\}\}$
$X \rightarrow Y \Leftrightarrow X \subseteq Y$
$X \oplus Y = X \cup Y$
$X \otimes Y = X \cap Y$
$L = \{\}$
$H = \{A,B\}$

FIGURE 4.3 A simple lattice-based policy derived from poset of $\{A,B\}$

An example of categories is the set of departments of an organization in which a resource can be accessible. Security labels assigned to active system entities such as users and processes are said to be bound to security *clearances* and system resources are assigned security *labels*.

The derivation of a lattice structure for an information-flow model can be extended to a Cartesian product of n lattices. The resulting flow relationship $\rightarrow$ is determined by $\rightarrow \equiv \wedge \rightarrow i, i = 1,...n$.

This means the flow relationship is computed as a logical AND over the flows in all of the participating lattices. The flow relationship therefore must hold in each of the lattices for it to hold in the lattice represented by their Cartesian product. For instance, when combining a linear ordering of security levels with a partial ordering as represented by the poset, the flow relationship is expressed as

$$A \geq B \Leftrightarrow B \rightarrow A, (B \rightarrow A) \Leftrightarrow A_{level} \geq B_{level} \text{ and } A_{categories} \supseteq B_{categories}.$$

The Bell-LaPadula Flow Model

Bell and Lapadula [BELL75, MCLE88] developed and formalized the concept of mandatory-access models, which falls in line with the information-flow model of Denning. It is worth noting that the model of Bell-Lapadula (BLP) preceded Denning's work on the information-flow model. The mandatory access-control policy as defined in BLP consists of assigning *security labels* (*classes*) to system subjects and objects. Labels assigned to objects are dubbed as *security classifications,* while those assigned to subjects are referred to as *security clearances.* BLP is stated in terms of two rules: the *simple security policy* and the **-property* (read as star property), both of which are mainly concerned with the flow of confidential information:

❏ Simple security rule This is also known as the *read-down* property. It states that information can be read only downward in the lattice structure representing the MAC policy. Subject s can read object o only if $S \geq O$ where S is the security label (class in Denning's formalism) of subject s, while O is the security label of object o. The security clearance of a subject has to dominate the security classification of an object so it can be read.

❏ **-property* This rule is also known as the *write-up* policy. It states that subject s can write object o only if $O \geq S$. This prevents leaking confidential information in that a subject can write only objects whose security classifications dominate the security clearance of the subject. Writing objects takes place in an upward fashion within the lattice structure of the BLP policy, while reading is performed downward, as illustrated in Figure 4.4.

As has been indicated the flow model in BLP is motivated by the confidentiality of information. Consequently, the ability to read objects upward in

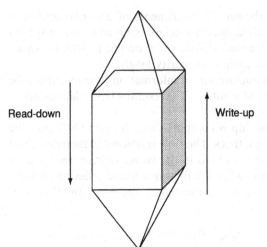

FIGURE 4.4 Information-flow direction in the BLP model as abstracted by a lattice structure

the lattice structure is not permitted. Similarly, the ability to write objects downward in the lattice structure is prohibited as both of these operations lead to transferring confidential information from higher-level entities to those having access to only lower-level objects.

The write-up property of BLP alone is not sufficient for preventing a subject from corrupting information at levels dominating those of the subject. Confidential information can be corrupted by subjects having lower security labels even when the read-down property prevents reading the information. To address this integrity problem, MAC policies have adopted a modified *-property that allows subject s to write object o only if the subject and the object are both bound to the same security class (i.e., $S = O$).

The integrity issue associated with the write-up property can in fact be addressed by the second component of the BLP model, which enforces a discretionary policy of resource-access control. In BLP the dominance relationship as stated by the MAC policy is augmented with a discretionary-access policy. An access decision therefore depends on both policies, MAC and DAC, being enforced at the same time. With this approach, corruption of confidential information by processes at lower security classes is prevented by specifically exposing resources that are intended to be receptacles of information from lower processes and disallowing access to the ones that contain confidential information through proper DAC policies. Similarly, the read-down property may also be controlled in this manner, although generally enforcing DAC controls around the write-up property is the main concern of many MAC policies.

The Biba Model

As has been noted, the goal of the BLP model is to prevent downgrading confidential information. The Biba model, on the other hand, is concerned with the integrity of information [BIBA77]. This model follows along the same ideas of the BLP model and as such does not present a fundamental departure from the concepts introduced by BLP. The underlying concept in Biba is that security classes are organized along a lattice structure in which each class corresponds to some integrity level with the highest integrity at the top of the structure and the lowest at the bottom. Information is allowed to flow from high-integrity objects to low-integrity objects only. In a similar way to BLP, Biba states its information flow policy using two rules: the *simple-integrity property* and the *integrity *-property*:

- ❏ *Simple-integrity property* This property states that subject s can read object o only if the security class of o dominates that of s (i.e., $O \geq S$).
- ❏ *Integrity *-property* This property states that subject s can write object o only if the security class of s dominates that of o (i.e., $S \geq O$).

Recall that a security class in Biba corresponds to an integrity label. A curious aspect of the Biba properties is that they are duals of their counterpart in BLP. For instance, while the policy in BLP is about read-down of information, the simple-integrity property of Biba states a read-up of information. Similarly, the integrity *-property of Biba states a write-down type of information flow as opposed to the write-up of the *-property in BLP.

Comparing Information Flow in BLP and Biba Models

The direction in which information flows in the BLP and the Biba models is driven by the nature of protections sought in each model. The BLP is motivated by confidentiality of information, and hence information in objects at higher levels is not allowed for read access by lower-level processes. Similarly, information at lower levels is allowed to flow to objects from higher security classes in the lattice structure. The write-up property of BLP represents an interesting aspect of information flow. It can be used to upgrade the classification of information from the bottom of the lattice all the way to its top as illustrated in Figure 4.5A. Once this information is copied to higher-level objects, there is no rule that enforces its deletion from lower-level objects where the information originates so that it can no longer be read by processes at those levels. Recall that the BLP as well as the Biba properties allow a process to simultaneously read and write objects at the same level in the lattice.

A process p_1 as depicted in Figure 4.5A reads object o_1 situated at its immediate lower level, writes it to object o_2 at the same level as p_1, then writes it to object o_3 located immediately above the level of p_1. Similarly, p_1 may also read o_1 and write it directly to o_3. Thus the flow of information between a lower level and any higher level may be achieved through a sequence of operations or simply in by a single sequence of read and write operations.

The direction of information flow in the Biba model is the opposite of that in the BLP model. As illustrated in Figure 4.5B information is allowed to flow from the top of the lattice all the way to its bottom in accordance with

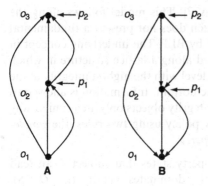

FIGURE 4.5 Scenarios of information flow in the BLP and the Biba models

the Biba properties. Although this flow does not imply modifying the security classes of objects involved, it somehow represents a downgrade of information as it yields a transfer of information from higher to lower security classes.

A curious reader may ask the question of why we need to enforce the read-up property in the Biba model as it does not seem to interfere with the integrity goal of Biba. Let us assume that in addition to the read-up capability, processes are also able to read-down objects in the lattice structure of a Biba integrity policy. As shown in Figure 4.6, process p_1 reads down an object o and writes it to object o_1 located at the same security label as p_1 (read and write at the same level are permissible due to the equality in the dominance relationship $\geq$). Now an upper level process p_2 reads down o_1 and writes it to object o_2 at the same level as that of p_2. Performing these steps in a bottom-up fashion along the lattice structure results in the flow of information upward, therefore conflicting with the intent of the Biba model.

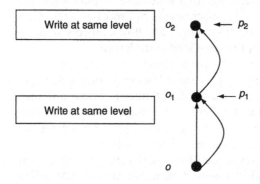

FIGURE 4.6 The need for read-up only in the Biba integrity model

Implementation Considerations for the BLP and the Biba Models

One implementation aspect that is worthy of mention for the BLP and the Biba models is the need to provide safety of concurrency. At any level in the BLP or the Biba policy lattice, objects have to be protected from concurrent writes by processes of that level. In the BLP model, objects situated at level l need to be further protected against concurrent writes by processes at levels $\leq l$ (Figure 4.7A).

It is also desirable to prevent against a simultaneous read and write of the same object. In the Biba model, objects situated at level l should be protected against concurrent writes by processes at levels $\geq l$ as illustrated in Figure 4.7B. Like in the BLP case, it is also desirable to prevent against simultaneous read and write of the same object.

Combining the BLP and the Biba Models

Protected entities of a computing system (resources, subjects, and programming agents or processes) can be subjected simultaneously to the BLP and Biba policies. We distinguish two ways in which such coexistence may take shape. In the first scenario we draw the security classes for the combined confidentiality and integrity lattices from a single set SC in which every security

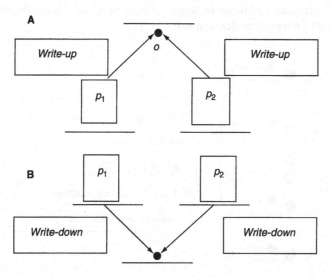

FIGURE 4.7 Synchronization requirement for concurrent reads and writes in the BLP and Biba models

class applies as a confidentiality and an integrity label simultaneously. The write-up in BLP requires the security class of the writing subject to be dominated by that of the receptacle object, while the write-up property of Biba requires the opposite. Hence writing an object in this scenario is confined to processes that are all at the same level as that of the object to be written. This amounts to the trivial isolationist policy where no information flows across security levels of a lattice. From the standpoint of information flow analysis, this model is equivalent to using a single security class. The isolated classes scenario is depicted in Figure 4.8.

The second and a more useful scenario of combining the BLP and the Biba models results from adopting independent confidentiality and integrity classes as shown by Sandhu [SAND93]. A composite model as such is the product of two lattices, which is in turn a lattice. Let $C = \{c_1,...,c_n\}$ be a lattice of confidentiality corresponding to the BLP model, and let $I = \{i_1,...,i_m\}$ be a lattice of integrity representing a policy based on the Biba model. Let α be a function that maps a system entity (subject or object) onto its confidentiality class (label), and let β be the function that maps an entity onto its integrity class. The composite BLP and Biba lattice is defined by the following constraints:

- Subject s can read object o only if $\alpha(s) \geq \alpha(o)$ and $\beta(s) \leq \beta(o)$.
- Subject s can write object o only if $\alpha(s) \leq \alpha(o)$ and $\beta(s) \leq \beta(o)$.

As has been noted, the composite model is the product of two lattices which reduces to one lattice. Figure 4.9 illustrates an instance of this lattice for $C = \{\alpha_L, \alpha_H\}$ with $\alpha_H \geq \alpha_L$ and $I = \{\beta_L, \beta_H\}$ with $\beta_H \geq \beta_L$, where L and H denote system Low and High, respectively. Note that while information in the BLP and Biba models flows in opposite directions, in the combined lattice (Figure 4.9) information flows upward.

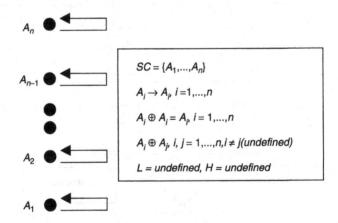

$$SC = \{A_1,...,A_n\}$$

$$A_i \rightarrow A_p\ i = 1,...,n$$

$$A_i \oplus A_i = A_p\ i = 1,...,n$$

$$A_i \oplus A_j,\ i, j = 1,...,n, i \neq j (undefined)$$

$$L = undefined,\ H = undefined$$

FIGURE 4.8 Combining BLP and the Biba models: The case of security classes that are used for both confidentiality and integrity

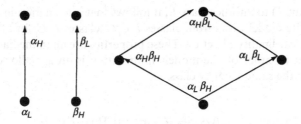

FIGURE 4.9 An example of combining BLP and the Biba models in the case of independent confidentiality and integrity classes

Figure 4.10 illustrates an access-control matrix representing the access policy of the product lattice of Figure 4.9. Rows of this matrix represent subjects, and the columns correspond to resources. Each row of the table specifies exactly the type of access a subject with a given label can have to a resource on the column. For example, a subject with label $\alpha_H \beta_H$ can read (r) information contained in resources with label $\alpha_L \beta_H$, and write (w) objects with labels $\alpha_H \beta_L$ but cannot (ϕ) read or write resources with labels $\alpha_L \beta_L$. The diagonal of this matrix represents access modes that subjects can have to the resources that are associated with the same levels as those of the subjects. Read and write accesses are thus shown along the diagonal.

One characterizing aspect of the composite BLP and Biba model is the fact that if information in the confidentiality-based model flows from one class (say, C_i) to another class C_j, then information in the composite model flows from classes $C_i I_k$ to classes $C_j I_k$ for all $k = 1,...,m$ (m being the cardinality of set I). Similarly, if information separately in the integrity model flows from

	$\alpha_L \beta_L$	$\alpha_L \beta_H$	$\alpha_H \beta_L$	$\alpha_H \beta_H$
$\alpha_L \beta_L$	rw	r	w	ϕ
$\alpha_L \beta_H$	w	rw	w	w
$\alpha_H \beta_L$	r	r	rw	r
$\alpha_H \beta_H$	ϕ	r	w	rw

FIGURE 4.10 An access-control table corresponding to the subjects and objects of the example of Figure 4.9

one class (say, I_j) to another class I_k, it follows that information in the resulting composite model flows from classes $I_j\ C_i$ to classes $I_k\ C_i$ for all $i = 1,...,n$ (n being the cardinality of set C). These properties are an immediate result of the fact that in either of the models information is always allowed to flow from and to the same security class.

On the Mandatory-Access-Control Paradigm

As has been noted, the development of the mandatory-access-control model was motivated mainly by the control policies found in military environments, specifically, in the United States Department of Defense (DoD). Within the DoD an information security policy assigns each system entity a linearly ordered classification level L and a set of categories C. The categories generally form a partial ordering along the poset relationship. The hierarchy of entities and resources as imposed by military policies is certainly amenable to the adoption of mandatory-access controls. In the commercial world, however, this is not generally the case, even when the categories are designed to reflect the organizational structure of an enterprise.

The authoritative policies of mandatory controls are inflexible and not amenable to sharing resources as warranted by the needs for information sharing. MAC policies are static in nature. They cannot be changed dynamically and without the intervention of an administrative authority whose immediate availability can be an issue. Resources of the same security class are undistinguishable with respect to the access controls applied at their level. For instance, all of the resources assigned the same confidentiality label in the BLP model can be read by every subject with a security label that dominates those resources. MAC policies do not support the concept of resource ownership and hence the inability to discern access rights to the resource in a discretionary fashion. Identification of resource ownership is a fundamental aspect of building access-control systems in modern commercial operating environments. With all these issues, Lipner [LIPN82] addressed optimum ways in which mandatory controls can be applied in the commercial nonmilitary world. He gave a detailed example in which confidentiality and integrity labels are simultaneously used as in the composite BLP and Biba models to achieve commercial uses.

Finally, it is worth noting that despite of the fact that BLP and Biba models are based on the confidentiality and integrity of information, respectively, they can be applied to any other types of information access. The semantics of access rights in the lattice-based models therefore can take various forms.

The Chinese-Wall Policy

The Chinese-wall policy (CWP) was developed by Brewer and Nash [BREW89] as an instance of lattice-based security models with applications in the commercial world. The intent of CWP is to enforce a conflict of interest policy in which a single user is prevented from having to simultaneously access information that represents a conflict of interest. Specifically, CWP was formulated to address a situation in which a financial institution provides market analysis as part of its consulting services to other businesses. Each analyst must not be able to advise a particular institution when he or she has knowledge of business information about a competitor of that institution. The analyst, however, is capable of advising any companies that are not in competition with each other. Thus, every subject that is affiliated with this consulting service must be confined to accessing information on businesses that are not competing with one another. For example, information about bank B should not be accessible to a subject that already has access to information about bank A. Unlike in BLP, where access to information is based on a static relationships between subjects and objects, in CWP access is constrained by what information the subject already has access to.

The elements of CWP are illustrated in Figure 4.11. A company maintains information about other businesses that is hierarchically divided along a set of conflict of interest classes. Within each class the company groups all information about a particular business in a dataset. In turn, each dataset consists of a number of individual objects containing data related to that business.

In a way similar to the BLP model, CWP is stated in terms of its own formulation of the simple security and the *-Property rules. It is also worth noting that Sandhu developed a scheme in which he shows how CWP is mapped to a lattice-based access-control model [SAND92a, SAND93].

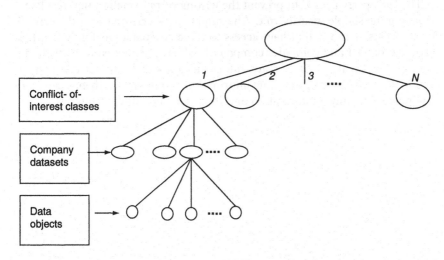

FIGURE 4.11 Dividing information along a Chinese-wall policy

Simple Security

This represents the basis of the CWP enforcing the fact that a user is allowed only access to information that is not in conflict with any information already accessible to that user. Access by a subject to an object is therefore granted only if

- ❑ The object is in the same company dataset that is already accessed by that subject (i.e., the object is within the wall), or
- ❑ The object belongs to an entirely different conflict of interest class.

As a result, Brewer and Nash establish the following theorems:

Theorem 1: Once a subject has accessed an object the only other objects accessible by that subject reside within the same company dataset or within a different conflict of interest class.

Theorem 2: A subject can at most have access to one company dataset in each conflict of interest.

Theorem 3: If for some conflict-of-interest class X there are X_Y company datasets, then the minimum number of subjects that will allow every object to be accessed by at least one subject is X_Y.

*-Property

This rule states that write access is permitted only if

- ❑ Access is permitted by the simple security rule, and
- ❑ Any object that is in a different company dataset with respect to the one for which write access is requested cannot be read.

The *-Property is used to prevent the writing of information that results in violating the simple security rule. An example of such scenario is the case of two subjects s_1 and s_2 that have access to three companies as follows: s_1 has access to bank 1 and computer company 1, while s_2 has access to bank 1 and computer company 2. If s_1 reads information about computer company 1 and writes it to objects containing information about bank-1, then s_2 can read computer company 1 information and thus yield a conflict of interest.

Chapter 5

Discretionary-Access Control and the Access-Matrix Model

Introduction

Contrary to the relatively static state implied by a lattice-based security model, *discretionary-access-control* (DAC) *systems* are characterized by unbounded protection states. It is for this reason that in many ways modeling access-control systems has historically been understood to implicitly relate to DAC. Although the access-matrix model, the subject of this chapter, applies to all security policies including those that are mandatory, it lends itself well to discretionary policies. The matrix model is concerned with the study of access control directly over the entities involved in an access policy—namely, subjects and objects. It reflects the access relationships that exist between these two at any point in time. Access relationships that are based on resource ownership and enable individual control over propagating access permissions are at the core of DAC systems.

We review the concepts defining the access-matrix model followed by a discussion of the corresponding implementation considerations. We reflect on the history of this access model by delving into the work of Harrison, Ruzzo, and Ullman. Subsequently, we introduce the reader to the foundation of safety in protection systems and describe relating results in detail.

Defining the Access-Matrix Model

The pioneering work of Lampson [LAMP71] followed by that of Harrison, Ruzzo, and Ullman (HRU) [HARR76, HARR78] has led to a generalized form of access-control modeling known as the access-matrix model. Three basic abstractions on which this model is built are

- ❑ Subjects,
- ❑ Objects (resources), and
- ❑ Access rights.

The two-dimensional matrix modeling a protection state has a row for every subject, an active entity, and a column for every object. Subjects form a subset of the objects. This leads to modeling access relationships that may exist among subjects as well as between subjects and objects. Furthermore, subjects may represent programming agents. Thus not all objects are passive resources. An example of such active resources is a stored procedure that in itself is a controlled shareable resource. When the procedure executes, it may assume an identity of its own or one corresponding to the subject that initiated it. Passive resources are those that are merely information containers, sometimes referred to as *data receptacles*.

Denoting A for an access matrix, S for the set of subjects, O for the set of objects available to a computing system ($S \subset O$), and R for the set of access rights defined by a particular policy, the value of a cell $A[s, o]$ represents the set of permissions $R_{so} \subset R$, confining the type of access subject s has to object o. An entire row s in the matrix is referred to as the *capability* of subject s. Similarly, a column corresponding to object o is called an *access-control list* (ACL) for that object. A snapshot of the access matrix at any point in time represents a protection state. The lifecycle of an access matrix follows that of a finite state machine model. Each snapshot of the matrix corresponds to a state variable, and the transition functions of the state machine correspond to the *processes* (also referred to as *commands*) of creating new subjects or objects, destroying them, as well as granting and revoking access rights. These processes or commands transform the matrix from one protection state to another. The transformations are driven by what is known as an *authorization scheme* or an *authorization policy*. Figure 5.1 shows an example of an access matrix that models a population of three subjects and four objects, all of which are files (a total of seven objects including the three subjects).

Implementation Considerations for the Access Matrix

The large number of resources that may potentially be available within a computing system may yield sparse access matrices. As a result, most

	File 1	File 2	File 3	File 4	Subject 1	Subject 2	Subject 3
Subject 1	Read, Write	Execute	——	Read	——	——	——
Subject 2	——	——	Read, Write, Execute	——	——	——	——
Subject 3	Append	——	Execute	Read, Write	——	——	——

FIGURE 5.1 Example of an access-matrix modeling access of three subjects to seven objects

implementations of the access matrix represent only the entries of the matrix that are relevant. For example, an entry corresponding to subject *s* that has no access to object *o* is omitted. The access matrix can be viewed in two different ways—from the resources and from the subjects perspectives.

Resource View of the Access Matrix: Access-Control Lists

Access-control lists (ACLs) are commonly used in implementing an access matrix. An ACL is a data structure that associates a resource identifier such as a file name with the list of subjects that have access to it. Each subject in the list is qualified by the access rights available to it. An ACL corresponds to a column of the access matrix with the empty entries removed. ACLs are generally maintained by the respective resource managers, although they can also be managed by a dedicated access-control service independently from the context of the resource. One of the advantages of using ACLs is the ease by which all the subjects having access to a particular resource can be determined. Revoking or updating access for a user is also an easy operation. Deleting an account or enumerating the list of resources accessible by a particular subject, however, require visiting all of the managed ACLs. ACLs provide one other advantage, and that is confining the scope of the semantics associated with the access permissions within the limits of the underlying resource manager or the access-control service that is acting as the reference monitor that mediates access to the resource. Such a local semantics scope prevents ambiguity and collision with similar permissions that have different semantics. However, the ability of the ACLs mechanism for scaling to a fine-grain level of resources may be challenging. Gladney [GLAD97] addresses this issue by aggregating subjects and objects into equivalence sets that can reduce the size of each ACL. These equivalence sets are known in access control as user groups and resource classes. Figure 5.2 illustrates the ACLs corresponding to the access matrix of Figure 5.1.

Subject View of the Access Matrix: Capabilities

Capabilities correspond to the rows of an access matrix. They represent a dual technique for ACLs. A subject's capability enumerates the list of resources accessible to the subject. Each entry identifies an object along with the set of access rights conferred on the subject. The main advantage of this mechanism is the ease by which one can determine all the resources accessible to a particular user (a simple traversal of the capability list). To determine all subjects that have access to a particular resource, or remove a resource, however, requires traversing all the capabilities. Capability lists combined with secure establishment of a networkwide security context are ideal for distributed computing. The semantics of permissions carried in a capability, however, will have to be uniquely defined over the distributed environment where they are used so that ambiguity can be prevented. Figure 5.3 depicts the capabilities associated with the access matrix in Figure 5.1.

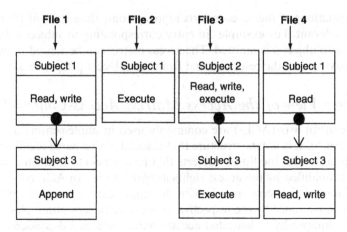

FIGURE 5.2 ACLs of the access matrix in Figure 5.1

Definitions from the HRU Access-Matrix Model

HRU [HARR76] characterizes the protection state of an access matrix model by the triple (S, O, A), where

❑ S is the set of subjects representing all active entities in a computing system (e.g., a user, a host system, or an application program).

❑ O is the set of objects (resources available to active entities of the system) (e.g., a file, a print server). S is a subset of O $(S \subset O)$. A system's monitoring program, for instance, can be a resource that is both an object and a subject. An application as such is a controlled resource in that its configuration and its execution may be granted to a particular system administrator only. While that same program is executing, it becomes an active entity of its own and thus may assume the identity and the privileges of an authorized system agent.

❑ A is an access matrix representing the protection state. Rows of the matrix correspond to subjects, while the columns correspond to objects. $A[s, o]$ contains the access rights that subject s is entitled to have for object o. Examples of access rights are read (r), write (w), execute (e), and *own*.

It is worth noting that in many cases the existing literature does not explicitly characterize a protection state with the applicable set of rights. Because the semantics of access rights have a direct impact on the propagation of rights in an access-matrix model, it is useful to add another dimension to the state of an access-matrix model—that of access rights. As such, we consider an access state to be defined as (S, O, R, A), where R is the set of permissions that are applicable to the elements of A. In what follows, however, we stick to the shorter notation of (S, O, A) instead.

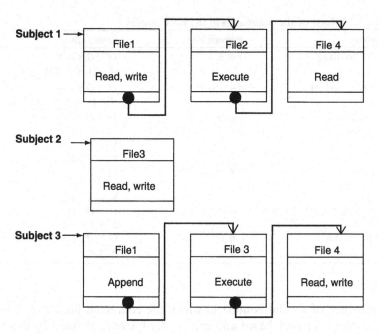

FIGURE 5.3 Capability lists of the access matrix in Figure 5.1

State Transitions in the HRU Access-Matrix Model

State transitions of the access-matrix model are the side effect of control commands that transform the matrix. Primitive operations affecting the states of an access matrix in the HRU model are defined as follows:

- Enter r into $A[s, o]$
- Delete r from $A[s, o]$
- Create subject s
- Create object o
- Delete subject s
- Destroy subject s
- Destroy object o

The side effects of these operations on an access matrix are summarized in Table 5.1.

Evidently the use of the primitive operations described in Table 5.1 needs to be controlled so that transforming the access matrix from one state to another is accomplished according to an authorization scheme. Entities can transform the matrix only if authorized by the policy. In practice, higher-level commands that encapsulate one or more primitive commands are provided for users to transform the access matrix. These complex commands are generally made of a precondition and a body. The precondition tests for

TABLE 5.1 Effects of the commands in the HRU model

Operation	Precondition	Postcondition
Enter r into $A[s,o]$	$r \in R$	$O' = O, S' = S$ $A' = [s, o] = A [s, o] \cup \{r\}$
Delete r from $A[s,o]$	$r \in A[s,o]$	$O' = O, S' = S$ $A' = [s, o] = A [s, o] - \{r\}$
Create subject s	$s \notin O$	$O' = O \cup \{s\}$ $S' = S \cup \{s\}$ $\forall_O \in O', A'[s,o] = \phi$ $\forall_S \in S', A[s,s] = \phi$
Create object o	$o \notin O$	$O' = O \cup \{o\}$ $S' = S$ $\forall_S \in S', A'[s,o] = \phi$
Destroy subject s	$s \in O$	$O' = O - \{s\}$ $S' = S - \{o\}$
Destroy object o	$o \in O$	$O' = O - \{o\}$ $S' = S$

the presence of a valid context in which the command body can execute. This context is policy based and can be, for instance, defined by the presence of certain rights in certain entries of the access matrix. One might therefore abstract the general form of a transformation command α as follows:

```
command α(X₁,X₂,..., Xₖ) {
if (condition)
then
      op₁;
      op₂;
      ...;
      opₙ
}
```

where X_i, $i = 1,...,k$ represent the formal parameters of the command that are drawn from the set of rights R and the set of objects O. The command syntax above is not limited to a single conditional flow of execution. Generally, it may contain a sequence of such conditional flows.

Example: create, confer and remove commands

Consider a protection system with a set of access rights
$R = \{read, write, append, execute\}$
and a set of commands $C = \{create_{file}, confer_r, remove_r\}$ where $confer_r$ allows subject s_1 to transfer right $r \in R$ to subject s_2; $s_1, s_2 \in S$, while $remove_r$ allows a subject to undue the action of the $confer_r$ command.

```
command create_file (subject, file) {
    create object file;
    enter own into A[subject, file];0
    enter read into A[subject, file];
    enter write into A[subject, file];
    enter execute into A[subject, file];
}

command confer_r (subject_1, subject_2, r, file) {
    if own in A[subject_1, file]
    then enter r into A[subject_2, file];
}

command remove_r (subject_1, subject_2, r, file) {
    if own in A[subject_1, file] and
            r in A[subject_2, file]
    then delete r from A[subject_2, file];
}
```

Modern access-control systems automatically retrieve the identity of the subject performing any of the above commands from the operating environment where an established security context is maintained. From the perspective of the subject that is performing the commands in this example, the formal parameters are

- ❑ $create_{file}$ (file)
- ❑ $confer_r$ (subject, r, file)
- ❑ $remove_r$ (subject, r, file)

Example: command effects

We now observe the effect of the following sequence of commands on an initial configuration of a protection system (S, O, A), where $S = O = \{s_1, s_2\}$.

$$create_{file} \ (s_1, \text{data});$$

$$confer_{read} \ (s_1, s_2, \text{data});$$

$$confer_{append} \ (s_1, s_2, \text{data});$$

We assume that the initial access matrix is empty. Figure 5.4 illustrates the states of the access matrix as the commands are being executed.

The Safety Problem of the Access-Matrix Model

The cumulative effects from transforming an access matrix are unbounded. Consider the $confer_{grant}$ command, an instance of $confer_r$ which discerns the permission to transfer access rights to other subjects via the $transfer_r$ command, which looks like

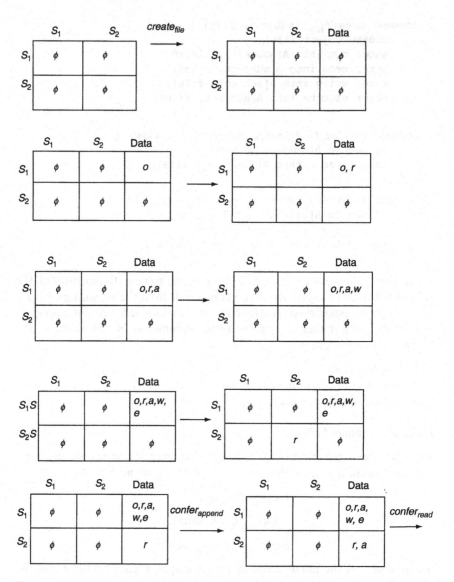

FIGURE 5.4 Snapshots of the access matrix transformed by the commands of the second example above

```
command transfer_r (subject_1, subject_2, r, file) {
    if grant in A[subject_1, file]
    then enter r into A[subject_2, file];
}
```

Applying random sequences of the *confer*$_{grant}$ and the *transfer*$_r$ commands along with others as permitted by the protection system may lead over a period of time to unwarranted effects. As a result, access to resources may take place without the concurrence of the owners. We now review a set of definitions as a prelude to discussing the safety problem that is characteristic of the access-matrix model and the DAC paradigm in general.

Definition 5.1: Given a protection system, we say command α leaks access right r from configuration $Q = (S,O,A)$ if the execution of α on Q results in a configuration Q' in which right r is entered into a cell of the access matrix A, which did not previously contain r. In this case, configuration Q' is said to be reachable from configuration Q through command α. We denote this by

❏ $Q \mapsto^{\alpha} Q'$

This definition is captured in Table 5.2.

Definition 5.2: A protection system is said to be unsafe or leaks right r with respect to an initial configuration Q_0 if

❏   There is a configuration Q that results from applying a series of transformations beginning with the initial configuration Q_0 (i.e., Q is reachable from Q_0), and
❏   A command α such that α leaks r from Q.

Definition 5.3: An initial configuration Q_0 of a protection system is said to be safe for a generic right r if Q_0 is not unsafe for r (i.e., Q_0 does not leak right r).

Definition 5.4: A security policy is the set of rules that govern the authorized states of a protection system. These rules should not translate into undesired leaks of rights. For instance, r access by subject s to object o in the Bell-LaPadula model is subject to the policy: $r \in A[s,o] \Leftrightarrow level(s) \geq level(o)$.

Definition 5.5: Let S be the set of all protection states, let P be the set of all authorized protection states, and let R be the set of all states reachable from some initial state:

❏   A system is said to be secure if $R \subseteq P$.
❏   A system is precise if $R = P$.
❏   A system is insecure if $\neg(R \subseteq P)$.

Figure 5.5 illustrates these definitions.

TABLE 5.2 Leaking an access right from a configuration of a protection system

Command	Precondition	Postcondition
$\alpha(X_1,...,X_k)$	$Q = (S,O,A)$ and for some $r \in R$ and $s \in O$, and $o \in O$, $r \notin A[s,o]$	$Q' = (S', O',A')$ $r \in A'[s,o]$

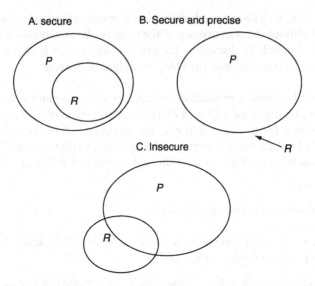

FIGURE 5.5 Illustration of secure, precise, and insecure systems, P being the set of authorized states and R the set of reachable states

Definition 5.6: A protection system is said to be mono-operational if the body of each command that it supports consists of a single primitive operation. For example a system containing commands $confer_r$, $remove_r$, and $transfer_r$ only is mono-operational. Command $create_{file}$ does not yield a mono-operational protection system. Note that in a mono-operational system the precondition part of each command can be arbitrarily complex.

Definition 5.7: A protection system is mono-conditional if the precondition part of each supported command has only one term. This implies that the test portion of the command involves the presence of a single right in a particular entry of the access matrix. Commands $confer_r$ and $transfer_r$ yield a mono-conditional protection system, while command $remove_r$ does not.

We are now ready to state the first theoretical result of Harrison, Ruzzo, and Ullman on the safety of protection systems:

Theorem 5.1: *There is an algorithm that decides whether a given mono-operational protection system as represented by an initial configuration is safe for a given generic right r.*

Sketch of proof: We summarize the proof of this theorem based on HRU [HARR76]. The goal is to establish that the length of the shortest leaky path of transformations for a given initial protection state is bounded. The assumption is that the protection system is mono-operational and hence that each supported command identifies in a one-to-one mapping with its corresponding primitive operation.

Let $Q_i = (S_i, O_i, A_i)$, and suppose that

$$Q_0 \mapsto^{c1} Q_1 \mapsto^{c2} \ldots Q_{m-1} \mapsto^{cm} Q_m \tag{5.1}$$

is a minimal length of a transformation path in which the reachable configuration Q_m leaks right r. The authors of the theorem use the technique of proof by contradiction in which the absurdity arrived at contradicts with the assumption that (5.1) is minimal. Now it is claimed that C_i, $2 \le i \le m$ is an enter command, and C_1 is either an enter or a create subject command. In other words the claim is that the sequence (5.1) contains at most one create subject command which can only be the first command. Suppose that this is not the case, and let C_n be the last nonenter command in (5.1). The proof proceeds by distinguishing three cases, each of which forms a leaky sequence that is shorter than (5.1):

❑ if C_n is a delete or a destroy command (either a right or an object is removed from the underlying protection state), then we can form a shorter leaky sequence (5.1') by simply removing command C_n from (5.1) as follows:

$$Q_0 \mapsto^{c1} Q_1 \mapsto^{c2} \ldots Q_{n-1} \mapsto^{c'_{n+1}} Q_{n-1} \mapsto \ldots Q'_{m-1} \mapsto^{c'_m} Q'_m \tag{5.1'}$$

where $C'_i = C_i$ and $Q'_i = Q_i$ augmented with the right, the subject or the object that C_n deletes or destroys. In other words, deleting a right or destroying a subject or an object from a configuration along the sequence (5.1) does not affect reaching configuration Q_m in which generic right r is leaked. One thing to note here is the fact that commands C_i, $n + 1 \le i \le m$ have no distinction between configurations Q_i and Q'_i. Therefore, C_n cannot be a delete or a destroy command since that contradicts the basic assumption that sequence (5.1) is the shortest leaky path for right r (length of (5.1') = length of (5.1) – 1 = $m - 1$).

❑ Now suppose that C_n is a create subject or object command. Because command α leaks r from configuration Q_m, therefore it must be an enter command. Since C_i, $i = n + 1,...,m$ are all enter commands by assumption, it follows that when C_n is a create object command that $|S_{n-1}| \ge 1$, where $|S_{n-1}|$ is the total number of subjects in configuration Q_{n-1}. Otherwise, command α that leaks right r in the sequence (5.1) will have no subject on which to operate. Let $s \in S_{n-1}$, and let o be the name of the object created by C_n. Sequence (5.1') now can be formed by removing command C_n from sequence (5.1) and using $C'_i = C_i$, $i = n + 1,...,m$, with s replacing all occurrences of o in C_i, and $Q'_i = Q_i$. This construction leads to the fact that any precondition of command C_i that is satisfied by o, the corresponding condition in C'_i is satisfied by s as well (due to the substitution for o by s). In particular, the preconditions in command α are satisfied by the actual parameters in which s replaces all occurrences of o. As a result, α leaks right r from configuration $Q'_i = Q_i$. Thus a contradiction of the fact that (5.1) is a minimal sequence. C_n, therefore, cannot be a create object command. If C_n is a create subject command then if $|S_{n-1}| \neq 0$ we generate a shorter leaky sequence from (5.1) by simply removing C_n and then substituting for the subject that C_n creates with an existing subject.

❏ The scenario considered in this case is the same as in the previous one but with $|S_{n-1}| = 0$. No subjects are created prior to configuration Q_n, and therefore C_n must be a create subject command resulting in $S_n = \{s\}$ and $n \geq 2$ due to the assumption. The sequence (5.1') can now be constructed by skipping commands preceding C_n. In doing so, we substitute s for any object o_j created by the skipped commands. All preconditions of commands C'_i satisfied by o_j will thus remain satisfied by s and in particular those contained in command α. Hence generic right r can be leaked in configuration Q'_m. The following is an instance of such a sequence.

$$Q_0 \mapsto^{c_n} Q'_n \mapsto^{c'_{m+1}} Q_{n+1} \mapsto \ \dots \ \mapsto Q'_{m-1} \mapsto^{c'_m} Q'_m \qquad (5.2)$$

In (5.2) we have $C'_i = C_i$ with subject s substituting for all objects in the initial configuration Q_0. Length of sequence (5.2) is (length of sequence (5.1)) $- (n-1) = m - n + 1$.

The creation of a shorter leaky path in each of the above cases contradicts the fact that the leaky sequence (5.1) is of minimal length. By removing duplicate commands from a leaky sequence (i.e., those with the same side-effect), we get an upper bound on the length of a leaky sequence as follows:

$$m \leq g * (|S_0| + 1) * (|O_0| + 1) + 1,$$

where g is the total number of generic rights, $|S_0|$ and $|O_0|$ are the total number of subjects and objects in the initial configuration of (S_0, O_0, A_0), respectively. Note that the final state in which right r is leaked via command α contains $|S_0| + 1$ subjects and $|O_0| + 1$ objects at most. This is because a leaky path contains at most one create subject command and one create object command.

The rational for the upper bound above reflects the total number of cells in the access matrix as well as the number of access rights that can be entered in each cell as a side-effect from applying a chain of mono-operational commands (no multiple enter commands that apply to the same parameters). Recall that each command has the effect of entering at most a single right in a particular position of the access matrix.

On the Safety of the Mono-Operational Protection System

The length of a shortest leaky path for the mono-operational case of a protection system is bounded. This leads to the feasibility of a brute-force algorithm for deciding the safety of such system where all possible sequences of enter commands are tried. This algorithm, however, is considered NP-complete in that it has an exponential complexity in the size of the access matrix. Furthermore, as noted by Sandhu [SAND92b], the mono-operation create object command is essentially useless in that there is no opportunity for the reference monitor to attach the identity of the owner to an object that is being created. Doing so requires the execution of two primitive operations in the body of a command, which by definition falls out of the scope of the mono-operational model. This aspect results in orphaned entries in the access matrix that will have no access rights associated with them. The mere absence of the owner privilege in an access matrix renders the protection system useless and makes it simply a theoretical model that does not map to systems of any practical benefits.

One other restriction that was applied to the HRU model is that of *monotonicity*. A monotonic protection system is one in which deletion of access privileges is not allowed once access rights are entered in a configuration. Safety in the HRU access matrix model is known to be decidable only in the case of monotonic commands, which are mono-conditional. Mono-conditional commands have only one term in the precondition part and thus can test only one cell of the access matrix. Monotonicity in the HRU model, however, does not help when the commands are allowed to have multiple terms for the precondition. It is established that safety is undecidable even for biconditional monotonic systems (with commands having exactly two terms for the precondition part).

Even when safety in the HRU model is decidable in the mono-conditional case of a monotonic system, it has little practical use. The ability to revoke access rights from users is a key element of secure systems. Indeed, there is a fundamental conflict between the expressive capability of a protection system and the decidability of the safety problem. The general safety problem dealing with unrestricted protection systems is undecidable. Nevertheless, a number of protection systems in which safety is proven to be decidable have been developed. Although these models are restricted in terms of expressive power, they lend themselves to practical implementations. We discuss two of these systems in the following two chapters.

The General Safety Problem of the Access-Matrix Model

We now turn our attention to the general case of the safety problem. The generalization is stated as follows:

Given a state of a protection system as represented by a corresponding configuration, decide whether or not the configuration leaks a given generic right.

Theorem 5.2: *It is undecidable whether a given configuration of a given protection system is safe for a given generic right.*

The proof of this theorem as given by HRU consists of reducing the general safety problem to the famous Halting problem described in the theory of computability and stated as follows:

Given a program and an input to the program, determine if the program will eventually terminate when it runs with the input data substituted for the actual parameters of the program.

The following steps are generally adopted when reducing a particular problem *P* to the Halting problem:

❏ Assume that you have an effective procedure to solve problem *P* (an algorithm for computing the answer to *P*).
❏ Show how to use the procedure solving *P* for the solution of the Halting Problem.
❏ Because the Halting problem is known to be unsolvable, one therefore concludes that problem *P* is in turn unsolvable.

The halting problem here corresponds to the Turing machine halting in a prescribed state during the computation of a solution to an arbitrary problem. Before we sketch the HRU proof for the undecidability of the general safety problem, we discuss the basic concepts behind the Turing machine.

The Turing Machine

Long before the advent of modern digital computing machines, several mathematicians (notably Alonzo Church and Alan Turing) began to think about what it means to state that a particular function is computable. In the 1930s Church and Turing independently arrived at equivalent conclusions. The common result of their work can be stated as follows:

A function is computable if it can be computed by a Turing machine.

This result stipulates that a Turing machine is capable of computing every function there is. Turing machines have become one of the key abstractions in modern theory of *computation*, the study of what computers can and cannot do.

A Turing machine abstracts a very simple computer. Its operations are limited to reading and writing symbols on a one-dimensional, linear tape virtually of unbounded size in both directions (i.e., it has no left end and no right end). The active part of the machine, a reading and writing head, can remain at the same position or move left or right by one position during any computation step. Each position on the tape can be conceived as a square that is either blank or contains a symbol from the finite alphabet of the particular Turing machine. At any point during a computation, the machine is capable of assuming any of a finite number of states. Depending on the content of the square over which the head is positioned as well as the state that the machine is in, the machine either halts or acts. It halts when there is no action defined for the state and the symbol being read. By the same token, the machine acts when the combination of the current state and symbol read is defined for the computation at hand. Any action performed by the Turing machine consists of at most four primitive operations defined by the following:

1. It may or may not erase the symbol that it reads at the square over which the head is positioned.
2. A symbol erased at the current or a blank found at the current position of the head may or may not be overridden.
3. The head of the machine may move by one position to the left, may move by one position to the right, or may remain at the current position.
4. The machine may change to a new state.

The interval of time in which a Turing machine completes an action is referred to as a time cycle. At most four and at least one primitive operation as described in the above are performed during a time cycle. The machine continuously performs action after action or comes to a halt when it reaches a state for which no action is defined. Such a state is also called a *final state*. The actions of a Turing machine are specified by a set of commands of the following form:

```
(current state, current symbol) ↦
(new state, new symbol, left/right/same),
```

where left/right/same indicates the fact that the machine either moves left (L), right (R), or maintains the same position. Omitting the direction of the move implicitly means the head maintains its current position. The state transitions of a Turing machine can be specified in a table as illustrated in the following example. The symbol B is used to indicate a blank square and, for simplicity, can be thought as being part of the machine alphabet.

Example: Actions of a Turing Machine

We define and illustrate the actions of a Turing machine that computes the sum of two integers. In the initial configuration of the machine, the tape contains the input to the computation. This consists of the two operands for the addition operator delimited with the symbol *. Each integer is represented by a sequence of "/" characters on the tape.

Actions of the Turing machine as illustrated in Table 5.3 are expressed by the following commands:

TABLE 5.3 Example of a Turing machine for adding two integers

State \ Symbol	B	/	*
q_1			Rq_2
q_2		R	Rq_3
q_3	Lq_4	R	
q_4		BLq_5	Bq_f
q_5		L	$/q_f$
q_f			

$$(q_1, *) \mapsto (q_2, *, R)$$
$$(q_2, /) \mapsto (q_3, /, R)$$
$$(q_3, B) \mapsto (q_4, B, L)$$
$$(q_3, /) \mapsto (q_3, /, R)$$
$$(q_4, /) \mapsto (q_5, B, L)$$
$$(q_4, *) \mapsto (q_6, B)$$
$$(q_5, /) \mapsto (q_5, /, L)$$
$$(q_5, *) \mapsto (q_f, *, /)$$

Figure 5.6 depicts the computation of $1 + 3 = 4$ by this Turing machine.

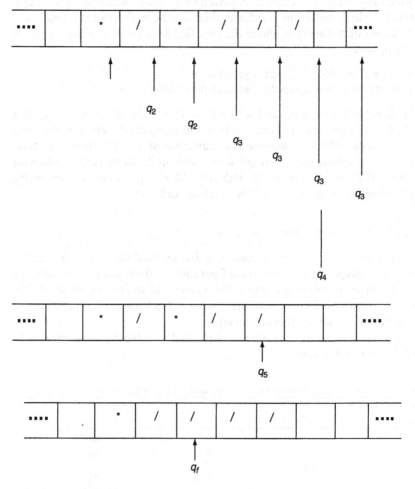

FIGURE 5.6 Illustration of the sum 1+3 processed by a Turing machine

Sketch of Proof for the Undecidability of the General Safety Problem

Harrison, Ruzzo, and Ullman [HARR76, HARR78] reduce the general safety question to the Halting problem as it applies to the Turing machine. The protection system as defined by HRU is shown to simulate the behavior of an arbitrary Turing machine. In this setting, leaking a particular generic right in the protection system becomes equivalent to the Turing machine halting at a designated final state.

Mapping an Arbitrary Turing Machine onto the Protection System

The input to this mapping is an arbitrary Turing machine computing the solution of a particular problem. The set of generic rights of the equivalent protection system include

- States of the machine and
- Tape symbols of the machine.

At any time during its computation, the machine will have scanned and processed some finite prefix of tape cells located to the left of its head, we number these cells $1, 2, ..., k$. as depicted in Figure 5.7.

Each such snapshot of the machine will be represented by a sequence of k subjects, $s_1, s_2, ..., s_k$ such that

- s_i corresponds to cell i.
- s_i is said to own s_{i+1} for $i = 1, 2, ..., k - 1$.
- Symbol X written on cell i corresponds to subject s_i having generic right X to itself in the protection system.
- The cell currently being scanned by the tape head at, say, position j, corresponds to subject s_j having generic right q to itself, where q is the current state of the machine (the state symbols are assumed to be distinct from the tape symbols so to avoid confusion).
- Subject s_k corresponding to the last position of the prefix string has a special generic right to itself called *end*. This indicates the fact that we have not yet defined subject s_{k+1}, which is to be owned by subject s_k.

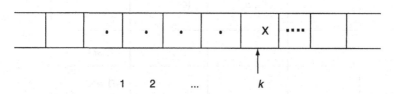

FIGURE 5.7 A snapshot of a Turing machine equivalent of deciding the general safety problem

Figure 5.8 shows the access matrix of a protection system corresponding to a snapshot of a Turing machine with a prefix string of "ABCD" at its current state q.

Mapping the Actions of the Turing Machine onto Protection Commands

Generic states and symbols are now used to map the actions of the Turing machine onto commands of the equivalent protection system. This generic notation underscores the generality of the mapping. Based on the direction in which the head of the machine moves after completing an action, we distinguish three scenarios as described below. But first we note that the tape head is assumed to move in either direction between two consecutive positions as shown in Figure 5.9 for the positions corresponding to subjects s and s'.

Moving to the Left

$$(q, X) \mapsto (p, Y, L)$$

Assume that the machine is in state q and that its head is positioned over a cell corresponding to subject s' with symbol X written on it. Overriding the cell with symbol Y and moving the head by one position to the left, changing into state p, means that subject s' no longer has rights q and X but instead has right Y to itself. Meanwhile, subject s, corresponding to the new position of the head, acquires right p to itself. This case is equivalent to the following:

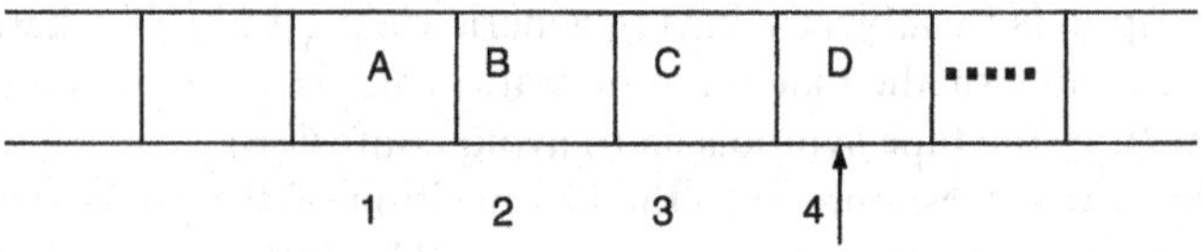

FIGURE 5.8 Correspondence between a Turing machine and an access matrix

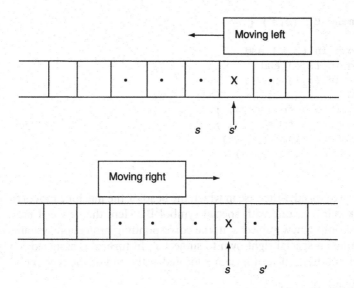

FIGURE 5.9 Moving the tape head in the Turing machine equivalent of a protection state

```
command C_qx (s, s' ) {
if
    own in (s,s') and
    q in (s', s') and
    x in (s', s')
then
    delete q from (s', s') ;
    delete x from (s', s') ;
    enter p into (s,s) ;
    enter y into (s', s') ;
}
```

Moving to the Right

$$(q, X) \mapsto (p, Y, R)$$

First we consider the case in which the machine moves into a cell that has been visited before and contains a symbol from the machine's alphabet (i.e., not a blank).

Assume that the machine is in state q, reads symbol X at the current position of the head corresponding to subject s, overrides X with Y, moves by one position to the left, and enters into state p. This means subject s no longer has rights q and X but instead has right Y to itself. Meanwhile, subject s', corresponding to the new position of the head, acquires right p to itself.

```
command C_qx (s,s') {
if
    own in (s,s') and
    q in (s,s) and
    X in (s,s)
then
    delete q from (s,s) ;
    delete X from (s,s) ;
    enter p into (s', s') ;
    enter Y into (s,s) ;
}
```

Now we consider the case in which the head of the machine moves right into a blank cell (i.e., one with special symbol B). Here the new cell needs to be mapped onto a new subject s' in the corresponding protection system. Subject s is granted a special right own to subject s'. In turn, s' is assigned the special right of end to itself as it becomes located at the end of the tape prefix:

```
command D_qx (s,s') {
if
    end in (s,s) and
    q in (s,s) and
    X in (s,s)
then
    delete q from (s,s) ;
    delete X from (s,s) ;
    create subject s' ;
    enter B into (s', s') ;
    enter p into (s', s') ;
    enter Y into (s,s) ;
    delete end from (s,s) ;
    enter end into (s', s') ;
    enter own into (s,s') ;
}
```

Maintaining the Same Position In this case, the action performed by the machine results in the head maintaining the same position on the tape but perhaps changing state.

If $(q, X) \mapsto (p, Y)$ then we have the following corresponding command in the protection system:

```
command D_qx (s) {
if
    q in (s,s) and
    X in (s,s)
then
```

```
        delete q from (s,s) ;
        delete X from (s,s) ;
        enter Y in (s,s) ;
        enter p in (s,s) ;
}
```

We note that this last scenario is not explicitly pointed out in the HRU proof. For this to become a special case of the command C_{qX} (s,s') when invoked with the actual arguments of C_{qX} (s,s), one has to assume that the special right of own $\in$ (s,s) for every subject s in order to satisfy the condition if own in (s,s').

Conclusion

The HRU proof shows that the mapping of an arbitrary Turing machine to the protection system as described is well defined and results in the protection system exactly simulating the actions of the Turing machine. Deciding whether the protection system, as represented by the commands above, leaks a generic right r is equivalent to the following:

❑ Map right r onto a final state (say, q_f) in the corresponding Turing machine.
❑ Deciding whether the Turing machine enters final state q_f becomes equivalent to deciding that the protection system leaks right r.

Due to the fact that generic right r is arbitrary and hence yielding state q_f is also arbitrary and given that answering the question of whether a Turing machine enters an arbitrary final state is undecidable, the general safety problem of HRU protection systems is therefore undecidable. Because each state of the machine corresponds to a generic right in the protection system, entering a final state corresponds to the protection system leaking the right.

Chapter 6

The Take-Grant Protection Model

Introduction

The *take-grant* (TG) *protection model* was introduced by Lipton and Snyder [LIPT77] in 1977 and subsequently analyzed in considerable detail by a number of authors [BISH79, BISH88, BISK84, SNYD81]. The name of this model is derived from the fact that it is based on two key-access rights—*take* and *grant*. These two rights control the propagation of other primitive permissions (such as read and write) and hence drive the flow of information among the protected entities of a system. Information flow in the take-grant model is elegantly modeled using directed graphs and can be viewed as a generalization of the transitive closure problems.

Unlike the Harrison, Ruzzo, and Ullman model that is discussed in the previous chapter, the take-grant model is simple and has linear time algorithms for deciding safety. But the take-grant scheme lacks the expressive capability exhibited in the HRU model. Nevertheless, it lends itself to various practical systems. In that respect, this model represents an interesting departure from the demarcation of decidable and undecidable protection systems set by the HRU model as noted by Sandhu [SAND92b]. Early analysis of the TG model dealt with the transfer of access rights under the assumption that active entities of the system cooperate in achieving the transfers. Such transfers are known as *sharing* or *conspiring*. Later analysis dealt with the conditions under which rights can be propagated without necessarily involving the cooperation of system subjects. The term *theft* is used to describe such transfers.

We begin by reviewing the basic definitions of the take-grant protection model. The governing rules of transforming protection states are described in detail with examples highlighting the underlying effects. We distinguish between two kinds of information flows—sharing and stealing of rights and—state the major results relating to the safety question of the take-grant model.

Definition of the Take-Grant Model

In the take-grant protection model, a system is represented by a finite, labeled directed graph whose nodes correspond to the entities of the protection

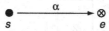

FIGURE 6.1 Directed graph modeling of access in the take-grant model

system. Active entities or subjects are represented by nodes of the form ●, passive entities, or objects are represented by nodes O; while entities that may correspond to either subjects or objects are represented by ⊗. A directed edge from subject s to an entity e (either an object or subject) represents the fact that s has access to e. The set of access rights that s has to e are in turn represented by the weight α associated with the edge as depicted in Figure 6.1.

Two special rights t for take and g for grant characterize the take-grant model. The semantics of these rights are summarized as follows:

- *Take* Subject s that has take right to entity e underscores the fact that s can assume any right that e has to other entities such as protected objects.
- *Grant* Subject s that has grant right to entity e can transfer any right it has for other entities to e.

Recall that the term *entity* is used to refer to either a subject or an object. We qualify an entity as a subject or an object whenever the context specifically applies to either one but not to both. Figure 6.2 illustrates the effects from exercising the take- and grant-access rights. Note the propagation of rights in opposing directions. The take right results in propagating rights forward, while the grant right disseminates rights backward with respect to the initiating subject.

The dynamic aspect of evolving the system from one protection state to another is driven by the application of a fixed set of graph-rewriting rules R. These rules transform the protection state of a system along a sequence of graphs, $G_0, G_1, ..., G_n$, such that G_i follows from G_{i-1}, $i = 1, ..., n$ by some rule in R. Analysis of the model focuses on answering the question of whether G_n has some property X. In the realm of protection systems, property X may, for instance, relate to an undesirable propagation of an access right, potentially leading to determine a protection violation. Property X is exhibited by an edge in graph G_n between two nodes p and q with the label α and is stated as p can $\alpha\, q$, meaning that entity p has access right α to entity q in the final protection state as represented by graph G_n. Note that generally α represents a set of rights.

The rewriting rules governing the transfer of rights in the take-grant model are known as the *dejure* rules. The take-grant model consists of four such rules defined as follows:

- *Take* Let x, y and z be three distinct nodes in a take-grant protection graph in which x is a subject. Let there be an edge from x to y labeled

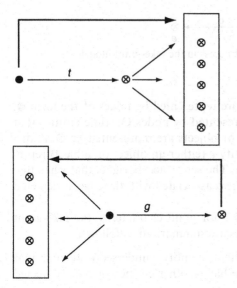

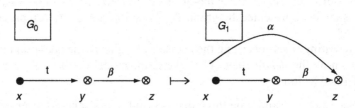

FIGURE 6.2 Propagation of rights in the take-grant model

γ with $t \in \gamma$ (i.e., x has take right to y in addition to perhaps other access rights). Let there be an edge from y to z labeled β. The take rule enables subject x to assume any subset of rights $\alpha \subseteq \beta$ to entity z. Figure 6.3 illustrates the effect of transforming a graph G_0 to graph G_1 using the take rule.

The take rule is written as x takes (α to z) from y.

❑   *Grant* Let x, y, and z be three distinct nodes in a take-grant protection graph G_0 in which x is a subject. Let there be an edge from x to y labeled γ with $g \in \gamma$ (i.e., x has grant right to y in addition to perhaps other access rights). Let there be an edge from x to z labeled β. Applying the grant rule to graph G_0 results in a protection graph G_1 by adding a new edge from y to z labeled α such that $\alpha \subseteq \beta$. Figure 6.4 depicts the effect from applying the grant rule.

FIGURE 6.3 Effect of the take rule

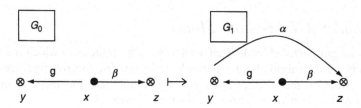

FIGURE 6.4 Effect of the grant rule

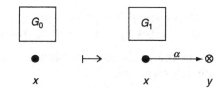

FIGURE 6.5 Effect of the create rule

The grant rule is written as *x* grants (α to *z*) to *y*.

❑ *Create* Let *x* be a subject in a take-grant protection graph G_0, and let $\alpha \subseteq R$, where *R* is the set of access rights defined in the systems. The create rule results in graph G_1 that contains a new node *y* and an edge from *x* to *y* labeled α as shown in Figure 6.5.

The create rule is written as *x* creates (α to new node) *y*.

❑ *Remove* Let *x* and *y* be two distinct nodes of a take-grant protection graph G_0 such that *x* is a subject. Let there be an edge from *x* to *y* labeled β (i.e., *x* possesses rights $\beta \subseteq R$ to entity *y*). The remove rule results in graph G_1 in which subject x has a lesser number of rights to y with the edge adjacency in G_1 maintained the same as in G_0. The remove operation is illustrated in Figure 6.6 in which a subset of rights α is removed from β. When all the rights that x has to y are removed, edge (*x*, *y*) becomes useless and thus is removed.

The remove rule is written as *x* removes α to *y*.

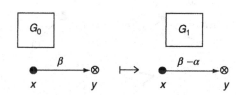

FIGURE 6.6 Effect of the remove rule

Example: A Take-Grant Model

The take-grant model lends itself well to security policies in which the set of subjects are organized along a hierarchy reflecting the control structure of an enterprise. Consider the application of this model to a five-member organization with a treelike structure as shown in Figure 6.7.

Note how subject s_5 acquires access to the resources directly under the control of subject s_4 as illustrated in the bottom portion of Figure 5.6. This follows from the transformations:

- s_2 grants t to s_4 to s_5, and
- s_5 takes right rwx to all the resources accessible to s_4.

On the other hand, subject s_4 cannot acquire access to the resources directly owned by s_5.

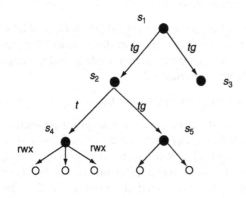

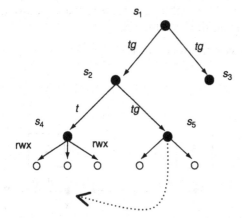

FIGURE 6.7 An example of transferring privileges using the take- and grant-control rights

Safety in the Take-Grant Model

The safety problem as it relates to the take-grant protection model asks the question of whether it is possible for any given subject to ultimately gain rights to a particular entity. Although the rules that define the take-grant scheme are simple and small in number, the ramifications from applying them can be quite surprising. The propagation of rights may not be obvious at first. Consider the scenario in which the initial protection state is represented by a simple graph G_0, as shown in Figure 6.8.

Despite the fact that there is no edge between nodes y and z in G_0, we ask the question is it possible for y to have t access to z as a result of transforming G_0 using the take-grant rules? The answer to this question is a surprising yes as depicted in the transformations of Figure 6.9.

The initial protection state as represented by graph G_0 of Figure 6.8 is transformed using the following rules:

- y creates (tg to new node) s $(G_0 \mapsto G_1)$
- x takes (tg to s) from y $(G_1 \mapsto G_2)$
- x grants (t to z) to s $(G_2 \mapsto G_3)$
- y takes (t to z) from s $(G_3 \mapsto G_4)$

The intent of this example is to demonstrate the abundance of transformations that can be applied to an initial configuration and that can result in unexpected flow of access rights among entities of the take-grant protection model. Although it may seem that these transformations can yield unbounded protection states, the work performed by Lipton and Snyder [LIPT77] as well as others [BISH88, SYND81] led to the formal determination of information flow in the take-grant model. We state those theoretical results here but first we begin with the definitions that characterize the results:

Definition 6.1: A tg-path is a nonempty sequence of distinct nodes $x_0, ..., x_n$ such that for all $i = 0,..., n - 1$, x_i is connected to x_{i+1} by an edge in either direction—i.e., (x_i, x_{i+1}) or (x_{i+1}, x_i)—and with a label containing either t, g, or both.

Definition 6.2: A nonempty set of nodes is said to be tg-connected if there is a tg-path that spans all of the nodes in the set. Nodes x and y are directly

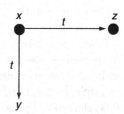

FIGURE 6.8 Example of an initial take-grant protection configuration with potentially a wider effect

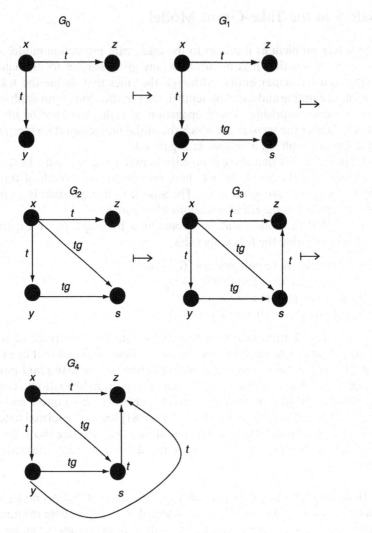

FIGURE 6.9 Effects of transforming the take-grant protection state of Figure 6.8

tg-connected if there is an edge between the two nodes with a label that includes either *t* or *g*.

Each *tg*-path can be associated with one or more words over the alphabet $\{\xrightarrow{t}, \xrightarrow{g}, \xleftarrow{t}, \xleftarrow{g}\}$. The notations t^*, and g^* are used to indicate one or more occurrences of the letters *t* and *g*, respectively. For example, instances of $t^* g$ can be the sequences *g*, *tg*, *ttg*. A *tg*-path of length 0 is referred to by the symbol *v*.

Definition 6.3: An island is a maximal tg-connected subject only subgraph.

Definition 6.4: A node x_0 is said to initially span to node x_n if x_0 is a subject and there is a tg-path between x_0 and x_n represented by a word in $\{\xrightarrow{\;t\;}{}^*\xrightarrow{\;g\;}{}^*\}\cup\{v\}$.

Definition 6.5: A node x_0 terminally spans to node x_n if x_0 is a subject and there is a tg-path between x_0 and x_n represented by a word in $\{\xrightarrow{\;t\;}{}^*\}$.

Definition 6.6: A bridge is a tg-path with endpoints that are both subjects and is represented by a word from the set

$$\{\xrightarrow{\;t\;}{}^*,\xleftarrow{\;t\;}{}^*,\xrightarrow{\;t\;}{}^*\xrightarrow{\;g\;}\xleftarrow{\;t\;}{}^*,\xrightarrow{\;t\;}{}^*\xleftarrow{\;g\;}\xleftarrow{\;t\;}{}^*\}$$

Definition 6.7: Given a set of rights α, and two nodes x and y of a take-grant protection graph G_0, the predicate $can.share(\alpha, x, y, G_0)$ is true if and only if there exist protection graphs $G_1, ..., G_n$ such that $G_0 \mapsto G_1 \mapsto ... \mapsto G_{n-1} \mapsto G_n$ using only the rewriting rules of the take-grant model, and in G_n there is an edge from x to y with label α.

Determinism of Sharing in the Take-Grant Model

The *can.share* predicate defines the potential for information flow in the take-grant model. This flow may take place with or without the direct cooperation of resource owners. The following theorem states the necessary and sufficient conditions for such a flow to happen:

Theorem 6.1: The predicate $can.share(\alpha, x, y, G_0)$ is true if and only if there is an edge from x to y in G_0 labeled α (i.e., the sharing is expressed in the initial state of the of the take-grant system) or if the following conditions are simultaneously satisfied:

- ❑ There is a node s in G_0 with an edge from s to y labeled α.
- ❑ There exists a subject x' such that $x' = x$ or x' initially spans to x.
- ❑ There exists a subject s' such that $s' = s$ or s' terminally spans to s.
- ❑ There exist islands $I_1, ..., I_n$ such that x' is in I_1, s' is in I_n, and there is a bridge from I_k to I_{k+1} for $k = 1, ..., n-1$.

Proof of this theorem is described in [LIPT77]. In what follows, we illustrate it for the special case where $x' = x$, $s' = s$, with s and x directly tg-connected. This scenario can be expressed as follows

The predicate $can.share(\alpha, x, y, G_0)$ is true if x is a subject and the following two conditions are satisfied:

- ❑ There is a subject node s in G_0 with an edge from s to y labeled α.
- ❑ s and x are directly tg-connected.

Case 6. 1a: { ──→ ──→ }
              t   α

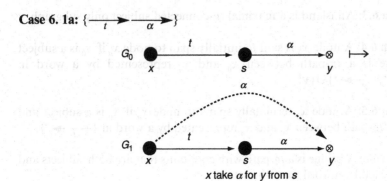

x take α for y from s

Case 6.1b: { ←── ──→ }
               g   α

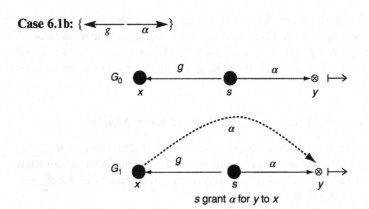

s grant α for y to x

Case 6.1c: { ──→ ──→ }
               g   α

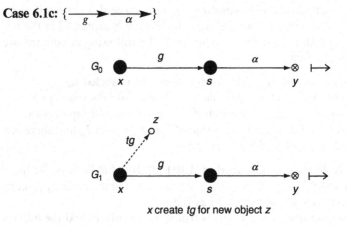

x create tg for new object z

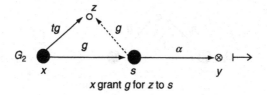

x grant g for z to s

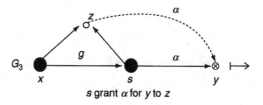

s grant α for y to z

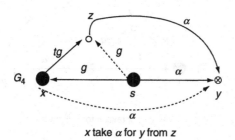

x take α for y from z

Case 6.1d: $\{\xleftarrow[t]{}\ \ \xrightarrow[\alpha]{}\}$

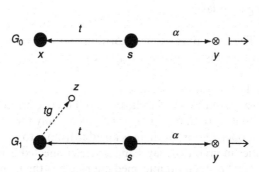

x create tg for new object z

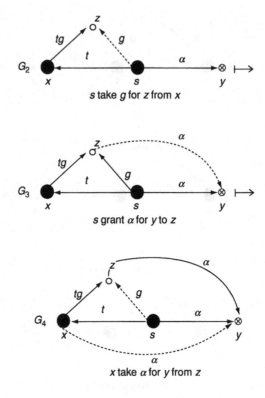

G_2

s take g for z from x

G_3

s grant α for y to z

G_4

x take α for y from z

Given any take-grant protection graph, it can be verified in linear time whether the conditions of Theorem 6.1 are simultaneously satisfied as stated by the following corollary:

Corollary 6.1: There is a linear-time algorithm in the size of a take-grant protection graph for testing the *can.share* predicate.

Definition 6.8: The predicate *can.steal*(α, x, y, G_0) is true if and only if there is no edge from x to y in G_0 that has label α, and there exist protection graphs $G_1, ..., G_n$ such that $G_0 \,\alpha\, G_1 \,\alpha\, ... \,\alpha\, G_{n-1} \,\alpha\, G_n$ using only the rewriting rules of the take-grant model, and in G_n there is an edge from x to y with label α, and if any two entities in graph G_0, say s and q, are connected with an edge from s to q that has label α, then no intermediate rule has the form s grants (α to q) to z for any node z in G_i for all $i = 1, ..., n-1$.

The last condition of Definition 6.8 characterizes the stealing of rights in the take-grant model. It states that for right α over entity y to be stolen it should not be explicitly disseminated by any entity that possesses it. Furthermore, as it is stated in Theorem 6.2 below, there has to be some entity in the initial protection graph that has right α to y. The act of stealing access rights corresponds to an information flow occurring without the cooperation of resource owners or in general terms the entities having control over the protected resources.

Theorem 6.2: The predicate $can.steal(\alpha, x, y, G_0)$ is true if and only if the following conditions are satisfied simultaneously:

- In G_0 there is an edge from x to y labeled α.
- There exists a node x' representing a subject such that $x' = x$ or x' initially spans to x.
- In G_0 there is a node s with en edge from s to y that includes α in its label.
- The predicate $can.share(t, x', s, G_0)$ is true.

Similarly, given a take-grant protection graph the conditions of Theorem 6.2 can be checked for validity with linear-time complexity.

Corollary 6.2: There is a linear-time algorithm in the size of a take-grant protection graph for testing the $can.steal$ predicate.

Chapter 7

The Schematic-Protection Model

Introduction

The access-matrix model of Harrison, Ruzzo, and Ullman (HRU) that we discussed in Chapter 5 is characterized by a rich expressive capability. HRU can be applied virtually to any access policies in existence. This generality, however, has led to the undecidability of the safety question in HRU due to the unbounded states of the protection system. Even when limiting the expressiveness of HRU to only mono-conditional and monotonic transformations of protection states, safety becomes decidable albeit nontractable. The take-grant model introduced in the previous chapter is unique in that it defines an information-flow model that is completely based on two control rights, take and grant. It has a limited expressive power but a solvable safety. Furthermore, safety in the take-grant model is efficiently computable with linear time complexity. One can think of the HRU and the take-grant models as being at opposing extremes of complexity in modeling protection systems.

The schematic-protection model (SPM) introduced by Sandhu [SAND88a, SAND90, SAND91] is intended by its inventor to fill the gap between the richness in expressive power of the HRU model and its intractability with respect to the safety question as compared with the limited applicability of the take-grant model but efficient decidability of safety. The key concept introduced in SPM is that of typed security entities. Each entity, subject or object, is statically associated with an invariable security type. All instances of a given security type are viewed and treated uniformly by the authorization scheme. This chapter introduces the novel concepts of SPM based on the work of Sandhu. We highlight some examples of access-control policies expressed in SPM constructs and summarize its safety results.

Overview of the Schematic-Protection Model (SPM)

Every SPM subject or object is designated to be an instance of a particular type that remains invariable throughout its lifetime. As such, the type of an entity needs to be determined by a thorough process during the initial setup of an authorization policy. A subject type may underscore some kind of position assumed by that subject, such as membership in a department or in a particular group. Similarly, an object type may represent its security classification as an information container—for example, a document that is company internal only or one that can be shared with entities external to the company. The set of types T in SPM is the union of types of subjects TS, and the types of system objects TO (i.e., $T = TS \cup TO$). It is assumed that the type of a SPM entity is given by the function *type*.

SPM characterizes all active entities of a protection system (i.e., subjects) using two parameters. The first, a static one, is the type associated with the subject. The second represents the dynamic aspect of that entity in that it enumerates the *capabilities* that can be exercised by that subject on other system entities, also called *tickets* or simply *privileges*. A ticket in SPM is denoted by Y/x indicating that the holder of the ticket has access right x to entity Y. The access right x may represent any abstraction of a set of operations that apply to entity Y. Its semantics are irrelevant to the analysis of SPM. But a distinction is made between access rights as they relate to the controls of the SPM in itself or simply inert rights such as the typical read, write, or execute. The set of access rights R is therefore divided into a subset of rights that are inert RI and a subset of control rights denoted by RC. Furthermore, right x is statically defined as either copyable (xc) or not copyable (simply x). The type of ticket Y/x:c is given by the value of the type function *type* ($Y/x:c$), which is the ordered pair *type* $(Y)/x:c$ meaning that the type of a ticket is determined by the type of the entity to which it applies and the right that it carries ($x:c$ denotes either x or xc).

More generally a ticket of the form Y/uvw indicates a capability to access entity Y via access rights u, v, and w and simultaneously denotes tickets Y/u, Y/v, and Y/w. Y/uvc is the union of Y/uc and Y/vc. The domain of a subject in SPM denotes the set of tickets granted to that subject. As stated above, every right x comes in two forms—x and xc where c is the *copy flag*. The difference between Y/x and Y/xc is that the former cannot be copied from the domain of one subject to the domain of another subject, while Y/xc allows the distribution of the ticket Y/x across subject domains provided other control elements are met in SPM. We describe the details of those elements in the next section.

The space of SPM entities is expandable through the *can-create* binary relationship denoted by $cc \subseteq TSxT$ that relates a subject type to an object type. A subject of type u can create an object of type v if and only the can-create relationship (u, v) is prescribed by the SPM policy (i.e., $(u, v) \in cc$). The can-create relationship is modeled by a directed graph, called the cc-graph, in which the nodes represent SPM protection types and an edge from u to v symbolizes the can-create relationship (u, v). SPM has decidable safety provided the can-create graph is acyclic (i.e., not containing cycles). When allowing arbitrary cycles in the can-create graph, however, SPM has undecidable safety. In summary, the schematic-protection model is based on the following elements:

- A finite set of entity types T that is the union of subject types TS and object types TO;
- A finite set of rights R partitioned into inert rights RI and control rights RC;
- The dissemination of access privileges through the generation and distribution of tickets, Y/x, based on a set of SPM rules to be discussed below;
- The can-create relationships $cc \subseteq TSxT$ is the means by which the system expands its space of entities.

SPM Rules and Operations

The protection state of a SPM can be transformed using three operations:

- Copy,
- Demand, and
- Create.

The copy and demand operations are concerned with the dissemination of tickets across SPM subjects, while the create operation introduces new subjects and objects into the system. Ticket distributions combined with gradually evolving the protection system with newly created entities result in a dynamic and perhaps unstructured aspect of the protection system. This makes the safety analysis a challenging task. The details of the SPM operations and rules are outlined in the next subsections.

The Copy Operation

The *copy operation* moves a copy of a ticket from the domain of one subject to the domain of another subject. The original ticket remains intact. The side-effect of the operation is that an additional subject in the system now becomes in possession of the ticket, which is the object of the copy operation. This operation is authorized by two rules:

- The copy flag attached to the ticket and
- The link predicate $link_i$ and its associated filter function f_i.

These rules are used by the policy setting officers and system administrators to enforce the conditions under which a ticket can be copied from one subject to another:

- *The copy flag* The presence of the copy symbol c in the ticket is a requirement for its copying to other user domains. Without this flag a ticket does not require any further policy checking to verify whether it can be transferred.
- *Link predicates* A link predicate takes two arguments, subjects X and Y, and evaluates to true or false. If true, it establishes a policy link

between subjects X and Y that can be used to copy tickets from the domain of X to that of Y. The presence of certain control tickets (those associated with control rights) in the local domains of X and Y, respectively, governs the evaluation of the link predicate. Because of this, it is termed the local link predicate. Link predicates are directional and thus are not commutative. The formal definition of the link predicate is stated by the following: Let dom(X) be the set of tickets in possession by subject X. A local link predicate $\text{link}_i (X, Y)$ is a function defined as an arbitrary Boolean expression using the conjunction or disjunction of the following basic terms for any control right $z \in RC$:

$$X/z \in \text{dom}(X)$$
$$X/z \in dom(\,Y)$$
$$Y/z \in dom(\,X)$$
$$Y/z \in dom(\,Y)$$
$$true$$

A link is established from subject X to subject Y if it is statically stated by the authorization policy in which case the link predicate for subjects X, and Y always evaluates to true. A link is also established dynamically from X to Y when there is a control ticket present in the domains of either subject. The control ticket is the mechanism by which a particular policy may state the rules for establishing the local links among its entities.

For generality, SPM makes use of a finite collection of local link predicates $\{\text{link}_i, \text{ for } i = 1,...,N\}$ that can be defined in a protection system. Dropping the subscript from the link predicate function means only one type of link function is defined in the entire system.

❑ *Filter functions* Each link function link_i is associated with a filter function $f_i: TS \times TS \to 2^{T \times R}$. Filtering here takes two subject types as input arguments and assigns them a subset in the space of ticket types. It is intended to put more restrictions on the types of tickets that can be copied when the link predicate is satisfied.

Finally, ticket Y/x:c can be copied from the domain of subject A to that of subject B if and only if the following conditions are satisfied for some link function (link_i) and its associated filter f_i:

$$Y/xc \in \text{dom}(A)$$
$$\text{link}_i = true$$
$$y/x{:}c \in f_i\,(a,b)$$

Thus, the combination of the copy flag, the link predicates, and the filter function is what governs a copy operation. The filter function is a means to strengthen policy rules and allows for finer control levels. Besides the discretionary information flows that can be enabled via the copy flag and the link predicates, the filter functions may be used to set mandatory controls beyond the powers of individual system subjects.

Examples:

The control rights t and g in these examples come from the take-grant protection model that is discussed in the previous chapter:

- ❑ Link(X, Y) ⇔ Y/g ∈ dom(X) OR X/t ∈ dom(Y): That means a link may be established between X and Y when either subject X has the grant right to subject Y or subject Y possesses the take right to subject X.
- ❑ Link(X, Y) ⇔ X/t ∈ dom(Y): A copyable ticket can be copied from the domain of subject X to that of subject Y if and only if Y has right t for X. Note the definition here is not commutative, in that Link(X, Y) does not necessarily imply Link(Y, X).

Figure 7.1 depicts the link rules that are used in the two examples above.

The Demand Operation

The *demand operation* allows subjects to acquire tickets ondemand. An SPM authorization scheme allows this ticket acquisition using the demand function

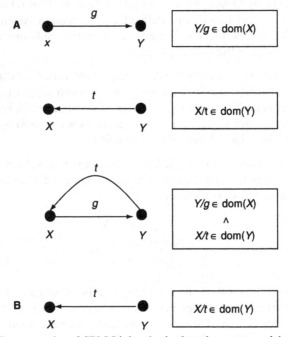

FIGURE 7.1 Two examples of SPM Link rules in the take-grant model

$$d{:}TS \rightarrow 2^{TxR}$$

that maps a subject type to a set of ticket types that can possibly be empty. A ticket of type a/x:c that is a member of $d(b)$ for some type b implies that every subject of type b can demand ticket A/x:c for every entity A of type a. This implies that every existing or newly created entity of type a is accessible immediately to any existing or new subjects of type b. Instead of having to explicitly distribute tickets, the demand operation allows for an implicit flow of tickets across system subjects.

The Create Operation

The *create operation* introduces new entities, subjects and objects, into the system. There are two aspects associated with this operation:

- ❏ Which entities are authorized to instantiate other entities and
- ❏ Which tickets are immediately introduced as a side-effect of the create operation.

Authorization

SPM entities are authorized to create new entities by way of the noncommutative binary relationship, can-create (cc). As was previously mentioned, this relationship is defined between an ordered pair of SPM entity types. The first is a subject type, while the second is an entity type that can represent either a subject or an object. The cc relationship can be thought of as a one-to-many mapping from the set TS to the set of all types T:

$$cc : TS \rightarrow T$$

or a one to one mapping

$$cc : TS \rightarrow 2^{T}$$

in which a subject type is related to a subset of T (the superset of types)

The cc relationship can be modeled using a directed graph $G(N, E)$ in which each SPM entity type is represented by a node (i.e., $N{=}T$). An edge e from node s to node v represents the fact that subject type s can instantiate entities of type v. By definition, there are no edges between object types. Only active subjects may instantiate SPM types into concrete entities. Thus a subject of type s may be able to instantiate subjects as well as objects of other types.

SPM restricts the cc graphs to those that are acyclic only (i.e., without cycles except for loops) (cycles of length 1). This restriction is very practical in that subjects should not be created directly or indirectly by other entities that they can create. The cc relationship naturally dictates some type of subject hierarchy. Figure 7.2 illustrates an example in which a top-down hierarchy represents the ability of higher authorities to instantiate profiles or accounts for new entities as they join an SPM authorization scheme.

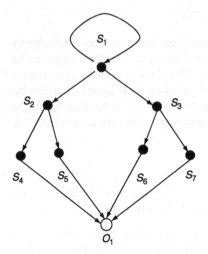

FIGURE 7.2 Example of a hierarchical cc relationship in SPM

Create Rules

For every pair of entities involved in the cc relationship, a SPM scheme specifies the tickets that can be generated when the underlying cc operation is applied. Every rule for ticket generation is expected to have a local effect meaning that tickets are generated for the entities involved in the cc relationship only. The target of a cc relationship is the second argument of the relation (i.e., target of $cc(a, b)$ is b). Depending on the type of the target, SPM distinguishes two scenarios governing ticket generation.

- ❏ *The target is of object type.* The creation of an object results in a set of inert tickets attached to the subject initiating the create operation. Formally, the create rule in this case is specified as $cr(a,b) \subseteq \{b/x:c \mid x:c \in RI\}$. This means when subject A of type a creates an object B of type b, A acquires tickets B/x:c if and only if $b/x:c \in cr(a,b)$.
- ❏ *The target is of subject type.* Recall that the initiator in the cc relationship is always a subject. In this case, both the initiator and the target are subjects, and the policy governing the create rule is specified in two parts. The first one is related to the subject initiating the create operation, denoted by *LEFT,* while the second is associated with the target subject, denoted by *RIGHT*. The operation is defined by $cr(a,b) = LEFT \mid RIGHT$. The *LEFT* part of the create operation relates to the tickets that are placed in the domain of subject A. The *RIGHT* part specifies the tickets to be placed in the domain of subject B, target of the operation. Formally, tickets contained in *LEFT* and *RIGHT* are subsets of $\{a/x:c,b/x:c \mid x:c \in R\}$. When both the initiator and the target are of the same type (case of $a = b$), this notation uses self to refer to the initiator. LEFT and RIGHT become subsets of $\{a/x:c,self/x:c \mid x:c \in R\}$. Here

self/x:c denotes tickets placed in the domain of the initiator, while *a/x:c* denotes tickets placed in the domain of the target subject.

Attenuating Create-Rule of SPM

In addition to the requirement that the graph modeling the can-create relationships in a SPM scheme be acyclic, the create rule is required to be attenuating for loops (i.e., rules of the form $cr(a, a)$). The attenuation restriction aids in the analysis of SPM and leads to a tractable decidability of its safety.

Consider subject A of type a such that $cc(a, a)$. Subject A can create subject A' of type a; recursively A' creates A" and so forth. The potential for long sequences of create rules that take place within the same type complicates the security analysis of SPM. To alleviate the effect of this complexity, the $cr(a, a)$ is constrained by the tickets it may introduce. The new restriction on $cr(a, a)$ is that after the create operation in which A instantiates A' is complete, the following condition must hold:

$$dom (A') \subseteq dom(A).$$

This means the set of tickets introduced by the $cr(a, a)$ operation is not extendable. A newly created subject is not allowed to acquire any more tickets than what is already in possession of the subject performing the create operation. Although this limitation may naturally exhibit itself in many practical policies, its introduction is mainly intended to ease the analysis of SPM. In that respect, all subjects of type a for which $cr(a, a)$ is allowed become equivalent from the standpoint of safety analysis. Furthermore, $cr(a, a)$ requires that if a ticket for A' is placed in the domain of subject A, the corresponding ticket for A is automatically placed in the domain of A. Formally, a $cr(a, a)$ rule is attenuating if

$$LEFT \subseteq RIGHT$$
$$a/\text{x:c} \in LEFT \Rightarrow self/\text{x:c} \in LEFT.$$

The second restriction underlines the fact that an entity that creates a subject of its type should possess all the privileges to itself as those it confers on the instantiated subject.

Application of SPM

In the following, we illustrate two SPM examples drawn from practical access policies as originally presented by Sandhu [SAND88a, SAND88b].

Sharing Across Resource Owners

In this scenario, SPM rules model a simple policy where a resource owner automatically grants access rights to all other users (complete sharing).

```
TS = {user}
TO = {file}
RI = {x:c | x is either r, w, or x (read, write, execute)}
RC = {}
link_u (X, Y) = true
f_u (user,user) = {file/xc}
d(user) = {}
cc(user) = { file }
cr{ user, file ) = {file/rc, file/wc, file/xc}
```

This scheme uses a single universal link function denoted by $link_u$ and its corresponding filter function f_u. Note that since the link function in this example evaluates to true for any given pair of users (X, Y), and because all tickets created are associated with a copy flag, this scheme defines a policy in which access to any created file is shared across the population of users in the system.

The Basic Take-Grant Model

In this basic take-grant model, there is only one subject type and one object type denoted by *sub* and *file*, respectively. We assume that inert right *x* allows appropriately meaningful access to *file* type of resource. To allow for the copy operation a universal link is established across subjects as follows:

$$link(X, Y) \Leftrightarrow Y/g \in dom(X) \vee X/t \in dom(Y)$$

A link from *X* to *Y* in SPM requires *X* to possess *g* right to *Y* or *Y* possess right *t* to *X* in the corresponding take-grant formulation. The can-create relationship is defined among subjects as well as between subjects and objects. Figure 7.3 represents the graph modeling this simple cc relationship. The creation of file *F* by subject *A* augments dom(*A*) by a new ticket *F/xc*. While the creation of subject *A'* by subject *A* results in *A* acquiring tickets of type *sub/tgc* that apply to the instantiated subject and ticket *self/tgc* for subject *A* itself. The latter is introduced so that the scheme maintains the attenuating create property. This basic take-grant model is specified by the following rules as defined in Sandhu [SAND88a, SAND88b].

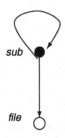

sub

file

FIGURE 7.3 Modeling the can-create rule in the take-grant example

```
TS = {sub}
TO = {file}
RI = {x:c}
RC = {t:c,g:c}
link (X, Y) ⇔ Y/g ∈ dom(X) ∨ X/t ⇔ dom(Y)
f(sub,sub) = TxR
d(sub) = {}
cc(sub) = {file,sub}
cr(sub,file) = {file/xc}
cr(sub,sub) = {sub/tgc,self/tgc} | {}
```

Chapter 8

Role-Based Access Control

Introduction

The access-matrix model directly manipulates access rights in that granting or revoking access to a resource explicitly refers to a particular permission. This approach yields a fine-grain level of control where each access type and its required permissions are related by a mapping that can be one-to-one at the finest level. For example, the *read* permission clearly means one can view the information contained in a resource but not modify it or add to it. To allow for updates, a new access right such as *write* or *append* is needed. Although this approach offers the advantage of fine-tuning an access control policy to accommodate any level of access needed, it can be costly to manage. The inherent cost factor becomes apparent with the increase in the number of managed users and resources. Furthermore, the effects from resources removed or added to the system as well as users leaving and joining an organization or simply changing job functions adds up to the complexity and overhead of maintaining such policy. For example, assigning an employee to a new function may require revoking his or her access rights to a large number of resources that are no longer needed for the tasks required by the new position. Similarly, functions of the new job may require access to various new resources. In this scenario, explicit revocation of access rights as well as the granting of new ones needs to span every old and new resource that is or used to be accessible to the user.

The notion of user groups was introduced to alleviate some of these issues. Users sharing similar access to the same resources become members of a single group. The group as a single entity is then granted or denied access to the managed resources. Access decisions take into account the fact that a user is a member of one group or another. Grouping users is certainly one important aspect in addressing the scale of manageability in access-control systems but alone is not sufficient.

In addition to user groups, another important dimension in the manageability of access controls is the grouping of access rights. Following on the concept of managing users that share similar access capabilities as a unit, role-based access control evolves around the idea of grouping access rights pertinent to a particular functionality into a role abstraction. Access

190

management as such is performed at a coarse-grain level than that of individual privileges. In our previous example of a person moving to a new function, he or she is simply assigned to the new role and removed from the old one when a role-based access control (RBAC) mechanism is in place. RBAC policies provide a natural and powerful way for an administrator to specify the privileges required by various job functions and efficiently manage user to role associations.

The appeal of RBAC is its inherent representation of real-world access-control processes. In many situations, people perform day-to-day functions based on the role in the organizations to which they belong, within a community of people, or in society at large. A role is a higher-level concept that can be better understood as opposed to individual access rights or operations. Roles are compatible with the hierarchical organizations found in real life, such as those in an enterprise. Roles can be easily mapped onto an already hierarchical structure of an organization. Higher-level roles are automatically granted the roles associated with lower level organizational entities. It is for these reasons RBAC is being touted as the generalized form of access-control models.

The underlying RBAC foundations are

- Permissions are assigned to roles,
- Users are assigned to roles, and
- Access decisions are based on users being members of applicable roles.

The premise of ease in managing an RBAC policy is based on the fact that user assignments to roles tend to change over time, while permission assignments to roles are relatively stable. The privileges associated with a particular role may remain unchanged over a long period of time due to the fixed semantics of the functions assigned to that role. Users can be easily reassigned to new roles as the need arises. Basing security administration on roles rather than on permissions provides simplicity, is easier to understand, and enables better scalability. Roles support the data-abstraction principle in systems design and can be viewed as higher-level encapsulations of lower-level privileges and permissions.

Roles have been adopted in many environments and contexts, at times with varying semantics. An early reference to roles can be found in [LOCH88], where they are defined in a generalized hierarchy and agents representing users are assigned to roles. Ting [TING88] describes the use of roles for application-level security controls. Baldwin [BALD90] named protection domains are similar to the roles as defined by Nyanchama and Osborn [NYAN94, NYAN99]. The embodiment of modern RBAC is described by Ferraiolo and Kuhn [FERR92], by Sandhu [SAND96], and in the proposed standard for RBAC [FERR01], to mention a few. In this chapter we present the RBAC model in its three major forms—basic RBAC, hierarchical RBAC, and constrained RBAC. We discuss all major aspects surrounding RBAC, including flow analysis and the simulation of DAC and MAC policies.

Basic RBAC

In its basic form, RBAC consists of managing a set of users, a flat set of roles, a set of resources, and a universe of access permissions. The idea is to encapsulate subsets of access rights within named roles. Assigning a user to a particular role implies that he or she is granted access to the resources that are in the confines of that role. A role can represent a competency in a particular area and does not necessarily have to have any users assigned to it. A role without any directly assigned users is referred to in the literature as a *virtual role* and sometimes is also called a *position* [MOFF99, SAND96]. For instance, the role of a health care provider can be used as a high-level abstraction for a physician or a nurse. Roles that are assignable to users embody a concrete scope of responsibility. One might have the competency necessary to be a supervisor for several work groups but have the responsibility for only the work group he or she actually manages.

At a lower level, each resource manager exposes a functional interface providing access to its resources. Each such interface is known as an *operation*. Based on the semantics of the operation performed on the resource, one or more permissions might be required for that operation to take place. Permissions can be discretely disjoint of one another or can be related through some hierarchical semantics or other relationships. For example, in the operations exposed via a file system, while the *read* and the *append* permissions are disjoint, they are both implied by the *write* permission. Similarly, the *control* permission, where applicable, implies all of the permissions read, append, and write. Depending on the access decision policy used, the list of permissions required by an operation may be further evaluated by the underlying access-control system using a predefined expression or rule before an access decision is made. For instance, the set of permissions required to access a particular resource can be evaluated using a disjunctive form (a single permission is needed) or using a conjunction in which all of the listed permissions are required for the operation to proceed. Figure 8.1 illustrates the basic relationships among roles, permissions, and operations.

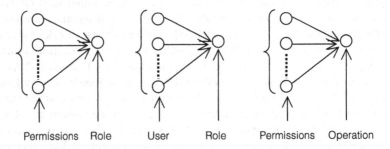

FIGURE 8.1 Basic relationships among roles, users, permissions, and operations

RBAC as a generalized access-control model supports two well-known security principles:

- *Separation of duty* Tasks requiring separation of duty are assigned to multiple users rather than to a single individual or one programming agent. This principle is used to formulate what is also known as a multiperson access-control policy.
- *Least privilege* A user is confined to a subset of roles based on the task being performed. In turn, each of these roles can be such that it encompasses only the privileges necessary for achieving the activities mandated by the role, not more and not less.

User, Role, and Permission Associations

Central to RBAC is the role concept around which access policies are formulated. Defining a set of roles is the first ingredient of RBAC. Users are assigned to roles in a many to many relationships. A single role can be assumed by multiple users, while each user can be assigned to multiple roles. Multiple roles that are assigned to a single user may be subject to further constraints such as the separation of duties where users are prevented from simultaneously being members of separated roles such as those with conflict of interest.

Roles can be discrete abstractions that are disjoint from one another or may adhere to a particular relationship such as a hierarchical containment in which one role may oversee several other roles and hence is automatically granted their permissions. Other forms of role relationship such as aggregations may also exist.

Permissions are assigned to roles in a many-to-many relationship. A single permission can be assigned to multiple roles. In turn, a single role can be designated to contain multiple permissions. Permission-to-role assignment can be constrained depending on restrictions imposed on the roles themselves. In the special case when role-to-permissions relationship is a one-to-one, the RBAC model does not offer the advantage of ease of management. In this worst-case scenario, RBAC becomes equivalent to the access-matrix model in its overhead and complexity. Assigning permissions to roles can be best implemented in line with the least-privilege principle, thereby avoiding the danger that a user may be granted more access to resources than is needed.

Conceptually, these assignments can be encapsulated by two Boolean matrices—UR (*USERS* × *ROLES*) and PR (*PERMISSIONS* × *ROLES*) defined as follows:

$$\begin{cases} UR[u,r] = true \Leftrightarrow u \to r \\ PR[p,r] = true \Leftrightarrow p \to r, \end{cases}$$

where $\to$ symbolizes an assignment operator mapping its left and right operands onto each other. *USERS, ROLES*, and *PERMISSIONS* are the sets of managed users, roles, and permissions, respectively.

In RBAC the concept of a session refers to the mapping between a user and an activated subset of roles that are assigned to the user. Each user can be associated with one or more sessions at a time. A role session is defined by the established security context of the user, and thus a session is associated with a single user. The number of user sessions and roles that can be simultaneously active varies based on the underlying security policies. In some instances, each user is serially confined to a single session that in turn remains associated with a single role. In other cases, a user-security context may acquire multiple concurrent sessions, and each is associated with multiple roles at a time. Associating multiple roles to a session allows selective activation and deactivation of roles. Widely acceptable RBAC implementations and policies limit a user's established security context to a single session but with multiple roles at a time.

The illustration of Figure 8.2 shows roles as defining the rows of two matrices. One matrix represents user to role assignments A, and another one representing permission to role assignments B. While the grouping of users has eased access-control management, a role is viewed not only as a collection of permissions but rather as a collection of both users and permissions. The view of a role as intermediary between privileges and users represents the major difference between roles and groups.

RBAC Relationship Reviews

Role reviews are an essential element in the administration of an RBAC policy. A reliable RBAC implementation supports bidirectional reviews of user-role relationships whereby the roles assigned to a particular user and the users assigned to a specific role can be determined. A comprehensive review capability also allows for permission-role reviews in which permissions assigned to a particular role as well as roles containing a specific permission can be determined. The rows and columns of the matrices in Figure 8.2A and B illustrate

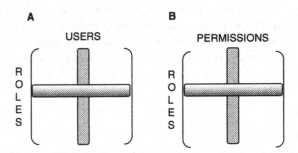

FIGURE 8.2 User-to-role and permission-to-role assignments as viewed in matrix forms

user-role and permission-role reviews, respectively. Formally, user-role reviews can be represented by a mapping *ur* and its inverse ur^{-1}, defined as

$ur : USERS \rightarrow 2^{ROLES}$,
$ur^{-1} : ROLES \rightarrow 2^{USERS}$.

The set of roles assigned to a given user is defined as
$user\_assigned\_roles(u) = \{r \in ROLES \mid UR[u,r] = true\}$.

The inverse mapping ur^{-1} yields role-user reviews that determine the set of users assigned to a particular role as
$role\_assigned\_users(r) = \{u \in USERS \mid UR[u,r] = true\}$.

Permission-role reviews can be represented by a mapping *pr* and its inverse pr^{-1} defined as follows:
$pr : PERMISSIONS \rightarrow 2,^{ROLES}$
$pr^{-1} : ROLES \rightarrow 2.^{\{PERMISSIONS\}}$

The set of roles to which a particular permission is assigned is given by
$permission\_assigned\_roles(p) = \{r \in ROLES \mid PR[p,r] = true\}$.

The set of permissions assigned to a particular role is given by $role\_assigned\_permissions(r) = \{p \in PERMISSIONS \mid PR[p,r] = true\}$.

Hierarchical RBAC

Role hierarchies are a natural means of structuring an organization's line of authorities. Support for hierarchical roles therefore is a key aspect of any role-based access-control implementation. Mathematically, a role hierarchy defines a partial ordering relationship among roles ($ROLES \times ROLES$) denoted by the symbol $\geq$. Each pair of related roles (i.e., $r_1, r_2 \in ROLES$) such that $r_1 \geq r_2$ is characterized by the following properties:

- r_1 is referred to as a *senior* role with respect to r_2.
- r_2 is referred to as a *junior* role with respect to r_1.
- r_1 acquires the permissions of r_2 in addition to its own permissions. This implies that the permission set assigned to r_2 is a subset of that assigned to r_1.
- r_2 acquires user membership of r_1 in addition to its own base of users. This means users with the senior role r_1 are automatically a subset of users in the junior role r_2.

Figure 8.3 illustrates the containment relationships corresponding to two hierarchical roles r_1 and its junior role r_2. Note the containment property with respect to users and permissions results in the senior user membership being part of the junior user membership, while the junior permissions are part of the senior permissions.

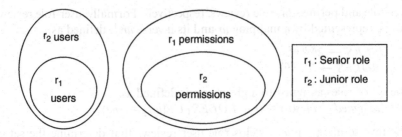

FIGURE 8.3 User and permission memberships in senior and junior role relationships

The partial ordering relationship ≥ defined among a set of hierarchical roles is also described as an inheritance relation. Role inheritance, in its most widely adopted definition, is expressed in terms of permissions whereby a senior role is said to inherit permissions of a junior role. A role r_1 inherits role r_2 if all permissions of r_2 are also permissions of r_1 and users of r_1 are automatically users of r_2. Role-inheritance modeling is functionally similar to class inheritance in object oriented systems.

Two forms of role inheritance are recognized, general, and limited role hierarchies.

General-Role Hierarchies

General-role hierarchies support the inheritance of privileges from one or more junior roles. Role inheritance here is analogous to the concept of inheritance in object-oriented programming languages where functions and data defined by a base class are inherited by a subclass, which, in turn, may further extend itself by defining additional data and functions. In the same manner by which instances of a subclass can be cast to the type of its parent class, a senior role can be cast to a junior role in that it automatically assumes the junior permissions. This analogy, however, does not apply when it comes to overriding functionality by a subclass that would correspond to overriding the semantics of an inherited permission.

The aspect of casting a specialized class of objects into a more generalized one is referred to in the literature by the *isa* relationship. Sandhu [SAND96] adopts the *isa* terminology in modeling role inheritance as illustrated in the example of Figure 8.4A. Roles with extended powers (i.e., those inheriting other roles) are better illustrated as higher than their juniors in the graphic representation of a role hierarchy. This visualization reflects the positions of lower level roles with respect to their senior roles. Figure 8.4B depicts the same inheritance relations as in Figure 8.4A but using the *isjunior* relation, thus graphically showing senior roles above their juniors. We adopt the *isjunior* relation in all of our illustrations of role hierarchies in the remainder of our discussion.

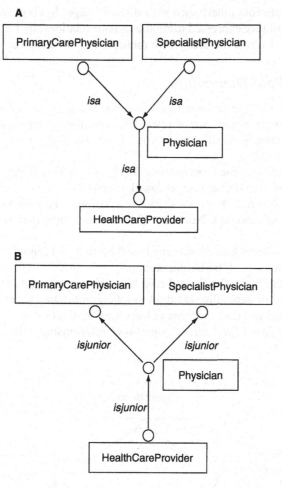

FIGURE 8.4 Representing role hierarchy using the *isa* relationship A and the *isjunior* relationship B

The *isa* and the *isjunior* relations are equivalent in the sense that

$$r_i \text{ isa } r_j \Leftrightarrow r_j \text{ isjunior } r_i.$$

Role-inheritance relationship is defined by the partial-order relationship denoted by $\geq$ such that $r_1 \geq r_2 \Leftrightarrow$ all permissions of r_2 are also permissions of r_1 and all users of r_1 are also users of r_2. This is expressed formally as

$$r_1 \geq r_2 \Rightarrow$$

role_assigned_permissions(r_2) $\subseteq$ role_assigned_permissions(r_1) $\wedge$
role_assigned_users(r_1) $\subseteq$ role_assigned_users(r_2).

We illustrate role inheritance with directed edges linking roles and representing inheritance expressed using the *isjunior* relationship. Figure 8.5 shows an example of a role hierarchy with multiple-role inheritance.

Limited-Role Hierarchies

This type of role hierarchy is restrictive over the general case in that it supports only single inheritance of roles. The semantics of inheritance, however, remain the same as in the general case. Formally, the limited-role hierarchy can be expressed as

$r_1 \geq r_2 \Rightarrow$ role_assigned_permissions$(r_2) \subseteq$ role_assigned_permissions$(r_1) \land$ role_assigned_users$(r_1) \subseteq$ role_assigned_users$(r_2) \land$

$\forall r, r_1, r_2 \in ROLES, r \geq r_1 \land r \geq r_2 \Rightarrow r_1 = r_2$ (single inheritance characterizing limited role hierarchies). Note that the $\geq$ relation here means direct inheritance only.

Figure 8.6 shows a role hierarchy based on that of Figure 8.5 but with single inheritance (i.e., a limited hierarchy).

Representation of the limited-role hierarchy corresponds to an inverted-tree structure or generally stated an acyclic graph. Once a limited-role hierarchy branches out (i.e., there are at least three distinct roles r_1, r_2, r_3 such that $r_2 \geq r_1$ and $r_3 \geq r_1$) (in a direct inheritance relationship), there cannot be a

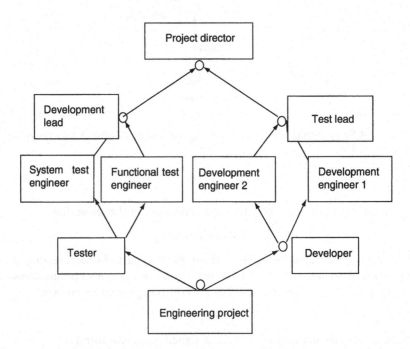

FIGURE 8.5 Example of a general-role hierarchy expressed by the *isjunior* relationship

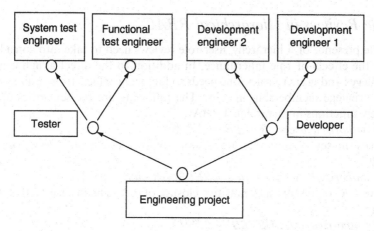

FIGURE 8.6 Example of a limited-role hierarchy (single-role inheritance)

single authoritative role *r* that encapsulates all privileges in the hierarchy. The absence of a *root* authoritative role is due to the single inheritance requirement imposed in the limited hierarchy. One exception to that is the linear hierarchy in which only a single role is defined at every level of authority as illustrated in the example of Figure 8.7.

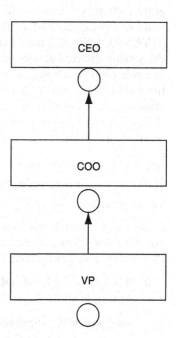

FIGURE 8.7 A linear-role hierarchy with three roles and a single root role (CEO)

Role Reviews in Hierarchical RBAC

In the presence of a hierarchy, user-role reviews need to take into consideration the effects of role inheritance. In addition to the direct assignment of privileges and users to roles, one needs to factor the effects from indirect user and privilege membership in roles. The following are the semantics of the review functions in hierarchical RBAC:

$role\_authorized\_users : ROLES \rightarrow 2^{USERS}$

returns the set of users that are authorized for a given role directly or indirectly.

$role\_authorized\_users(r) = \{u \in USERS|\ UR^* [u,r] = true\}$,

where UR^* represents the transitive closure of UR. The inverse of this mapping is

$user\_authorized\_roles:USERS \rightarrow 2^{ROLES}$

which returns the roles authorized for a given user, directly or indirectly:

$user\_authorized\_roles(u) = \{r \in ROLES|\ UR^* [u,r] = true\}$.

$role\_authorized\_permissions:ROLES \rightarrow 2^{PERMISSIONS}$

returns the set of permissions that are authorized for a given role either directly by way of assignment or indirectly through inheritance:

$role\_authorized\_permissions(r) = effective\_permissions(r)$.

Modeling Hierarchical RBAC Using Role Graphs

As has been mentioned, role inheritance can be modeled using directed graphs whereby a graph node represents a role and an edge from node r_1 to node r_2 represents the fact that r_2 inherits role r_1. Nyanchma and Osborn [NYAN99, OSBO02] have extensively studied the modeling of role hierarchies using directed acyclic graphs in what they refer to as *role graphs*. Roles in a role graph are bounded by *MaxRole* and *MinRole*. *MaxRole* represents the union of all privileges in the role set, and *MinRole* corresponds to the minimum set of privileges available to any role in the system (i.e., a common subset of privileges assigned to every role). In the absence of such a minimal privilege set, *MinRole* reduces to an empty set as stated below:

$role\_assigned\_permissions\ (MinRole) =$

$\begin{cases} \text{minimum required privilege set if defined} \\ \Phi \text{ otherwise} \end{cases}$

MaxRole is merely used for the formalism of role graphs and may or may not have any users assigned to it. As outlined by Nyanchama and Osborn [NYAN99], role graphs have the following properties:

❑ There is a single *MaxRole* whose set of privileges is given by the following formula:

$role\_assigned\_permissions\ (MaxRole) =$

$\cup$ *role_assigned_permissions* (r_i), $i = 1, ...,n$, where n is the cardinality of the *ROLES* set.

❏ There is a single *MinRole* containing the following set of privileges: *role_assigned_permissions* (*MinRole*) = I *role_assigned_permissions* (r_i), $i = 1,...,n$, which could result in an empty set.

❏ There is a path from *MinRole* leading to every role r_i, $i = 1,...,n$. This follows directly from the definition of the *MinRole* being at the bottom of an inverted tree of the role graph. This also follows from the fact that by definition *MinRole* is inherited by every role (i.e., $r_i \geq MinRole$, $i = 1,...,n$). The relationship $\geq$ here can be either direct or indirect by way of transitivity.

❏ The graph is acyclic. Assuming a role graph is allowed to contain cycles, by definition of the inheritance relation, it follows that each cycle of the graph can be reduced to a single node (role). The presence of a cycle in a role graph therefore is useless. Role graphs should not contain any cycles other than loops, which do exist by definition of $\geq$ since $r_i \geq r_i$, $i = 1,...,n$.

❏ The set of junior roles of a given role r, denoted by *juniors(r)*, consists of all roles represented by nodes r_i such that there is a path of length 1 or more from r_i to r. Immediate juniors of r are roles r_i such that (r_i, r) is an edge in the role graph.

❏ The set of senior roles of a given role r, denoted by *seniors(r)*, consists of all roles represented by nodes r_i such that there is a path of length 1 or more from r to r_i. Immediate seniors of r are roles r_i such that (r, r_i) is an edge in the graph. Note that by definition of role inheritance, a role can be either a senior or a junior to another role but cannot be both at the same time. Also note the fact that seniority relationship is the inverse of the junior relationship and vice-versa.

❏ For any two roles r_i and r_j, if *role_assigned_permissions* $(r_i) \subset role\_assigned\_permissions$ (r_j) then there exists a path from r_i to r_j. This property enforces the hierarchical structure of role graphs. By definition a role encompasses a set of privileges accumulated along the path starting at *MinRole* and leading up to that role. Therefore any role r_i whose set of privileges is part of the privileges of another role r_j is considered a junior role to r_j. A path exists between a senior role and all of its juniors.

Effective and Direct Privileges

Nyanchama and Osborn [NYAN99] introduced the notion of effective and direct privileges of a role. The direct privileges of role r are those privileges associated with r but are not assigned to any of its junior roles. On the other hand, the effective privileges of r are the union of all privileges accumulated from the junior roles of r augmented with the direct privileges of r itself. The set of effective privileges of any role r is expressed by the following recursive form:

$$\begin{cases} \textit{effective\_ privileges } (r) = \textit{direct\_ privileges}(r) \cup \\ \textit{effective\_ privileges } (r_i) : i = 1, \ldots, m \\ \textit{effective\_ privileges } (MinRole) = \\ \textit{direct\_ privilges} (MinRole), \end{cases}$$

where m is the total number of immediate junior roles of r. Recall that a role r_i is an immediate junior to r if and only if in the role graph there is an edge from r_i to r.

Direct privileges of a role can be an empty set. An example of that is a scenario in which a particular role is used to join multiple other roles. The privileges associated with a role created as a result of this role-join operation are the union of the effective privileges of its junior roles. Formally,

$$\textit{effective\_ privileges } (r) = \cup_{i=1,\ldots,m} \textit{effective\_ privileges } (r_i),$$

where r_i, i $= 1, \ldots, m$ is the set of immediate junior roles of r. Similarly, some roles in a hierarchy may have no users assigned to them. These virtual roles are defined only to capture competencies of some kind and are not assignable. For instance, an educator role is simply used to encapsulate the generic tasks that are common to every educator. A physical educator role that inherits from educator can be an elementary teacher, for instance.

Role-Graph Modeling of Generalized Role Inheritance

Direct role inheritance is a role-to-role relationship that can be viewed as happening in three different ways:

- ❑ *One-to-one* A role is inherited by a single role only. Therefore, propagating the privileges of the inherited role in one direction along the upper hierarchy. This case yields a linear role hierarchy.
- ❑ *One-to-many* A single role is inherited by multiple other roles and hence propagating the privileges of the inherited role in multiple directions. This scenario can be viewed as a split in the hierarchy in that different inheriting roles will have to exist at the level immediately above the level of the inherited role.
- ❑ *Many-to-one* Here multiple roles are inherited by a single role. This case can be viewed as a join operation in which multiple lower-level roles are inherited by a single upper role.

Figure 8.8 depicts the generalized role-to-role relationships and their implication on privilege sharing. For simplicity we refer to roles R_1, R_2 and R_3 to describe each of the scenarios illustrated. Case A is meaningful only when *effective_privileges* $(R_1) \subset$ *effective_privileges* (R_2). This implies that

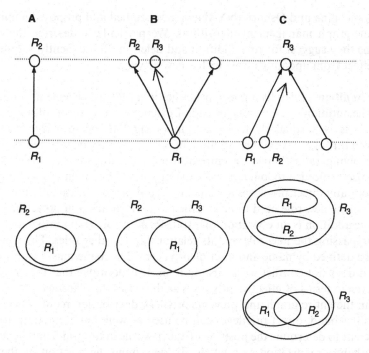

FIGURE 8.8 Scenarios of role-to-role relationship cardinality in the generalized RBAC model

direct_privileges(R_2) ≠ Φ. Role R_2 therefore has to be assigned permissions that are not in the effective permission set of R_1. The same applies to case B. In case C role R_3, however, does not need to introduce new privileges. This case assumes that *effective_privileges* (R_1) and *effective_privileges* (R_2) are disjoint sets; otherwise, there is no use from joining two identical roles. Role R_3 is used to join the authoritative powers of R_1 and R_2 into a single role and may in turn acquire new direct privileges.

Role-Graph Operations

The modeling of role hierarchies using acyclic directed graphs leads to the application of various graph-theoritic algorithms for manipulating and analyzing them. Given a role graph, one can deduce a corresponding graph that has no redundant edges by computing the transitive closure of the graph [AHO72, CHAR96]. For a particular role r, we compute the set of its junior roles by simply executing a breadth or a depth first search beginning at node r. Similarly, the set of *seniors(r)* can be computed by reversing the direction of edges in the role graph then computing a breadth or a depth first search starting at node r. Reversing the direction of edges is easily accomplished by making a copy of the original adjacency matrix then transposing it.

Nyanchama and Osborn [NYAN94] have studied and proposed a number of role-graph management algorithms. We particularly describe the algorithms they suggest for role addition and deletion. Subsequently, we discuss the effect from updating a role with a new privilege.

Role Addition   Introducing new privileges in an RBAC scheme may necessitate the addition of new roles instead of extending the controls of an existing one. This is particularly useful in supporting the least-privilege principle enabled through RBAC. The addition of a new role may be required to reflect the evolving authoritative structure of a particular organization. A new role may also be needed to join multiple existing roles into a single supervising role without any direct privileges assigned to it and in which case only the junior roles of the new role need to be specified to perform the join operation.

Role addition is an operation that transforms a role graph into a new state encompassing the new role and its relationship to other roles. The new role can be defined by name and a set of privileges. The name must be unique so that it does not conflict with existing roles. It is desirable that the privileges be given in terms of effective privileges as this eases the placement of the role within the entire graph and prevents privilege distribution redundancies. On the other hand, direct privileges can be used as well, but alone they are not sufficient to determine the position of the new role in the graph and hence the underlying organization as a whole. To determine the position of the new role, say r, we compute the sets of its senior as well as junior roles. The junior roles are those with an effective privilege set that is contained in the effective privileges of r; while the senior roles are those with effective privileges containing those of r. The result of this computation determines the edges incident to r (i.e., (r_i, r)) and those that are outgoing from r (i.e., (r, r_j), $i \neq j$), thus shaping the state of the new graph.

Finally, we need to perform privilege resolution to update direct and hence effective privileges of the nodes leading from r to all of its seniors. The direct set of privileges of the new role is decreased by any privileges that may be inherited along the paths leading up to the specified set of juniors of r. Similarly, any redundant direct privileges along the paths leading from r to all of its seniors are removed. In a well-formed role graph, the privilege resolution step should not result in removing an existing role; otherwise, the newly added role introduces an inconsistency in the graph, or it may indicate the fact that the addition of the new role is useless.

Another approach for adding roles as outlined by Nyanchama and Osborn [NYAN99] is to specify the new role with its direct privileges, the set of its junior roles, and the set of its senior roles. These parameters are sufficient for the placement of the new role in the graph. The following are the processing steps needed to transform the graph:

- ❑ Update edges of the role graph. We identify a subset of edges to be removed from the role graph based on the new role relations as derived from the set of senior and junior roles of the new role, r. This step concerns the removal of all edges (r_i, r_j) such that $r_i \in juniors(r)$, $r_j \in seniors(r)$ and the addition of edges (r_i, r) and (r, r_j).

❏ Perform privilege resolution as outlined before.

Figure 8.9 illustrates the effect of adding a role to a role graph.

Role Deletion This operation involves the elimination of a role from the role graph and is determined simply by the name of the role r to be deleted. Once the corresponding node in the graph is deleted, role relations are updated such that all immediate juniors of r are now joined with the immediate seniors of r prior to the deletion taking place. Formally, we build all edges (r_i, r_j) into the new graph where r_i is a member of the immediate set of juniors of r; while r_j is a member of immediate seniors of r. This process is termed as short-circuiting role r.

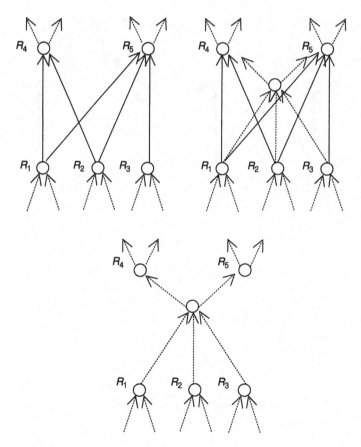

FIGURE 8.9 Inserting a role in a role graph

The privileges associated with the deleted role can either be eliminated or distributed across senior or junior roles of r. Eliminating the privileges of r affects only the effective privileges of its superior roles. Each may now account for a decrease in privileges. Retaining the privileges, however, is policy dependent in that they may be distributed across the senior roles of r in accordance to organizational needs and requirements. To make role deletion as much a transparent operation as possible, the privileges of the deleted role can simply be reassigned to each of its immediate senior roles or can all be reassigned to its junior roles. Other policies may elect to reassign the privileges of the deleted role to a combination of immediate senior or junior roles. A more complex policy may redistribute the deleted privileges arbitrarily across junior and senior roles that are not necessarily immediate to the deleted role. Figure 8.10 depicts the role-deletion operation.

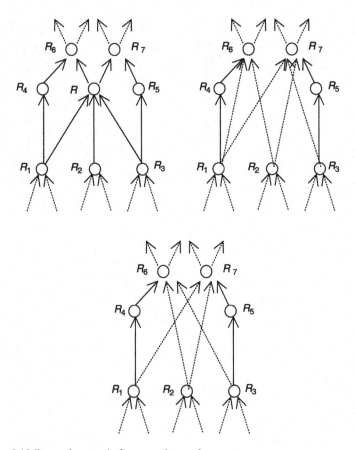

FIGURE 8.10 Removing a role from a role graph

Role-Privilege Update Role-privilege update is concerned with the changes made to the direct privileges of a given role r. These privileges may increase or decrease depending on the update operation performed. Removal of privileges may alter the structure of the underlying role graph in two ways.

❏ In the first scenario, the privilege deletion operation leaves the affected role (say, r) with no direct privileges of its own. We distinguish two cases: *The affected role has no senior roles*. If r has the same set of effective privileges as any of its immediate juniors, then it is considered redundant and thus can be deleted. As a result of the role deletion, the appropriate updates of the graph are applied as previously discussed. Otherwise r is left connected to the smallest set of incident nodes whose union of effective privileges yields the set of effective privileges of r. This step is used to optimize the structure of the graph and is evidently applicable only when r has one or more junior roles.
The affected role has one or more senior roles. Since this role no longer contributes any direct privileges to its seniors, it can be short-circuited by deleting it.

❏ In the second scenario, the delete operation leaves the affected role with a nonempty set of direct privileges. The newly updated role can be examined against other roles to determine any potential for overlaps. Overlapping roles are those with identical effective roles. An optimization process can be applied to the role graph to remove any redundancies in edge connectivity as a result of the new effective privileges of all seniors of r.

In addition to the automatic updates of a role graph as a result of a privilege deletion, one certainly should consider the effect on the entire role hierarchy, particularly as it relates to the senior roles of the affected role. This has to be taken in light of the fact that the deleted privilege may no longer be available to any superior roles of the affected role.

Increasing the direct privileges of a role implies an increase in its effective privileges. This operation, therefore, is useful only when the new set of effective privileges for the affected role is not identical to that of any other role; otherwise the affected role is considered redundant. In addition to the updates of the effective privileges of all seniors of the affected role, the graph structure may require changes to any eliminate potential redundancies.

Role graph updates may also be the result of modification to the sets of junior or senior roles of a particular role. The effects from such changes have to be accounted for throughout all nodes in the graph that are reachable from the affected node.

Optimizing Role Graphs The transformation of role graphs using role- and privilege-level operations may result in arbitrary graphs with redundant paths. A path p, $MinRole \rightarrow r_1 \dots \rightarrow r$ leading to node r is said to be redundant if there is one or more other paths starting at $MinRole$ and terminating at r such that the union of their effective privileges contains the set of effective privileges accumulated along path p. Figure 8.11A shows a role subgraph in which path $r_1 \to r_4 \to r$ is by definition redundant with the combination of two other paths $r_2 \to r_5 \to r$ and $r_3 \to r_6 \to r$. This is due to the fact that the set of privileges inherited by role r along the first path $\{p_1, p_2, p_3\}$ is a subset of that inherited along the union of the two other paths, which is $\{p_1, p_2, p_3, p_4, p_5\}$. Edges of the graph are labeled with the direct privileges associated with the source node. The subgraph of Figure 8.11B shows edge (r_4, r) eliminated as a result of this redundancy.

RBAC: A Comparative Discussion

RBAC has been touted as a policy-neutral access-control model. This implies that it can be used to model various access schemes such as discretionary and mandatory policies. Although the neutrality aspect of RBAC with respect to various security policies is not evident, researchers have shown its viability as a generalized access-control model encompassing both commercial as well as military access policies [SAND98, OSBO00].

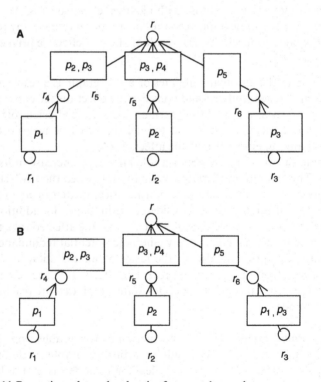

FIGURE 8.11 Removing edge redundancies from a role graph

Performing access decisions based on user groups pales in comparison to the benefits of RBAC for the main reason that user grouping is one-dimensional. RBAC, on the other hand, is viewed as a two-dimensional grouping of users and privileges. A role, by definition, is an encapsulation of a set of users and at the same time a set of privileges. Because members of the same role have common privileges, simulating user groups using roles is a straightforward exercise. Each designated group is mapped to a separate role with user to role assignments that are identical to the membership in the group. Assigning privileges to roles is not needed here because user groups are not directly concerned with privilege grouping. This construction is very simple and unnecessary since it does not exploit the benefits brought forth by RBAC—namely, encapsulation of privileges, arbitrary role hierarchies, and role constraints.

Discretionary access policies are founded on the notion of user ownership of resources and hence the unconditional access to the resource by its owner. The owner may further grant other users access to his or her resources on a discretionary basis. RBAC can be configured to emulate a DAC policy by simulating the owner-centric view of resources as well as the power of granting access to others on a discretionary basis. We discuss this simulation shortly. To impart the benefits of RBAC on a DAC policy, however, it might be better to redesign an existing DAC policy so that it is effectively modeled by an entirely new RBAC scheme.

Mandatory access-control (MAC) policies evolve around the concept of a one-directional flow of information in a lattice of security classes. In its basic confidentiality scheme, a MAC policy is concerned with preventing the flow of information from higher levels of the lattice to the entities that are lower. Hierarchical and constrained RBAC has been formally shown to simulate various MAC policies, the details of which are discussed in the next section.

Mapping of a Mandatory Policy to RBAC

The work done by Osborn, Sandhu, and Munawer (OSM) [OSBO00] is an excellent proof that RBAC deserves to be described as a generalized framework for articulating various access-control policies rather than its limitation to one scheme or another. In particular, mandatory-access control referred to as a lattice-based-access control (LBAC) can be formally expressed using RBAC. The essential element of mapping an LBAC policy onto a corresponding RBAC model as noted by Osborn et al. lies in the similarity between an activated session role in RBAC and the security classification associated with a login session of LBAC. Another aspect that contributes to the similarity between these two models is the hierarchical nature of roles and security classifications. Nonetheless, the similarities alone are not sufficient to establish an evident mapping between LBAC and RBAC or to demonstrate that LBAC is indeed an instance of RBAC. The development of this mapping eliminates the barriers that have for long separated mandatory policies, in use mainly by the military, and the commercial access-control policies as described by many implementations of RBAC and DAC. In that respect, this mapping along with others can be considered a major step in unifying access control models.

At the core of a mandatory security policy is a set of *security labels*, also referred to as *security classes*, assigned to system users and resources in a static fashion by authorized system administrators. These assignments remain invariant, an aspect known in LBAC systems as *tranquility*. A confidentiality LBAC is defined as a finite lattice of security classes *SC* with a partially ordered relationship denoted by $\geq$ satisfying the simple security property, also known as the *read-down rule*, and the liberal *-property, known as the *write-up rule*. Both of these rules are formally defined by

❑ *Simple security property* Subject s can read object o only if $\lambda(s) \geq \lambda(o)$.
❑ *Liberal *-property* Subject s can write object o only if $\lambda(s) \leq \lambda(o)$.

λ represents the procedure by which an association is made between a particular security class and a system entity, a subject or an object. This LBAC confidentiality policy as we have known imparts a dual property on the governed entities in that a higher entity can read a lower entity but cannot write it and vice versa.

The OSM construction is based on the following two observations:

❑ A higher-level subject in an LBAC lattice has complete power with respect to the read operation over objects that it dominates but has no authority with respect to the write operation over the same objects.
❑ A subject that is higher in an RBAC hierarchy always has more control over entities lower in the hierarchy. Specifically, when the privilege set of an RBAC system is reduced to the read operation only, a higher subject can read all of the objects that are lower in the hierarchy. Similarly, when the privilege set of an RBAC model is reduced to the write operation only, subjects higher in the hierarchy can write all objects governed by roles that are lower in that hierarchy.

The dual aspect of an LBAC lattice with respect to the read and write operations led to the use of two role hierarchies in the equivalent OSM construction that maps LBAC onto RBAC. The first hierarchy simulates the read operation, while the second one simulates the write authority. Consider the basic confidentiality LBAC of Figure 8.12A in which $SC=\{L, M_1, M_2, H\}$, with H and L being the highest and the lowest security labels, respectively. M_1 and M_2 are two disjoint labels that both dominate L but dominated by H. The equivalent RBAC of this lattice is represented by two role hierarchies as shown in the role graphs of Figure 8.12B.

The duality of the two role hierarchies of Figure 8.12B is apparent. The highest read role H_R is able to read all objects, while the lowest write role can write them all. Meanwhile, intermediary read roles M_{1R} and M_{2R} are each able to read objects at their respective levels and those readable by role L_R corresponding to the lowest security label in LBAC. On the other hand,

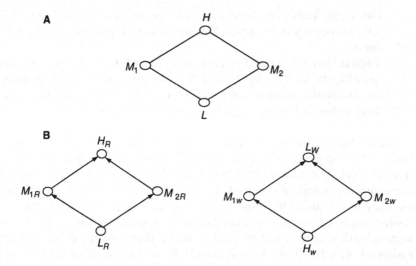

FIGURE 8.12 A basic LBAC model A and its RBAC equivalent B

intermediary roles M_{1W} and M_{2W} are able to write objects at their respective levels, and those that are writable by H_W (the highest security label in the LBAC model). The OSM construction results in each security label x being modeled as two roles x_R and x_W for read and write at level x, respectively.

OSM Mapping of a Confidentiality-Mandatory Policy

Given a confidentiality LBAC system defined by a finite set of security labels $SC = \{L_1,...,L_n\}$ and a partial ordering relationship among the labels denoted by $\geq$, an equivalent RBAC system is formulated by the following OSM construction, referred to as Construction 1:

❑   Two disjoint role hierarchies RH and WH for read and write, respectively, are defined as $RH = \{L_1R,...,L_nR\}$ and $WH = \{L_1W,...,L_nW\}$. Each security label L_i, $i = 1,...,n$ is mapped onto two roles L_iR with the same partial order as $\geq_{LBAC}$ and L_iW with a partial order that is the inverse of $\geq_{LBAC}$. The notation $\geq_{LBAC}$ is used herein to explicitly refer to the dominance relationship in the LBAC model as opposed to role inheritance.

❑   Because an LBAC object o has a single security label (say, x) associated with it, in RBAC o is accessible through read and write permission-to-role assignments on object o such that (o, r) is assigned to role xR ⇔ (o, w) is assigned to role xW. This enforces the policy that at security label x the objects that can be simultaneously read and written are those at level x only. It represents the duality of a security label with respect to read and write operations. Coupled with this constraint is the requirement that permission *(o, r)* be assigned to exactly one role *xR*. This constraint is equivalent to the use of a single security label for *o*.

❑ Each subject is assigned to exactly two roles *xR* and *LW*, where *x* is the security label of the subject and *LW* is the write role that corresponds to the lowermost security label in accordance with the relationship $\geq_{LBAC}$.

❑ Each active session has exactly two roles *yR* and *yW*.

The last two constraints allow for user sessions that are bounded by the *xR* role for the read privilege and the *LW* role for the write privilege, *x* being the security label associated with the user activating the session. Since each session must have a matching pair of roles *yR* and *yW*, these roles must be junior roles of *xR* and *LW*, respectively. A special case arises when the user session consists of the pair of roles *LR* and *LW*, thereby allowing the user to write all other objects but to read none of them, except those that are assigned to role *LR*. This case corresponds to the bottom of the lattice in the LBAC model.

Note that the constructed-role hierarchy is a special role graph in which the effective privilege set and the direct privilege set of each role are equal. The difference among roles, however, lies in the scope of objects accessible to each. Higher roles evidently have access to more objects than lower roles. For the *RH* hierarchy, the constant effective privilege set contains the read permission, while that of the *WH* hierarchy consists of the write permission. The effect of role inheritance in this construction is the widening scope of objects that can be read or written by a particular senior role. This construction leads to the formal proof of the following theorem:

Theorem 8.1: *An RBAC system defined by Construction 1 satisfies the simple security property and the liberal *-property of an LBAC system.*

Given an object *o* whose security label is $\lambda (o) = x$, and a subject *s* simulated by an active session corresponding to user *u* whose security label is $\lambda (u) = z$, for user *u* to read object *o*, permission *(o, r)* must be assigned to role *zR* or one of its juniors (i.e., one corresponding to a security label *y* such that $z \geq_{LBAC} y$, which in turn corresponds to the user's active session role *yR*). Hence, $\lambda (u) \geq_{LBAC} \lambda (s)$ and $\lambda (s) \geq_{LBAC} \lambda (o)$, which is the simple security property.

Similarly, for user *u* to write object *o*, *(o, w)* must be among the permissions assigned to *u* directly or indirectly through role inheritance. Since *u* is assigned to role *LW* with *L* corresponding to the lowest security label, and *LW* being at the top of the write role hierarchy, *(o, w)* is therefore within reach of role *LW*. However, user *u* can only have a session activated with the pair of roles *zR* and *zW* or one such as *yR* and *yW*, where *yR* and *yW* are junior roles of *zR* and *zW*, respectively. Since the write role hierarchy is the inverse of the LBAC lattice, it follows that $\lambda (o) \geq_{LBAC} \lambda (s)$.

OSM Mapping of an Integrity-Mandatory Policy

The integrity of a security lattice, also referred to as the *strict *-property*, mandates that subject s is able to write object o only if s and o are both at the same level in the lattice—i.e., $\lambda(s) = \lambda(o)$. The OSM mapping of the integrity LBAC policy onto an equivalent RBAC model, herein called Construction 2, follows exactly the same construction as we saw with the confidentiality-based LBAC but with the following two exceptions:

- The write roles $L_1 W, ..., L_n W$ are all disjoint—i.e., there is no hierarchy relation between any two roles $L_i, L_j, i, j = 1, ..., n, i \neq j$.
- Each user is assigned exactly two roles xR and xW, where x is the security label of that user in the LBAC system.

The result of the mapping above is expressed by the following theorem:

Theorem 8.2: *An RBAC system defined by Construction 2 satisfies the simple security property and the strict *-property of an integrity-based LBAC system.*

The simple security property follows immediately from the construction of theorem 8.1. The strict *-property is evident in that each object is writable by a single role only. For user u to write object o, u must activate session s with the pair of roles (yR, yW), where y corresponds to a security label that is dominated by $\lambda(u) = z$ and (o, w) is assigned to role yW. Since u is assigned to a single role zW and because the roles are disjoint, the session will always consist of the pair of roles (zR, zW); therefore, $\lambda(s) = \lambda(o)$.

Figure 8.13 represents the read and write role hierarchies resulting from the OSM mapping onto RBAC of the basic integrity LBAC model with four security labels $SC = \{L, M_1, M_2, H\}$ layered as shown in Figure 8.12A.

RBAC Correspondence to a Mandatory Policy

The OSM constructions are concerned with a mapping that formulates an existing mandatory policy into a corresponding new role-based policy. Given

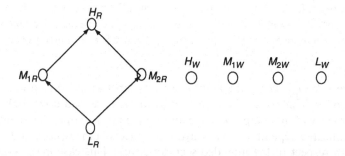

FIGURE 8.13 The OSM mapping of a basic integrity LBAC onto corresponding RBAC

a RBAC system, however, one might be interested in knowing whether the role-based policy in fact satisfies a mandatory policy over the same set of subjects and objects if they were to be assigned security labels. Such an analysis was first undertaken by Osborn [OSBO97] in which it was shown that the structure of an RBAC hierarchy that at the same time corresponds to an LBAC scheme is constrained in many ways. We discuss some of these scenarios here.

For example, a role with permissions to write a low-level object and read a high-level object is not assignable to any subject for the obvious reason that it yields a conflict with the mandatory policy. Similarly, a role with permissions to simultaneously read and write a mixture of high-level and low-level objects cannot be assigned to a user with a high security label. Doing so violates the write-up-mandatory policy. In the meantime, that same role cannot be assigned to users at lower labels as it results in the violation of the read-down-only policy. On the other hand, if a particular role is assigned read permissions for objects that are at intermediary security levels only and write permission is assigned only to higher-level objects, a user with the corresponding security label can be assigned to that role.

The analysis of Osborn reduces the set of privileges assignable to each role in an existing RBAC scheme to read (r) and write (w) operations only, calling it the *modified privilege set*. Given a role R, any object o such that (o, r) is in the modified privilege set of R is considered to be in the *r-scope* of R. Likewise, an object o that is writable by R (i.e., (o, w) is in the modified privilege set of R) is said to be in the *w-scope* of R.

Consider a write-only role R (i.e., one with an empty *r-scope*). For subject s to be assigned this role, the security label of s has to be dominated by the security labels of all objects that are members of the *w-scope* of R so that s adheres to the write-up mandatory rule as illustrated in Figure 8.14A. Thus, the constraint

$$w\_level_{min} (R) \geq \lambda (s),$$

where $w\_level_{min} (R)$ is the lowest security label assigned to objects in the *w-scope* of R. This constraint enforces the write-up policy. Similarly, when R is a read-only role (i.e., the w-scope of R is empty), for subject s to be assigned to this role, the security label of s has to dominate the security labels of all objects in the *r-scope* for R as illustrated in Figure 8.14B. Thus, the constraint

$$\lambda (s) \geq r\_level_{max} (R),$$

where $r\_level_{max} (R)$ is the highest security label assigned to objects in the *r-scope* of R. This constraint is needed to enforce the read-down policy.

For roles with nonempty r-scope and nonempty w-scope, the analysis can be complicated depending on the layout of objects in the r-scope and w-scope sets with respect to the intended security lattice. This case may range from simple scenarios to situations where it cannot be possible for a given role R to be assigned to any subject. The simplest of such cases arises when all objects in the r-scope and the w-scope of a role R have the same security

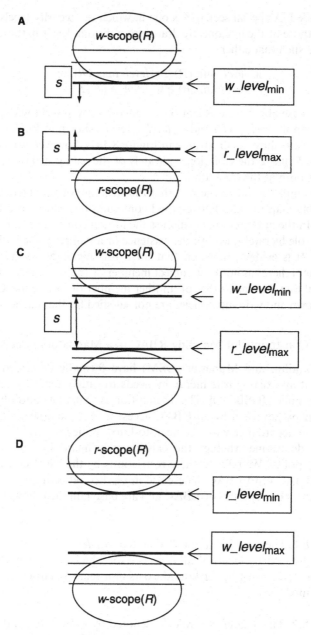

FIGURE 8.14 Scenarios of mapping a role hierarchy onto a mandatory policy

label. This role can therefore be assigned to any subject whose security label is equal to that of objects in the r-scope or the w-scope of R.

In the case of the r-scope and the w-scope of R being assigned security labels that arbitrarily span multiple levels in a security lattice, the combinations can be unbounded. A special scenario is one in which the security labels of the r-scope and those of the w-scope are drawn from disjoint levels in the lattice and are ordered such that either

$$w\_level\_min\ (R) \geq r\_level\_max\ (R),\ or$$
$$r\_level\_min\ (R) \geq w\_level\_max\ (R).$$

In the first case above, role R can be assigned to any subject with a security label between $w\_level_{max}\ (R)$ and $w\_level_{min}\ (R)$ as shown in Figure 8.14C. In the second case above as illustrated in Figure 8.14D, however, no user can be assigned to R due to the violation separately of the read-down rule and write-up rules or both at the same time.

These examples point to the fact that the structure of role hierarchies that may possibly map to valid lattice-based configurations can indeed be greatly restricted. In the next section, we discuss the formal constraints that when satisfied by a role hierarchy, lead to the existence of a mapping to an LBAC configuration. It is evident, however, that for a role hierarchy to map onto an LBAC system there cannot be an object member of the w-scope for any role R with a label that dominates that of another member of its r-scope. Otherwise, the read-down and write-up policies are not satisfied for that particular object.

The OSM Constraints for Mapping RBAC to a Mandatory Policy

Osborn, Sandhu, and Munawer (OSM) have formally described the constraints that an existing role hierarchy needs to satisfy for it to map onto a mandatory policy [OSBO00]. The assumption is that users and objects of a system already governed by an RBAC access model are now assigned security labels in accordance with the need-to-know policy of LBAC. The question is to determine whether the existing role hierarchy serves the new mandatory policy. We refer to these restrictions by the OSM constraints for mapping RBAC onto LBAC. These are in essence reflecting the read-down and the write-up properties of LBAC and are based on the following two definitions:

Definition 8.1: The *r-level* of a role R, denoted by *r-level(R)*, is the least upper bound of the security labels of all objects o for which (o, r) is in the r-scope of R. Because the least upper bound exists in a security lattice, the *r-level* is always defined.

Definition 8.2: The *w-level* of a role R, denoted by *w-level(R)*, is the greatest lower bound of the security labels of all objects o for which (o, w) is in the w-scope of R. When such a bound does not exist, the *w-level* is undefined. The following theorem by OSM follows directly from these definitions.

Theorem 8.3: *An authorization scheme that is governed by a role hierarchy satisfies the read-down and the write-up mandatory properties if the following constraints on the user-to-role assignments (UA) hold:*

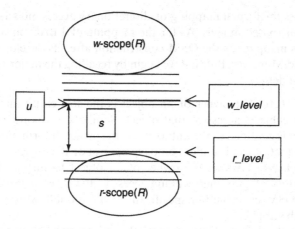

FIGURE 8.15 OSM constraints mapping an existing RBAC policy onto a mandatory policy

$$\forall R \in UA, w - level(R) \text{ is defined}$$
$$\forall (u, R) \in UA, \lambda (u) \geq r - level(R)$$
$$\forall (u, R) \in UA, \lambda (u) \leq w - level(R),$$

where for all user u and object o, $\lambda(u)$ and $\lambda (o)$ represent the security labels of u and o, respectively. The last two constraints define the range of security labels to which role R can be mapped. User sessions are as always confined within the bounds of the security label assigned to the user—i.e.,

$$\forall s \in sessions, \lambda (s) \leq \lambda (u).$$

Figure 8.15 illustrates the constraints outlined of theorem 8.3.

Mapping Discretionary-Access Control to RBAC

RBAC has been shown by Osborn, Sandhu, and Munawer to be capable of simulating discretionary policies [OSBO00]. Recall that the central theme of DAC is that of resource ownership. The owner of an object has the authority over who else can access that object. Information flow in DAC is therefore driven by owner-based administration of access rights. Overlooking the role of a super administrative user, generally all variations of the DAC policies share the following characteristics:

- ❑ The creator of an object, such as a file in a file system, automatically becomes the owner of that object.
- ❑ An object can be destroyed only by its owner.
- ❑ While an object is automatically owned by its creator, ownership may optionally be shared with other subjects as well.

We discuss the formal mapping of discretionary access models into corresponding role-based models. As for the mapping of LBAC onto RBAC, we refer to this mapping as the OSM construction after its developers Osborn, Sandhu, and Munawer. But first we begin by recalling the major variations of the DAC models.

- ❏ *Strict DAC* The owner of an object is the sole entity that may grant other subjects access to that object. Similarly, revoking access to the object is confined to the authority of the owner. Information flow from or to that object is under complete control of the owner.
- ❏ *Liberal DAC* Allows the owner of an object to further delegate the authority of granting/revoking access to the object by other subjects. The OSM construction specifically treats the following variations of the liberal DAC:

  One-level grant: Delegation of the grant/revoke authority is limited to one level only. The owner may delegate grant/revoke authority to other users but they cannot further delegate this power.

  Two-level grant: The chain of delegating the grant/revoke authority is limited to a maximum of two levels. Besides the owner delegating his or her authority to another user, the latter can further delegate that authority to other users. For instance, Elyes can delegate the grant/revoke authority over his files to Aicha. In turn, Aicha can delegate the same authority to Alice. But Alice has no control over further delegating this authority to other users.

  Multilevel grant: The power to delegate the grant/revoke authority can be propagated down to multiple levels. Elyes can authorize Aicha, who can authorize Alice, who can further authorize Fatima, and so forth.
- ❏ *DAC with change of ownership* This variation allows a user to transfer ownership of an object to other users.
- ❏ *DAC with grant-independent revocation* In this variation revoking access can be performed by any subject with the appropriate authority, not necessarily the one who granted access in the first place.
- ❏ *DAC with Grant-Dependent Revocation* Revocation can be performed only by the granter of access. The entity performing the grant access is required to be the same as that revoking it.

The Elements of the OSM DAC to RBAC Mapping

The central aspect of the OSM DAC to RBAC mapping is the simulation of the owner-centric and delegated information flow exhibited in the DAC model. For simplicity, the OSM construction is described for a DAC policy with a single *read* operation. Construction for DAC with multiple operations follows in the same way.

The creation of an object O in a DAC system corresponds to the creation of a role hierarchy consisting of three administrative roles and one regular role in the corresponding RBAC model. This hierarchy consists of the following roles in which READ_O is the regular role (i.e., one with no privileges affecting properties of other roles):

- ❑ *READ_O* This role encapsulates the privilege to read object *O*. It is assigned the canRead_O permission. An entity assigned to this role has the authority to read object *O*.
- ❑ *PARENT_O* This role represents the authority to assign and remove users from role READ_O. It is assigned permissions addReadUser_O and deleteReadUser_O. PARENT_O captures the authority of granting access in the DAC model.
- ❑ *PARENTwithGRANT_O* This role is used to express the delegated powers of grant and revoke down in a DAC chain. It is used to administer the PARENT_O role via two permissions (addParent_O and deleteParent_O) and represents the recursive grant and revoke in DAC.
- ❑ *OWN_O* This role is used to simulate the concept of resource ownership in DAC. It is assigned two permissions for administering the PARENTwithGRANT role via addParentWithGrant_O and deleteParentWithGrant_O which add and remove users from the PARENTwithGRANT_O role, respectively. Additionally, OWN_O is assigned the privilege destroyObject_O, making it the only role with the power to destroy object *O*. Destruction of *O* automatically results in the deletion of all the roles above.

These roles are structured in a linear inheritance hierarchy, at the bottom of which is the READ_O role inherited by PARENT_O, which in turn is inherited by PARENTwithGRANT_O. The latter is further inherited by the OWN_O role positioned at the top of the hierarchy. Privileges are therefore inherited along this hierarchy in such a way that OWN_O has the authority of assuming all of the permissions defined in the above. Figure 8.16 depicts this hierarchy.

Note that that role OWN_O has the power to add and remove users from role PARENTwithGRANT_O, which in turn is capable of adding and removing users from role PARENT_O. This construction embeds the recursive property of delegating authorities and is needed to allow for multiple levels of grant and revoke down the stream of discretionary controls governing a particular object.

Simulating Strict DAC This policy can be enforced by the corresponding role hierarchy of Figure 8.16 by simply imposing the following cardinality constraints on the administrative roles:

- ❑ Cardinality of 1 for OWN_O,
- ❑ Cardinality of 0 for PARENTwithGRANT_O, and
- ❑ Cardinality of 0 for PARENT_O.

Strict DAC is thus simulated using only two roles OWN_O and READ_O as shown in Figure 8.17 with OWN_O assigned the privileges addReadUser_O, deleteReadUser_O, and destroyObject.

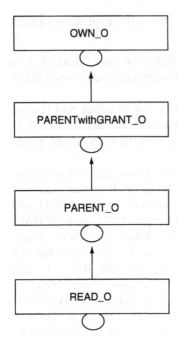

FIGURE 8.16. The OSM hierarchy of roles corresponding to resource ownership in the DAC model

Imposing cardinality of 1 restriction over role OWN_O prevents multiple ownership of object O. The owner in this case is the sole entity that grants access to the protected object.

Simulating Liberal DAC   In this case, the OSM construction distinguishes three scenarios based on the level of the grant authority as follows:

One-level grant   This policy can be simulated by imposing the following cardinality constraint: Cardinality of 0 for PARENTwithGRANT_O.

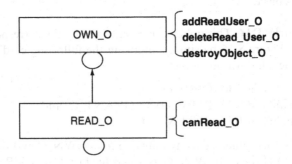

FIGURE 8.17. Simulating strict DAC by an RBAC policy

Here the construction requires only three roles: OWN_O, PARENT_O, and READ_O as illustrated in Figure 8.18. The one-level grant can be achieved by way of the owner adding a user to the PARENT_O role. The latter becomes capable of adding other users to the READ_O. A user that is added to the READ_O role only cannot further delegate the grant authority to other users.

Two-level grant No cardinality constraints are set on any of the three administrative roles to achieve the semantics of this policy. The owner can assign users to role PARENTwithGRANT_O, which is in turn used to assign users to PARENT_O thereby realizing a two-level grant. Note that a n-level grant can be similarly achieved using n roles:

PARENT_O,
PARENTwithGrant_O$_1$,
PARENTwithGRANT_O$_2$,...,
PARENTwithGrant_O$_{n-2}$,
PARENTwithGrant_O$_{n-1}$

Deeper n-level constructions performed in this way, however, are not amenable to a larger degree of scalability.

Multilevel grant Recursive nesting of the grant authority is achieved by removing all cardinality constraints on the three administrative roles and furthermore assigning the addParentWithGrant privilege to the role PARENTwithGRANT_O. To couple the grant and the revoke authorities the deleteParentWithGrant_O privilege is also assigned to the role PARENTwithGRANT_O. The permissions addParentWithGrant_O and deleteParentWithGrant_O therefore become direct privileges of role

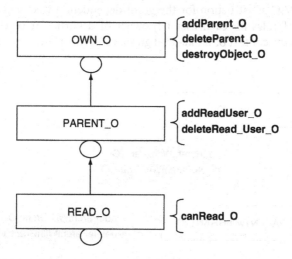

FIGURE 8.18 Simulating a one-level grant DAC policy by RBAC

PARENTwithGRANT_O and are simply inherited by role OWN_O as part of its effective set of privileges. This recursive pattern is depicted in Figure 8.19.

An example of a three-level grant follows. Aicha, being the owner of object O, assigns user Elyes to role PARENTwithGRANT_O. Hence Elyes is automatically granted read access to object O through privilege inheritance from role READ_O. In his role, Elyes invokes the privilege addParentWithGrant_O to assign user Alice to the PARENTwithGRANT_O role and thereby gives Alice read access to object O. In turn, Alice invokes the privilege addParentWithGrant_O to assign user Bob to role PARENTwithGRANT_O. At this point, Bob decides not to disseminate any further grant privilege and thus maintains a three-level grant.

Simulating DAC with Changes to Ownership   Resource ownership can be transferred by redefining the administrative authority of role OWN_O. This can be accomplished by assigning a new privilege—say, changeOwner_O to role OWN_O. The owner of an object O may invoke this privilege to change ownership to another user. Due to the cardinality constraint over role OWN_O being 1, ownership of the object transfers solely to the new user. Multiple owners can be accommodated by simply increasing the cardinality of role OWN_O.

Simulating Grant-Dependent Revoke   In all previous constructions, revocation of access is independent of the granter. The roles considered allow for user A to grant access to user B, while a third user, C with the appropriate authority, may revoke access to B. Grant-dependent revoke enforces a policy whereby only the user who granted access in the first place is capable of revoking it. In essence, grant-dependent revoke draws distinct administrative domains across the entities governed by a DAC policy as such.

OSM RBAC construction for the grant-dependent revoke enforces a strict separation of roles for each user Ui, owner of a particular object O, and is described in the context of a one-level grant authority. Here the one-level grant

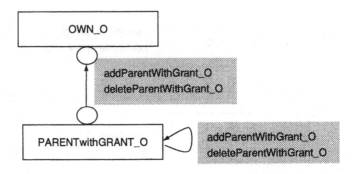

FIGURE 8.19 Simulating a multi-level grant DAC policy by RBAC

policy is simulated by creating a different administrative role Ui_PARENT_O and a different regular role Ui_READ_O for each user authorized by the owner to perform a one-level grant. Each role Ui_PARENT_O is assigned two permissions used to manage user assignments to role Ui_READ_O as follows:

- addU_ReadUser_O is used to add a user to role Ui_READ_O.
- deleteU_ReadUser_O is used to remove a user from role Ui_READ_O.
- The key to the separation of these administrative tasks however is the constraints: Each role Ui_PARENT_O has cardinality of 1.
- Membership in role Ui_PARENT_O remains unchanged once it is assigned.

A single user Ui, therefore, will be the only one granting read access to users and the only one capable of revoking it by invoking addU_ReadUser_O and deleteU_ReadUser_O, respectively, on role Ui_READ_O.

In this one-level grant construction, each role Ui_PARENT_O is automatically created by the owner invoking the administrative privilege addParent_O for user Ui. Figure 8.20 depicts the association between each Ui_READ_O and its corresponding Ui_PARENT_O role. Note that all of these roles are juniors to role OWN_O.

A Note About the OSM DAC to RBAC Mapping

It is quite apparent that OSM constructions for mapping DAC onto a corresponding RBAC policy do not scale to any average size of resource inventory

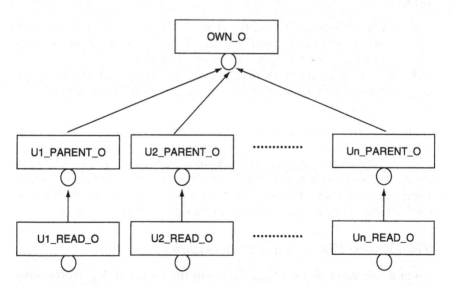

FIGURE 8.20 RBAC Simulation of a grant-dependent revoke in one-level grant DAC policy

in a computing system. The lack of scalability is due to managing separate role hierarchies for each object owned by entities of a system such as users, programming agents, processes, and hosts. The overhead incurred from setting these role hierarchies becomes prohibitive particularly when contrasted with the cost and scalability of a simple DAC mechanism such as access-control lists that can be readily used to protect resources. The OSM construction for mapping DAC onto RBAC therefore may be regarded as only theoretical proof of concept. Indeed, such mapping is yet another demonstration that role-based access control deserves to be viewed as a unified access-control model now that mandatory policies can also be modeled using RBAC.

RBAC Flow Analysis

The modeling of role hierarchies using role graphs provides a formal way of studying and analyzing RBAC. The fact that directional edges of role graphs correspond to privilege hierarchies translates immediately into the paths of an RBAC information flow. Osborn used the role-graph modeling process as a tool to analyze the flow of information across objects of an RBAC system [OSBO02].

Given a role graph, the Osborn analysis constructs a flow graph representing all potential information flows across objects. This analysis is based on the ability of copying the content of one object into another object. The copy operation usually takes place using a combination of read r and write w privileges. As such, the Osborn RBAC flow analysis is based on the following elements:

❑ If the privileges (o_1,r) and (o_2,w) are in the same role R, then a user assigned to R has the ability to cause the flow of information from object o_1 to object o_2 by way of a copy operation.

❑ Regardless of the roles to which the privileges (o,r) and (o,w) are assigned information will always be considered to flow from any object o to itself.

The first element corresponds to a directed edge from node (o_1,r,R) to node (o_2,w,R) in the flow graph, while the second one is represented by potentially multiple bidirectional edges from (o,r,R_i) to (o,w,R_j) and (o,r,R_j), where R_i,R_j are any two roles to which either of the privileges (o,r) and/or (o,w) is assigned. These edges essentially represent the flow of information from an object to itself irrespective of the permissions and roles controlling that object.

The Osborn Flow-Analysis Algorithm

Given a role graph $RG = (N_{RG}, E_{RG})$ with the set nodes N_{RG} representing modeled roles and the set of directed edges E_{RG} corresponding to the role hierarchy relationships, the Osborn flow-analysis algorithm outputs a flow graph $FG = (N_{FG}, E_{FG})$ in which a node in N_{FG} represents an object that is controlled by some role R_i through privilege r or w, or both. Edges E_{FG} represent the flow of information across the protected objects. Figure 8.21 describes the details of this algorithm.

In the following, we discuss two examples of the Osborn flow analysis.

Example 1: Flow Analysis of a Simple LBAC Scheme   We map an LBAC with strict *-property to an RBAC model and then apply the Osborn algorithm to determine the paths of information flow in the resulting RBAC system. We consider a simple LBAC scheme with four security labels $\{L, M_1, M_2, H\}$ as we illustrate in Figure 8.12A. The strict *-property states that subject s can write object o only if o is at the same security label as s—i.e., $\lambda(s) = \lambda(o)$. Recall also that two role hierarchies are created by the OSM mapping construction in which the read hierarchy has a partial order identical to that of LBAC, while the write roles are completely disjoint. We select an object as a representative of every security level as follows:

o_L for level L

o_{M1} for level M1

o_{M2} for level M2

o_H for level H

The RBAC construction results in eight roles—four for the read hierarchy $RH = \{L_R, M_{1R}, M_{2R}, H_R\}$ and four for the write hierarchy $WH = \{L_W, M_{1W}, M_{2W}, H_W\}$. Because users assigned the privilege of writing an object at level L for instance are also able to read the same object, role L_W automatically

---

for each role $R_k \in N_{RG}$ do

  for each privilege $p = (o, r/w) \in Effective(R_k)$ do

    construct node $n \in N_{FG}$ and label it with role R_k and privilege p;

  for every pair of privileges in $Effective(R_k)$ that is of the form (o_i, r)

  (o_j, w)

    construct a directed edge $e \in E_{FG}$ from node (R_k, o_i, r) to node

    (R_k, o_j, r);

for each object o do

  for each pair of nodes $n_i, n_j \in N_{FG}$ whose labels refer to the common

object o

    construct edges $n_i \to n_j, \; n_j \to n_i \in E_{FG}$;

FIGURE 8.21 The Osborn algorithm for the information-flow analysis in role graphs

inherits privilege (O_L, r). Similarly, role H_W inherits privilege (O_H, r), while roles M_{1W} and M_{2W} inherit privileges (O_{M1}, r) and (O_{M2}, r), respectively. Due to this inheritance structure we rename the write hierarchy as follows: $WH = \{L_{RW}, M_{1RW}, M_{2RW}, H_{RW}\}$. The resulting read and write hierarchies are now combined into a single hierarchy as represented by Figure 8.22. The effective privileges associated with each role are shown.

To simplify the Osborn algorithm and add to the clarity of the resulting flow graph, we omit the evident information-flow paths from an object to itself. This relevant omission yields a simplified version of the algorithm as described in Figure 8.23.

The application of the simplified Osborn algorithm directly to the graph of Figure 8.22 yields the simplified flow graph shown in Figure 8.24. Note how the labels in the final graph are reduced to the names of objects, thereby expressing the flow of information among the set of objects irrespective of the roles responsible for that flow.

Example 2: Reduction of a Role Hierarchy Governing Read and Write Access We now consider a role hierarchy governing read and write access to three objects o_1, o_2, o_3 via roles R_1, R_2, R_3, R_4 as shown in Figure 8.25A. The resulting flow graph is illustrated in Figure 8.25B. In turn, the final reduction of this graph yields a flow graph that is equivalent to a single node as depicted in Figure 8.25C. This indicates that all of the objects modeled by the

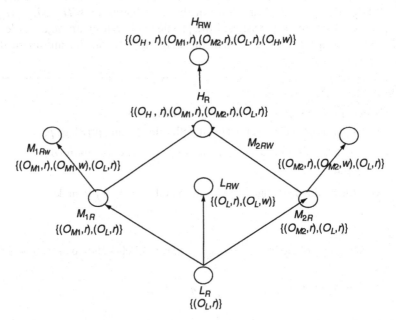

FIGURE 8.22 Application of the Osborn flow analysis to a role graph corresponding to an integrity LBAC model

> for each role $R_k \in N_{RG}$ do
>
>   for each privilege $p = (o, r/w) \in Effective(R_k)$ do
>
>   construct a node $n \in N_{FG}$ and label it with role R_k and
>
>   the privilege p;
>
>   for every pair of privileges in $Effective(R_k)$ that is of the form
>
> (o_i, r) (o_j, w), $i \neq j$
>
>   construct a directed edge $e \in E_{FG}$ from node (R_k, o_i, r) to node
>
> (R_k, o_j, r);
>
> remove all nodes $n \in N_{FG}$ that are not connected to any other nodes;

FIGURE 8.23 A simplified version of the Osborn flow-analysis algorithm

initial role graph are equivalent with respect to information flow (i.e., information received by each of these objects is visible to the rest of objects).

Flow graphs are not acyclic. The graph of Figure 8.25B is a complete directed graph and thus is cyclic. Nodes comprising a cycle are identical with respect to information flow. As such, each cycle in the flow graph is logically equivalent to a single node. In other terms, each strongly connected component of a flow graph reduces to a single node as shown in Figure 8.25C.

Separation of Duty in RBAC

RBAC lends itself to enforcing the *separation-of-duty* (SoD) *principle*. Recall that the goal of SoD is to guard against internal fraud and errors by limiting the powers of individuals. As a result, accountability becomes automatically built in the governing policy of an enterprise. We refer to this fact as *autonomous accountability*. The classical example expressing assurance in

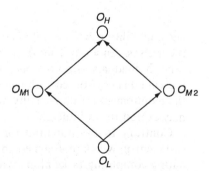

FIGURE 8.24 Application of the simplified Osborn algorithm to the role graph of Figure 8.22

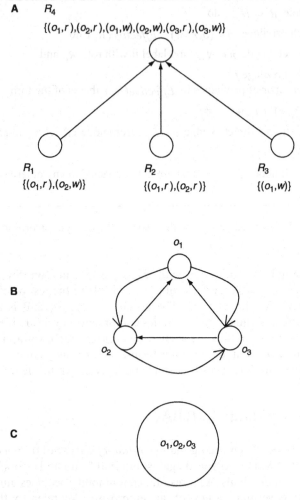

FIGURE 8.25 A: Example of a role hierarchy governing access to objects o_1, o_2, o_3. B: its information flow graph. C: and the final reduced flow graph.

accountability based on SoD is the rule that prohibits auditors for auditing themselves. An auditor must be designated to perform audits on actions of other individuals. Auditing oneself yields a conflict of interest in which the individual is confronted with two semantically exclusive interests. The first is the requirement for impartiality, while the second is the natural bias that one may exhibit toward oneself.

Contrary to the potential for singlehandedly perpetrating fraud when sufficient powers are assigned to individuals, SoD is achieved by disseminating computing tasks along with associated permissions among multiple individuals. This is usually accomplished by first breaking a business process that presents a conflict of interest when viewed as a single set of transactions into its basic tasks that are free of conflict of interest. Once independent sub-tasks are identified, separate individuals are then authorized to perform each subtask. For instance, a role that evaluates a procurement process in an organization and one that authorizes payment represent a conflict of inter-est. An SoD policy that may remedy the potential for fraud in this case would assign different individuals to each of these two roles. Early work on SoD was described by Clark and Wilson [CLAR87], Sandhu [SAND88b], and Brewer and Nash [BREW89], to mention a few.

SoD, however, cannot protect against a deliberate collusion in which indi-viduals trusted with the enforcement of a policy collaborate in performing the tasks required but in a fraudulent manner. To alleviate this concern, SoD policies can be best implemented when the separated roles are assigned to individuals with divergent interests, with no relationships to one another and perhaps even with no knowledge that the other role exists. Separated roles as such become discrete entities that are disconnected with respect to the indi-viduals assigned to them.

SoD is achieved in RBAC by first recognizing roles that are associated with conflicts of interests. A set of constraints are then established over user-to-role assignments in a way that no individual can assume the powers of any two or more conflicting roles at the same time. Two broadly defined cate-gories of separation of duty are in common use, *static* and *dynamic*. The static separation of duty encapsulates an invariant role-assignment policy that is maintained under any execution context. The dynamic separation of duty, however, can be represented by an unlimited number of variants. Each is characterized by the constraints it imposes on role activation. We discuss the details of each type in the following sections.

Elements of Role Conflicts in RBAC

Conflict of interest is the key element in any separation of duty policy. Even though the goal is always to prevent a conflict of interest from taking place through fraud, the origins of the conflict can be attributed to a number of factors.

Conflicting Permissions

One or more permissions that when exercised together (i.e., are members of the effective privileges of any single role) have the potential to cause fraud are said to be *conflicting permissions* (CP). In the simplest case, such permissions can be organized as unordered pairs that conflict with one another. Formally, $CP \subseteq PERMISSIONS \times PERMISSIONS$ with

$$(p_i, p_j) \in CP \Leftrightarrow (p_j, p_i) \in CP, i \neq j \text{ and } (p_i, p_i) \notin CP.$$

Conflicting permissions may also arise when a combination of certain permissions becomes a subset of the effective privileges associated with any one single role. A permission set may yield a conflict of interest whenever a combination of n or more permissions from the set results in a conflict situation. Formally, the set of conflicting permissions in this case can be described as $CP \subseteq 2^{PERMISSIONS} \times N$, which is a collection of pairs (ps, n), where each ps is a permission set and n an integer ≥ 2 with the property that any combination of n or more permissions from ps yields a conflict. The special case of mutually conflicting permissions results from $n = 2$.

The basic safety condition associated with conflicting permissions is that they must not be a subset of the effective privileges of any single role in the role set. On the other hand, nonconflicting permissions (those that do not represent a conflict of interest of some sort) are allowed to be part of the privilege set of any role.

Conflicting Users

A set of users that are likely to conspire for one or more social or any other reason is said to be a *conflicting user set*. When separation of duty policies are being formulated, any such set of users is reduced to a single user from the perspective of safety analysis and thus cannot be assigned to conflicting roles. Formally, a pair of conflicting users (CU) is defined as $CU \subseteq USERS \times USERS$ with

$$(u_i, u_j) \in CU \Leftrightarrow (u_j, u_i) \in CU, i \neq j \text{ and } (u_i, u_i) \notin CU.$$

The extension to a set of conflicting users may formally be described as: $CU \subseteq 2^{USERS} \times N$, which is a collection of pairs (us, n), where each us is a user set and n an integer ≥ 2 with the property that any combination of n or more users from us yields conflicting users. The special case of mutually conflicting users results from $n = 2$.

Conflicting Tasks

A collection of tasks representing a particular business process as a unit and that require conflicting permissions to complete are considered conflicting tasks. Pairs of conflicting tasks (CT) are formally described by $CT \subseteq TASKS \times TASKS$ with

$$(t_i, t_j) \in CT \Leftrightarrow (t_j, t_i) \in CT, i \neq j \text{ and } (t_i, t_i) \notin CT.$$

The extension to a set of conflicting tasks can be formally described as $CT \subseteq 2^{TASKS} \times N$, which is a collection of pairs (ts, n), where each ts is a task set and n an integer ≥ 2 with the property that any combination of n or more tasks from ts yields a conflict. The special case of mutually conflicting tasks arise when $n = 2$.

Because conflicting tasks require conflicting privileges, they are assigned to different roles. Nonconflicting tasks, however, can be assigned to conflicting or nonconflicting roles.

Safety Condition from the Perspective of Conflicting Tasks A safety condition can be formulated as an indicator of correctness in processing conflicting tasks governed by a separation-of-duty policy. First, we map the tasks required by the business processes at hand onto their respective sets of privileges, which in turn translates into roles required by the tasks. Formally, $S(t)$: $TASKS \rightarrow 2^{PERMISSIONS}$.

We then determine the set of mutually conflicting tasks CT based on a predefined policy. The safety condition for processing the set of mutually conflicting tasks is to ensure that no single person can be assigned all of the privileges required to perform each pair of conflicting tasks t_1, $t_2 \in CT$. Formally,

$$\forall u \in USERS, \forall t_1, t_2 \in CT, \neg (S(t_1) \cup S(t_2) \subseteq effective\_rivileges(u)).$$

The safety condition above extends in the same way to any conflicting set of tasks $t_1,..., t_i$. The union in this case is performed over the sets $S(t_1),...,S(t_i)$. Note that this safety property is a sufficient condition but not a necessary one.

Static Separation of Duty

Static separation of duty (SsoD) is also known in the literature as *authorization-time separation of duty* and sometimes is referred to as *strong exclusion*. SSoD places constraints on the assignment of users to roles in the context of an overall security policy independently of time or any other constraints. The effect of SSoD is limiting user-to-role in that membership in a particular role may prevent a user from becoming a member of one or more other roles. A wide variety of rules may govern SSoD policy. Most basic and common of these rules is the identification of mutually disjoint roles by the permissions assigned to each of them. Two roles require static separation when assigned permissions that result in a conflict of interest at all times. As such, a user is prohibited from being simultaneously a member of both roles. For instance, an individual assigned to the role of billing should not be assigned to the role of account receivable at any time.

Various implementations of the SSoD policy have adopted constraints on user-to-role assignments by simply identifying mutually exclusive role pairs. Each user is then assigned to at most one role in every such conflicting pairs of roles. A generalized model as proposed by Ferraiolo et al. [FERR01] defines SSoD relations as constraints over arbitrary sets of role sets instead of simply role pairs. Each such relation consists of a set of two or more roles along with a cardinality number for the lack of a better term. This cardinality integer, which must be greater than one, indicates the smallest number of roles from the constrained set that requires separation of duty (i.e., not assignable to a single user). For instance, an organization with five defined roles may require that no single user be assigned three or more roles. This constraint is denoted by the pair: $(rs, 3)$, where rs is the role set over which the constraint is defined, $rs = \{R_1, R_2, R_3, R_4, R_5\}$ in our example. The assignment of roles R_1, R_2, and R_3 to any particular user would constitute a violation of the separation of duty relation expressed by the policy $(rs, 3)$.

The formal definition of SSoD relations in this generalized model is expressed as follows:

❑ The SSoD relations are $SSoD \subseteq 2^{ROLES} \times N$ consisting of pairs (rs, n) where each rs is a set of roles involved in the separation of duty, and n is an integer ≥ 2.

❑ No user is assigned to a combination of n or more roles from each set rs such that $(rs, n) \in SSoD$. This is formally expressed as

$$\forall\, (rs, n) \in SSoD, \forall e \subseteq rs\text{:}\, |e| \geq n \Rightarrow$$

$$\underset{r \in e}{\cap}\, role\_assigned\_users\,(r) = \Phi \quad \cdot$$

The constraint $(rs, 3)$ in our example above limits the simultaneous assignment of a user to each of the following role sets only: $\{R_1, R_2\}$, $\{R_1, R_3\}$, $\{R_1, R_4\}$, $\{R_1, R_5\}$, $\{R_2, R_3\}$, $\{R_2, R_4\}$, $\{R_2, R_5\}$, $\{R_3, R_4\}$, $\{R_3, R_5\}$, and $\{R_4, R_5\}$. Note that a mutually exclusive role set rs results from $(rs,2)$. The assignment of any two roles from rs to a user violates the SSoD policy. The mutual exclusion of roles underscores the fact that the user sets denoting memberships in mutually excluded roles are completely disjoint as formally expressed by the following property:

$$\forall u \in USERS, \forall R_1, R_2 \in ROLES\, |\, R_1 \neq R_2$$

$$(\{R_1, R_2\}, 2) \in SSoD \Rightarrow u \in role\_authorized\_users(R_1) \Rightarrow$$

$$u \notin role\_authorized\_users(R_2).$$

Static separation of duty has the advantage of simplicity but exhibits a degree of rigidity that may present itself in some situations as a handicap rather than a control feature. Many real-life controls require the assignment of restricted roles to the same individual. Controls over which role can be assumed by the user at one time are dynamically applied based on context.

The Effect of Role Hierarchy

Mutually exclusive roles are established due to the conflict in one or more permissions that are assigned to those roles. The extension to an arbitrary constraint (rs, n) follows for the same reason that two or more mutually exclusive permissions end up being assigned to any combination of n or more roles. The effective permission set of each role is therefore a determinant factor of whether a pair of roles represents a conflict of interest in the case of mutual exclusion and similarly whether a particular set of roles exhibits a conflict in the general case. It is evident that if role R_1 is in conflict with role R_2 and role R_3 inherits from R_2 then R_3 is also in conflict of interest with R_1 due to the fact that $Effective(R_2) \subseteq Effective(R_3)$. Furthermore, R_2 and R_3 as well as any role that inherits either of them will remain in conflict of interest with any roles that inherit R_1. The separation-of-duty relations are thus inherited along a role hierarchy. The following two properties characterize the static separation-of-duty relationships in the presence of role hierarchies:

❑ The inheritance hierarchy implies that the static separation of duty is defined in terms of users authorized for a role instead of users directly assigned to that role. Recall that the set of users authorized for a role includes all users inheriting that role directly or indirectly. As such, SSoD can be formally expressed as

$$\forall (rs, n) \in SSoD, \forall e \subseteq rs \colon |e| \geq n \Rightarrow$$

$$\bigcap_{r \in e} role\_assigned\_users(r) = \Phi$$

❑ Any two roles that are assigned to the same user directly or indirectly, through inheritance, are not members of any static separation-of-duty relation. Formally,

$$\forall u \in USERS, \forall R_1, R_2 \in ROLES, R_1, R_2 \in$$

$$user\_authorized\_roles(u) \Rightarrow (R_1, R_2) \notin SSoD$$

This can be further generalized as

$$\forall u \in USERS, \forall R_1, R_2, \ldots, R_i \in ROLES, R_1, R_2, \ldots, R_i \in$$

$$user\_authorized\_roles(u) \Rightarrow$$

$$(R_1, R_2, \ldots, R_i) \notin (rs, i)$$

for any integer i and role set rs for which $(rs, i) \in SSoD$.

Dynamic Separation of Duty

Dynamic separation of duty (DsoD), also known as *runtime separation of duty* and sometimes referred to as *weak exclusion*, is intended for the same reasons SSoD is. The distinction between these two policies, however, is related to the runtime context. While an SSoD policy remains invariant throughout all execution environments, DSoD policies place constraints on the roles that can be activated within a user's session during system operation. Furthermore, the restrictions are enforced across multiple, simultaneous sessions initiated by the same subject. Two roles that are designated to be mutually exclusive in a user session cannot be simultaneously activated by the user logging to multiple sessions.

The main goal of DSoD is to provide a dynamic and variable method of setting the scope of authorized session roles based on the execution context.

This flexibility is used to remove the rigid constraints of SSoD. For instance, while a static policy separating a procurement role that initiates a payment from one that authorizes payment, prohibits an individual initiating payment ever from authorizing any payment. A dynamic separation-of-duty policy may allow the same subject to act in a payment initiation and a payment authorization roles provided no individual is able to authorize payments that he or she had initiated.

The flexibility of DSoD is intended to decrease the overhead incurred by the adoption of a static security policy. A user can be assigned to two roles that have a DSoD relationship, but a user cannot be assigned to two roles that have an SSoD relationship. While time of activation is usually what restricts roles in a DSoD policy from being activated simultaneously, it is not always the sole criterion. In the example of payment initiation and authorization roles, the rule governing role activation in DSoD is related to the identity of the user performing payment initiation and that authorizing it. The applicable execution context here is related to the parameters of the transaction performed, the subject performing the action, and the object of the transaction. This scenario illustrates the potential for various rules and application-oriented policies that may govern DSoD relations. DSoD can be viewed as a finer means of enforcing the principle of least privilege, where it is referred to by the terms of *timely grant* and *revocation of trust*. The formal definition of DSoD can be expressed as follows:

❑ DSoD relations are $DSoD \subseteq 2^{ROLES} \times N$ consisting of pairs (rs, n), where each rs is a set of roles involved in the dynamic separation of duty, and n is an integer ≥ 2.

❑ No subject may activate n or more roles from the set rs in each relation $dsod = (rs,n) \in DSoD$. This is stated formally as

$$\forall rs \in 2^{ROLES}, n \in N, (rs,n) \in DSoD \Rightarrow n \geq 2 \wedge |rs| \geq n, \text{and}$$

$$\forall s \in SESSIONS, \forall rs \in 2^{ROLES}, \forall role\_subset \in 2^{ROLES},$$

$$\forall n \in N, (rs,n) \in DSoD,$$

$$role\_subset \subseteq rs, role\_subset \subseteq session\_roles(s) \Rightarrow$$

$$|role\_subset| \leq n.$$

As a special case, the DSoD mutual role exclusion for a given session s has the following property:

$$\forall u \in USERS, \forall s \in SESSIONS, \forall R_1, R_2 \in ROLES| R_1 \neq R_2,$$

$$session\_user(s) = u$$

$$\{(R_1,R_2),2)\} \in DSoD \Rightarrow u \in role\_authorized\_users(R_1) \wedge u \in$$

$$role\_authorized\_users(R_2) \Rightarrow$$

$$R_1 \in session\_active\_roles(s) \Rightarrow R_2 \notin session\_active\_roles(s).$$

The semantics of dynamic separation of duty are much broader than those of static classification of separated roles. DSoD is amenable to encompassing a richer set of policies that exist in real organizations and manifest in many day-to-day tasks. Simon and Zurko [SIMO97] describe a number of variants of DSoD policies, which are outlined below. The term *restricted role* was rightly used by Simon and Zurko to mean any role that participates in a dynamic separation of duty. This indicates that DSoD virtually does not concern itself as much with user assignment to roles as it does with the constraints imposed on those assignments in the form of one or another dynamic policy. We use the terms *restricted roles* and *separated roles* interchangeably. DSoD is tightly related to application semantics and thus is not amenable to formal classifications at a broader level. Nevertheless, a number of well-defined policies have emerged. Below is a discussion of some broadly categorized dynamic separation of duty policies.

Simple Dynamic Separation of Duty

The simplest case of a DSoD policy calls for the separation of roles during run-time using a basic rule: no user can activate two restricted roles in two or more sessions at the same time. Recall, however, that separated roles as such may still have common members assigned to them. The dynamic aspect is the execution context, which in this case is defined by a user session. The majority of existing literature equates this variation to the dynamic separation of duty itself. The reason for this might simply be chronological since this is the first and simplest variation of DSoD devised.

Object-Based Separation of Duty

In this variation, separated roles may share user members but with the constraint that a user assigned to two separated roles may assume both roles at the same time but cannot act on an object that he or she has already acted on. An example is the commonly adopted policy in which one cannot approve a purchase order that he or she had initiated but can approve one that someone else did. In this case, a user may perform two functions: approve an order that another entity had initiated or initiate one that some other individual will have to approve. If we abstract the set of available privileges in this example to *order* and *approve*, an object encapsulating a purchase transaction may be ordered or approved only by any one individual but not ordered and approved by the same individual. This variant was first identified by Nash and Poland [NASH90]. Note the dynamic aspect of this policy is due to the user being capable of performing all operations exposed by an object instead without limitation but restricted in terms of objects on which to act.

Another criterion for object-based restriction of roles is the situation in which a user is capable of acting on all objects of some type (e.g., one representing a banking transaction), except for those that apply to the user performing the action. For instance, a teller is not allowed to act on his or her bank account. The constraint in this case may be driven by any policy-based rule governing the relationship between the user and a business object.

The semantics of yet another object-based separation of duty variant can be stated as follows: restricted roles are allowed to have common users, and those users are authorized to assume the authorities of the restricted roles in a single session, but no user may act on an object that another user authorized for the restricted roles had acted on. In essence, this partitions roles across the set of controlled objects but in a dynamic fashion, meaning roles restricted as such may interchangeably be used to act on the controlled objects but only once. Further actions on an object controlled as such have to be performed by users that are not common members of the restricted roles. Figure 8.26 illustrates this case. The intersection of roles R_1 and R_2 represents users assigned simultaneously to two restricted roles. An arrow from a user to the controlled object represents an action performed by that user. Once a user

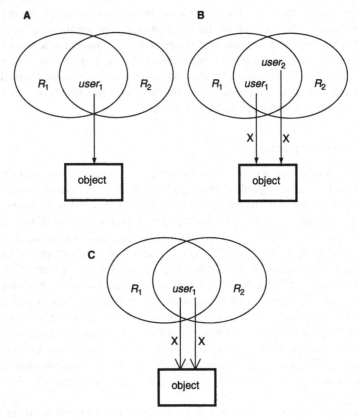

FIGURE 8.26 A variant of DSoD based on role partitioning across controlled objects

concerned with this policy has acted on an object as in case A, no further actions are allowed by any users that are participants in this policy as illustrated in cases B and C.

Operational Separation of Duty

Ferraiolo, Cugini, and Kuhn first introduced the paradigm of *operational separation of duty* [FERR95]. Here business processes or more generically computing tasks are broken into subtasks each is associated with its own required operations. The operational controls in this case are such that no single role may have sufficient privileges to perform all the tasks of a particular business process. Instead, subsets of the total privileges that are needed by a business process are disseminated across multiple roles, not all of which can be assigned to a single individual. The intent is to prevent any one person from performing all of the tasks of a business process controlled as such. Note the fact that an operational separation of duty applies to every object governed by such policy and hence the difference with the object-based DSoD policy.

This policy at first seems to equate the static separation of duty. The subtle difference between the two lies in the fact that users under the operational separation of duty can be shuffled across the role set in a dynamic fashion as long as the principle of this policy is not violated. In the static case, user to role assignment is quite rigid and remains strictly attached to the user. Operational separation of duty is well suited for the security of workflow processes in which at least two distinct roles are required for the completion of a business function. Long-running processes in workflow environments move from one state to another and may require various roles to be assumed at different stages. The classical example is that of the purchasing process, which can be separated into five tasks:

- Initiating a purchase order,
- Authorizing a purchase order,
- Processing an invoice,
- Processing the arrival of an item, and
- Authorizing payment.

Assigning each of these tasks to a distinct role and ensuring that no user is assigned to more than one of these roles diminish the likelihood of fraud. In this example, any possibility for fraud requires the conspiracy of all five parties. This raises the risk of disclosure and thus capture. The overhead incurred by this policy is dependent on the granularity of subdividing larger business processes.

History-Based Separation of Duty

This policy is essentially a combination of object-based and operational policies. Object-based separation of duty alone limits a user to performing only a single action on any one particular object. Some real-life policies may require the flexibility of performing further actions by the same individual. Similarly, an operational separation-of-duty policy alone does not allow a single person to perform all actions required by a particular business process to different objects. The combination of both policies makes the object-based policy borrow the ability to perform multiple actions on the same object from the operational policy (e.g., a complex transaction), while the operational policy borrows the aspect of distinguishing among various objects based on the actions required by each. The combination allows a single individual to perform all actions required by a particular business object but not on any single object in what is known as *history-based* separation of duty. This variant of DSoD requires tracking the individual histories of users in two ways:

❑ The list of objects acted on by any one user is maintained, and
❑ The actions performed by a user on any particular object are also kept.

The tracking process is used to determine if a user is in violation of the history-based separation-of-duty policy. An attempt to violate such policy occurs when a user tries to single handedly perform all tasks required by a particular business object. On the other hand, a user performing all tasks but on different business processes is considered in line with the policy. Overhead due to maintaining histories may be incurred in this policy, although history information may serve another security purpose—that of maintaining audit trails. Depending on the context in which a history-based separation of duty policy is implemented, history trails associated with each object may require strong integrity checks. Figure 8.27 illustrates this policy.

Example: Dynamic Separation of Duty in a Workflow Activity
We consider a business process dealing with the reimbursement of travel expenses in an organization that we abstract as consisting of three roles—a manager, a regular employee, and a secretary. The hierarchy corresponding to these roles is depicted in the graph of Figure 8.28. It reflects the fact that a manager role is empowered with all privileges assigned to the roles of a regular employee and that of a secretary. The controlled business process consists of four steps driven by the activities of an expense reimbursement workflow process as follows:

❑ An employee fills out a form to apply for the reimbursement of his or her expenses incurred by a business travel.
❑ The form is sent to two managers for approval.
❑ Both managers signal their approval.
❑ The secretary transfers money to the employee's bank account.

Despite the fact that from a static policy perspective, a manager is authorized to perform all these workflow steps, a meaningful dynamic separation of duty can be instituted, subject to the following constraints:

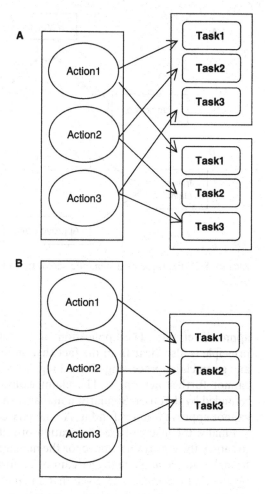

FIGURE 8.27 Illustration of history-based dynamic separation-of-duty policy

- ❏ A manager is not allowed to approve his or her own travel-reimbursement claim.
- ❏ A single manager is not allowed to perform both approval tasks on any one claim.
- ❏ A manager cannot refund a claim that he or she approved.
- ❏ A secretary is not allowed to transfer reimbursement funds for his or her own travel expenses.

The most apparent type of dynamic separation-of-duty principle in this example is the operational one. An object representing a particular reimbursement claim cannot be acted on entirely by one individual. A single manager can at most perform the actions {approve, refund} out of {initiate,

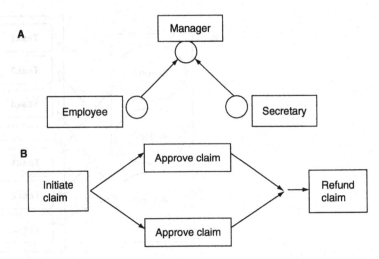

FIGURE 8.28 Example of a dynamic separation-of-duty policy involving a workflow process

approve, refund}. The application of the object-based separation-of-duty principle is also clear from the fact that an individual may act only once on any given claim processing. Once a regular employee initiates a claim, he/she cannot further act on it. The claim cannot be reinitiated, approved, or refunded by that user. Similarly, a manager that initiates his or her own claim cannot approve it nor refund it. A secretary can refund a claim only once.

Finally, the history-based separation-of-duty principle should be enforced to satisfy the constraints above for the manager role. This history is used first to make sure a single manager cannot perform two approval tasks required by any claim. Second, and given that a manager is empowered with all privileges {initiate, approve, refund}, an activity history for every claim is maintained so that a manager cannot perform all three actions on any one particular claim in light of the fact that a manager cannot approve or refund a claim of his or her own.

Role Cardinality Constraints

The *cardinality constraint* limits the number of users that can be members of a particular role. This constraint naturally fits with certain roles that may exist within an organization. For instance, only one person can fill the role of a department chair in an educational institution. Conversely, the number of roles that an individual user can be assigned to could be limited. The cardinality constraints can thus be applicable to the user as well as to the role sets.

In some cases this constraint may be applicable to lower or upper bounds for user memberships. For example, a role may be required to be assigned to a defined minimum number of individuals. To increase the assurance of a separation-of-duty policy, an organization may decide to require that the auditor role have a minimum of three members. The maximum and the minimum cardinality constraints are formally defined by

$$cardinality_{maximum} : ROLES \rightarrow N \cup \{\infty\}$$

$$cardinality_{minimum} : ROLES \rightarrow N \cup \{\infty\}.$$

The set $\{\infty\}$ denotes an unbounded condition, which basically underscores the fact that the cardinality constraint is not applicable.

RBAC Consistency Properties

In this section we look at 13 properties that should hold throughout the lifetime of an RBAC system. This is mostly based on the work of Serban et al. [SERB98].

Property 8.1   Imposing a maximum cardinality constraint on a given role means the number of authorized users for that role at any time should not exceed its cardinality. Formally,

$$\forall R \in ROLES, |role\_authorized\_users(R)| \leq cardinality_{max}(R).$$

Property 8.2   Imposing a minimum role cardinality constraint means the number of users authorized for that role should not be lower than the cardinality requirement for that role. Formally,

$$\forall R \in ROLES, |role\_authorized\_users(R)| \geq cardinality_{min}(R).$$

Note the use of authorized users here due to the effect of a hierarchical RBAC. In the case of a flat RBAC, authorized users are identical to the assigned users.

Property 8.3   To maintain consistency and avoid useless cyclic scenarios, no role should inherit itself directly or indirectly. Formally,

$$\forall R \in ROLES, \neg (R \rightarrow^+ R).$$

$\rightarrow^+$ denotes an inheritance path of length one or more.

Property 8.4   Any two roles authorized for the same user are not in any static separation-of-duty relationship. Formally,

$$\forall u \in USERS, \forall R_1, R_2 \in ROLES, R_1, R_2 \in$$

$$user\_authorized\_roles(u) \Rightarrow R_1, R_2 \notin SSoD.$$

Property 8.5   Any two roles explicitly assigned to a user should not inherit directly or indirectly from each other. Formally,

$\forall u \in USERS, \forall R_1, R_2 \in ROLES, R_1, R_2 \in user\_assigned\_roles(u) \Rightarrow$
$\neg (R_1 \rightarrow R_2) \wedge \neg (R_2 \rightarrow R_1).$

Property 8.6 No role can be in a static or dynamic mutual exclusion relationship with itself. Formally,

$\forall R \in ROLES \Rightarrow (\{R, R\}, 2\}) \notin SSoD \wedge (\{R, R\}, 2) \notin DSoD.$

Property 8.7 The static and the dynamic separation-of-duty relations are symmetric. Formally,

$\forall R_1, R_2 \in ROLES, (R_1, R_2) \in SSoD \Rightarrow (R_2, R_1) \in SSoD,$ and

$\forall R_1, R_2 \in ROLES, (R_1, R_2) \in DSoD \Rightarrow (R_2, R_1) \in DSoD$

Property 8.8 Any two roles in a static or dynamic separation of duty do not inherit one another either directly or indirectly. Stated in terms of the role graph, this property means there is no path between any pair of nodes (roles) that are in separation of duty relation. Formally,

$\forall R_1, R_2 \in ROLES, (R_1 \rightarrow^+ R_2) \vee (R_2 \rightarrow^+ R_1) \Rightarrow (R_1, R_2) \notin SSoD.$

The same holds for DSoD:

$\forall R_1, R_2 \in ROLES, (R_1 \rightarrow^+ R_2) \vee (R_2 \rightarrow^+ R_1) \Rightarrow (R_1, R_2) \notin DSoD.$

This means two roles can be in a mutual separation-of-duty relation only when they are incomparable with respect to the partial ordering relationship representing role inheritance.

Property 8.9 Two roles that are in separation-of-duty relationship cannot be both inherited directly or indirectly by another role. Formally,

$\forall R, R_1, R_2 \in ROLES, (R_1 \rightarrow^+ R) \wedge (R_2 \rightarrow^+ R) \Rightarrow (R_1, R_2) \notin SSoD,$ and

$\forall R, R_1, R_2 \in ROLES, (R_1 \rightarrow^+ R) \wedge (R_2 \rightarrow^+ R) \Rightarrow (R_1, R_2) \notin DSoD.$

The implication of the above property is that a role graph can have a "root" role (i.e., a role that inherits from every other role) only when no pair of roles in the entire role hierarchy is in any separation of duty relation. Formally, a role hierarchy can have a root super user only if

$\forall R_1, R_2 \in ROLES, (R_1, R_2) \notin SSoD \wedge (R_1, R_2) \notin DSoD.$

Property 8.10: The static and dynamic separation-of-duty relations are inherited along a role hierarchy chain. Formally,

$\forall R, R_1, R_2 \in ROLES, (R_1 \rightarrow^+ R) \wedge (R_1, R_2) \in SSoD \Rightarrow (R, R_2) \in SSoD.$

Similarly,

$$\forall R, R_1, R_2 \in ROLES, (R_1 \to^+ R) \wedge (R_1, R_2) \in DSoD \Rightarrow (R, R_2) \in DSoD.$$

Property 8.11 In a dynamic separation-of-duty context, the active role set of any user is bounded by his or her set of authorized roles. Note that in the case of an SSoD policy the active role set is identical to the set of roles for which the user is authorized. Formally,

$$\forall u \in USERS, user\_active\_roles(u) \subseteq user\_authorized\_roles(u).$$

Property 8.12 Any two roles that are in a dynamic mutual-exclusion relation cannot be both in the active set of roles for a user. Formally,

$$\forall u \in USERS, \forall R_1, R_2 \in ROLES, R_1, R_2 \in user\_active\_roles(u) \Rightarrow$$

$$(R_1, R_2) \notin DSoD.$$

Property 8.13 The dynamic separation of duty and the static separation-of-duty relations form disjoint sets. Formally,

$$\forall R_1, R_2 \in ROLES, (R_1, R_2) \in SSoD \Rightarrow (R_1, R_2) \notin DSoD,$$

and

$$\forall R_1, R_2 \in ROLES, (R_1, R_2) \in DSoD \Rightarrow (R_1, R_2) \notin SSoD.$$

The proof of this property is by absurdity. Assume that R_1 and R_2 are two roles that are in a static separation of duty relation. By definition, this means no user can be authorized for both roles R_1 and R_2. Hence there is no further need to dynamically constrain the two roles—i.e., $(R_1, R_2) \notin DSoD$. Now assume that R_1 and R_2 are in a dynamic separation-of-duty relation. By definition, this means a user can be authorized for both roles but cannot have both roles active at the same time. This implies that these two roles do not represent a static separation-of-duty relation.

The Privileges Perspective of Separation of Duties

Separation of duty yields separation of roles, which in turn inevitably implies separation of privileges. While the premise of separation-of-duty policies is to not assign two or more separated roles to the same individual, care also must be taken to ensure that the same individual is not empowered with the separated privileges through a combination of multiple roles that may not be participating directly in any separation of duty relations.

Suppose there are two roles R_1 and R_2 that are mutually exclusive and R_1 has access to a total of two privileges a and b—i.e, $Effective\_privileges(R_1) = \{a, b\}$. Assume that role R_3 has privilege a and another role R_4 has privilege b. Although access to privilege a or b alone by role R does not yield a separation of duty with R_2, a user assigned to R, which when simultaneously inherits directly or indirectly from R_3 and R_4, results in a conflict of interest with R_2.

Any separation-of-duty policy therefore must take into account the incremental effects from the propagation of individual privileges across roles.

Kuhn [KUHN97] outlines four scenarios for sharing privileges in a mutual separation-of-duty policy. He presents his view along two dimensions. The first is the privilege sharing among separated roles only, while the second one is the sharing of privileges with roles that are not part of any separation-of-duty relations.

❑ (*Disjoint, Disjoint*) Denoted by (D,D), this indicates the fact that if two roles are designated to be mutually exclusive, then each privilege is assigned to at most one of the roles. Furthermore, these two roles share no privileges with any other role with which they have no separation-of-duty relations. Each pair of mutually exclusive roles has unique individual privileges that are not assigned to any other role. Formally,

$$\forall R_1, R_2, R_3 \in ROLES, \forall p \in PERMISSIONS, \ (R_1, R_2) \in SoD \Rightarrow$$

$$p \in Effective\_privileges(R_1) \Rightarrow$$

$$p \notin Effective\_priveleges(R_2) \land$$

$$p \notin Effective\_privelges(R_3).$$

In this scenario, each two roles in a mutual exclusion relationship is completely disjoint and does not inherit from any other role in the role set. The effective set of privileges of each such role is therefore identical to its direct set of privileges. Alternatively, the property above can be stated as

$$\forall R_1, R_2, R_3 \in ROLES, \forall p \in PERMISSIONS, (R_1, R_2) \in SoD \Rightarrow$$

$$p \in Direct\_privileges(R_1) \Rightarrow p \notin Effective\_privileges(R_3).$$

❑ (*Disjoint, Shared*) Denoted by (D,S), this indicates the fact that the privilege sets of each pair of roles that are mutually exclusive are completely disjoint but can be shared with other roles outside of the mutual exclusion relationship. Formally,

$$\forall R_1, R_2 \in ROLES, \forall p \in PERMISSIONS, \ (R_1, R_2) \in SoD \Rightarrow$$

$$p \in Effective\_privileges(R_1) \Rightarrow p \notin Effective\_priveleges(R_2)$$

❑ (*Shared, Disjoint*) Denoted by (S,D), this means privileges may be shared between two roles that are in a mutual exclusion relationship but are not shared with any other role outside of this relation. Note that for the separation-of-duty relation to hold in this case, each role must have at least one privilege that is not available to the other role. Formally,

$$\forall R_1, R_2, R_3 \in ROLES, \exists p \in PEMRISSIONS \mid \forall q \in$$

$$PERMISSIONS, (R,R) \in SoD \Rightarrow$$

$p \in Effective\_privelges(R_1) \Rightarrow$

$p \notin Effective\_priveleges(R_2) \wedge$

$(q \in Effective\_priveleges(R_1) \vee$

$q \in Effective\_priveleges(R_2) \Rightarrow$

$q \in Effective\_privileges(R_3))$

❑ (*Shared, Shared*) Denoted by (S,S), this represents a situation in which each two mutually exclusive roles are allowed to share privileges, provided that each role must have at least one privilege that is not available to the other role. Additionally, a privilege assigned to a role that is mutually exclusive with another role may be assigned to other roles outside of the mutual exclusion relationship.

Figure 8.29 is an illustration of the four scenarios outlined above. It is easier to manage and maintain the safety of a separation-of-duty policy in the completely disjoint case (D,D). One only needs to ensure that each privilege is uniquely assigned to any role in the mutual exclusion relationship and never assign the same privilege to any other role. We also need to maintain the isolation of any roles participating in mutual exclusion relationships such that they

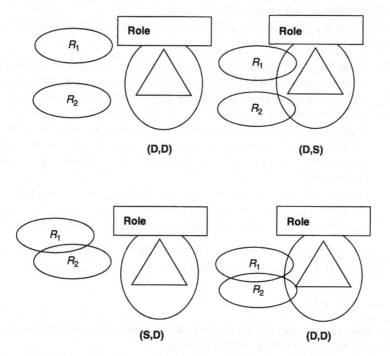

FIGURE 8.29 Illustration of the privileges view of separation-of-duty relationships

remain discrete and not participate in role inheritance. The manageability of the (S,D) scenario is more or less similar to that of the (D,D) case, although its safety might be slightly more complex to maintain. In the (D,S) and the (S,S) cases, one has to be concerned about the possibility that mutually exclusive privileges may be acquired through the combination of other roles. One way of avoiding this situation is to carefully handle assignment of mutually exclusive privileges to roles outside any mutual exclusion relationship.

Functional Specification for RBAC

In their proposed RBAC standard, Ferraiolo et al. [FERR01] have described a set of functional interfaces for the implementation of RBAC. These interfaces not only are expressed syntactically but have defined semantics, albeit at a higher level. The key benefit of adopting a standard interface across various RBAC implementations is the decoupling of applications using RBAC security controls from the components providing and managing those controls. One should not, however, expect a perfect portability of applications across RBAC implementations. For one thing, the policies may differ in the semantics of roles and their authoritative scope. Standard interfaces are also useful in implementing RBAC administrative tools such as graphical interfaces. This enables portability of such tools across RBAC policies and can be easily reusable as independent components.

The proposed specification addresses RBAC functionality from three perspectives:

- *Administrative functions* These concern the instantiation of various element sets of USERS, ROLES, OPS (operations), and OBS (objects) and the management of relationships across these elements (e.g., assignment of users to roles).
- *Supporting system functions* These concern the processing entailed by an RBAC implementation in supporting various constructs such as sessions and in enforcing the underlying RBAC policy via access decision making.
- *Review functions* These functions facilitate the review of an RBAC policy state as it evolves through the administrative functions. An example would be reviewing which entities have been assigned to a particular role.

We review the proposed functions for core RBAC, hierarchical RBAC, and constrained RBAC (separation of duty).

Core RBAC Functions

Functions in this category represent basic functionality aspects and as such are applicable to all RBAC implementations.

Administrative Functions

Tthese are concerned with the management of various RBAC element sets including USERS, ROLES, OPERATIONS, and OBJECTS. Users and roles evolve dynamically during the lifetime of an RBAC system. Operations may evolve but with a lesser frequency. Likewise, objects are usually predefined by the underlying computing system and evolve slowly over the lifetime of a policy. The following functions are needed:

- ❏ *AddUser*   Creates a new user in the RBAC repository,
- ❏ *DeleteUser*   Deletes an existing user from the RBAC repository,
- ❏ *AddRole*   Creates a new role in the repository,
- ❏ *DeleteRole*   Deletes an existing role from the repository,
- ❏ *AssignUser*   Assigns a user to a role,
- ❏ *DeAssignUser*   Removes a user from a role,
- ❏ *GrantPermission*   Grants a role the permission to perform an operation on an object, and
- ❏ *RevokePermission*   Removes a permission from the set of permissions assigned to a role.

Supporting System Functions

These are functions necessary for managing user sessions and enforcing underlying RBAC policies. They provide the runtime required for tracking active roles of each user session and RBAC policy management functionality. In broad terms, these functions are responsible for the runtime management of RBAC-based user-security contexts. The following is a set of functions supporting basic system RBAC functionality:

- ❏ *CreateSession*   Creates a new session with a given user as session owner and an associated set of active roles,
- ❏ *DeleteSession*   Removes an existing session associated with a given user,
- ❏ *AddActiveRole*   Adds a role to an active user session,
- ❏ *DropActiveRole*   Deletes a role from the active role set of a session, and
- ❏ *CheckAccess*   Performs an access decision related to a subject associated with a given session and attempting to perform an operation on a particular object.

Review Functions

These functions provide the sense of control over the various relationships that may exist among users, roles, permissions, operations, and objects. The proposed standard makes a distinction here between the review functions that are mandatory in any basic RBAC implementation and those that are optional. The following is the list of mandatory review functions:

- ❏ *AssignedUsers*   Returns the set of users assigned to a given role, and
- ❏ *AssignedRoles*   Returns the set of roles assigned to a user.

These are the optional review functions:

- ❑ *RolePermissions* Returns the set of permissions granted to a given role,
- ❑ *UserPermissions* Returns the set of permissions a user is granted through his or her assigned roles (this is essentially the set of effective privileges),
- ❑ *SessionRoles* Returns the active roles associated with a user session,
- ❑ SessionPermissions: returns the permissions assigned to the active roles of a given session, and
- ❑ *RoleOperationsOnObjects* Returns the set of operations a given role is allowed to perform on an object.
- ❑ *UserOperationsOnObjects* Returns the set of operation a given user is allowed to perform on an object.

Hierarchical RBAC Functions

Hierarchical RBAC includes the functionality of core RBAC and further adds functions necessary to establish and manage role hierarchies. The semantics of some core RBAC functions are modified to account for role hierarchy.

Administrative Functions

The semantics of DeAssignUser poses an issue in the presence of a role hierarchy and gives rise to two possibilities:

- ❑ Apply the DeAssignUser function to a role that is directly assigned to the user, or
- ❑ Apply the DeAssignUser function to any role that a user may inherit.

In the first case, the implementation is simplified and reduces to that of the core RBAC. The second case, however, is more complex as the impact could affect the entire role hierarchy. While the first case is more restrictive, the second one responds to the practical needs of an organization in a more accommodating fashion. Additional administrative functions needed by hierarchical RBAC are as follows:

- ❑ *AddInheritance* Establishes a new immediate inheritance relationship between two existing roles,
- ❑ *DeleteInheritance* Deletes an existing immediate inheritance relationship between two roles,
- ❑ *AddAscendant* Creates a new role and places it in an existing role hierarchy as an immediate ascendant of a particular role, and
- ❑ *AddDescendant* Creates a new role and places it in an existing role hierarchy as an immediate descendant of a particular role.

Supporting System Functions

These are the same as the supporting functions for core RBAC. The presence of role hierarchies, however, impacts the semantics of functions CreateSession and AddActiveRole. Two implementation scenarios can be possible:

- ❑ An active session role automatically activates the roles it inherits, or
- ❑ A role has to be explicitly activated within a session or else is not considered active.

Although implementations may choose to implement either of these scenarios, explicit activation of an inherited role can be considered a drastic change to the semantics of role inheritance. Access decisions can be complicated by supporting the inheritance of certain permissions only as opposed to the effect from inheriting the entire permissions assigned to inherited roles.

Review Functions

In addition to the functions supported by core RBAC, the following is a list of review functions needed to support role hierarchies:

- ❑ *AuthorizedUsers* Returns the set of users authorized for a given role,
- ❑ *AuthorizedRoles* Returns the set of roles authorized for a given user,
- ❑ *RolePermissions* Returns the set of all permissions in the form of (operation, object) that are granted to a given role rather directly or through inheritance,
- ❑ *UserPermissions* Returns the set of permissions granted to a given user through his/her authorized role set,
- ❑ *RoleOperationsOnObjects*   Returns the set of operations a given role is allowed to perform on an object, and
- ❑ *UserOperationsOnObjects*   Returns the set of operations a given user is allowed to perform on a particular object.

Functional Specification for Static Separation-of-Duty Relations

All of core RBAC as well as hierarchical RBAC functions remain in effect where applicable.

Administrative Functions

The first thing to note is a change in semantics for the AssignUser and GrantPermission functions. Assignment of a user or granting a permission to a particular role must take into consideration any conflict of interest constraints. A user must not be simultaneously assigned to conflicting roles, and similarly conflicting permissions must not be assigned to nonconflicting roles. Aside from this, administrative functions for managing static separation of duty relations are all related to the definition and maintenance of sets of conflicting roles. The following is a list of such functions:

- ❏ *CreateSsdSet*   Creates a named set of roles participating in a SSoD relationship with a given cardinality number,
- ❏ *DeleteSsdSet*   Deletes an existing SSoD role set,
- ❏ *AddSsdRoleMember*   Adds a role to a named SSoD role set (no change is effected in cardinality of the SSoD relationship),
- ❏ *DeleteSsdRoleMember*   Removes a given role from an SSoD role set (the cardinality of the SSoD relationship remains unchanged; however, the relationship will not have any semantics when the total number of roles remaining in the role set drops below the designated cardinality of the relationship), and
- ❏ *SetSsdCardinality*   Sets the cardinality associated with a given SSoD relationship.

Supporting System Functions

These functions are the same as those of core RBAC.

Review Functions

The following is the list of review function needed for tracking existing static separation-of-duty relations of an RBAC system:

- ❏ *SSDRoleSets*   Returns the list of all existing SSoD role sets,
- ❏ *SSDRoleSetRoles*   Returns the set of roles associated with a given SSoD relationship, and
- ❏ *SSDRoleSetCardinality*   Returns the cardinality associated with a given SSoD role set.

Functional Specification for Dynamic Separation-of-Duty Relations

All of core RBAC as well as hierarchical RBAC functions remain in effect where applicable.

Administrative Functions

The semantics of administrative functions for DSoD are similar to those of SSoD. The difference as we know relates to the enforcement of DSoD constraints being done at time of activation for session roles, while for SSoD it is performed during the process of user assignment to roles. Below are the administrative functions for DSoD following their counterparts in SSoD:

- ❏ *CreateDsdSet*   Creates a named DSoD set of roles with a given cardinaltity,

- *DeleteDsdSet*   Deletes an existing DSoD role set,
- *AddDsdRoleMember*   Adds a role to a named DSoD role set (the cardinality associated with the DSoD relationship remains unchanged),
- *DeleteDsdRoleMember*   Deletes a role from a named DSoD role set (the cardinality of the DSoD relationship remains unchanged but may not be meaningful when the total number of remaining roles drops below the cardinality), and
- *SetDsdCardinality*   Sets the cardinality associated with a given DSoD role set.

These functions are based on the definition of separation-of-duty relations as described in the proposed RBAC standard. Based on this definition, separation-of-duty relations are expressed in terms of conflicting role sets qualified with a cardinality number beyond which a conflict of interest arises. As we have discussed dynamic separation of duty relations can be expressed in various other means including rule and time-based constraints.

Supporting System Functions

These functions are the same as those of core and hierarchical RBAC but with a slight change in semantics, as follows:

- *CreateSession*   Creates a new session owned by a given user and associated with a given role set,
- *AddActiveRoles*   Adds a role as an active role of a given session associated with a particular user, and
- *DropActiveRole*   Drops a role from the active role set of a session.

Review Functions

Additional functions needed specifically for supporting DSoD relations are similar to their counterparts for SSoD as summarized below:

- *DsdRoleSets*   Returns the list of all existing DSoD role sets,
- *DsdRoleSetRoles*   Returns the set of roles of a given DSoD role set, and
- *DsdRoleSetCardinality*   Returns the cardinality of a given DSoD relationship.

References

[ABAD93] Abadi, M., Burrows, M, Lampson, B., and Plotkin, G., A Calculus for Access Control in Distributed Systems, *TOPLAS*, vol. 15, no. 4, pp. 706–734, 1993.

[ABRA95] Abrams, M., Jajodia, S., and Podell, H., *Information Security: An Integrated Collection of Essays*, IEEE Computer Society Press, Los Alamitos, CA, 1995.

[AHO72] Aho, A. V., Garey, M. R., and Ullman, J. D., The Transitive Reduction of a Directed Graph, *SIAM Journal of Computing*, pp. 13–137, 1972.

[ANDE80] Anderson, J., *Computer Security Threat Monitoring and Surveillance*, P. Anderson Co., Fort Washington, PA, 1980.

[BALD90] Baldwin, R., Naming and Grouping Privileges to Simplify Security Management in Large Databases, *Proceedings of the 1990 IEEE Symposium on Research in Security and Privacy (Oakland, CA)*, IEEE Computer Society Press, Los Alamitos, CA, pp. 116–132, 1990.

[BDTI91] British Department of Trade and Industry, *Information Technology Security Evaluation Criteria*, 1991. Can be found at http://www.itsec.gov.uk/.

[BELL75] Bell, D. E., and LaPadula, L. J., *Secure Computer Systems: Mathematical Foundations and Model*, M74-244, Mitre Corporation, Bedford, MA, 1975.

[BELL92] Bellovin, S. M., and Merritt, M., Encrypted Key Exchange: Password-Based Protocols Secure Against Dictionary Attacks, *Proceedings of the 1992 IEEE Computer Society Conference on Research in Security and Privacy*, IEEE Computer Society Press, Los Alamitos, CA, pp. 72–84, 1992.

[BENA02] Benantar, M., *Introduction to the Public Key Infrastructure for the Internet*, Prentice Hall, Upper Saddle River, NJ, 2002.

[BERN98] Berners-Lee, T., *Uniform Resource Identifiers (URI) Syntax*, IETF RFC 2396, 1998.

[BIBA77] Biba, K. J., *Integrity Considerations for Secure Computer Systems*, Mitre TR-3153, Mitre Corporation, Bedford, MA, 1977.

[BISH02] Bishop, M., *Computer Security: Art and Science*, Addison Wesley, Reading, MA, 2002.

[BISH79] Bishop, M., and Snyder, L., The Transfer of Information and Authority in a Protection System, *Proceedings of the Seventh ACM Symposium on Operating Systems Principles*, Pacific Grove, CA, pp. 45–54, 1979.

[BISH88] Bishop, M., *Theft of Information in the Take-Grant Protection Model*, *Proceedings of the Workshop on Foundations of Computer Security*, MITRE TR M88-37, Franconia, NH, pp. 194-218, 1988.

[BISK84] Biskup, J., Some Variants of the Take-Grant Protection Model, *Information Processing Letters*, vol. 19, no. 3, pp. 151–156, 1984.

[BLAZ96] Blaze, M., Feigenbaum, J., and Lacy, J., Decentralized Trust Management, *Proceedings of the IEEE Conference on Security and Privacy*, Oakland, CA, USA, 1996.

[BLAZ99] Blaze, M., Feigenbaum, J., and Keromytis, A. D., KeyNote: Trust Management for Public-Key Infrastructures, *Lecture Notes in Computer Science*, pp. 59–63, 1999.

[BREW89] Brewer, D. F. C., and Nash, M. J., The Chinese Wall Security Policy, *Proceedings of the IEEE Symposium on Research in Security and Privacy*, Oakland, CA, pp. 206–214, 1989.

[CALL98] Callas, J., Donnerhacke, L., Finney, H., and Thayer, R., *OpenPGP Message Format*, IETF RFC 2440, http://www.ietf.org, 1998.

[CANA93] Canadian System Security Centre, *The Canadian Trusted Computer Evaluation Criteria*, Version 3.0e, 1993.

[CHAR96] Chartrand, G., and Lesniak, L. M., *Graphs and Digraphs*, Chapman and Hall, 1996.

[CLAR87] Clark, D. D., and Wilson, D. R., A Comparison of Commercial and Military Computer Security Policies, *Proceedings of the IEEE Symposium on Security and Privacy*, Oakland, CA, pp. 184–194, 1987.

[DENN76a] Denning, P., Fault-Tolerant Operating Systems, *Computing Surveys*, vol. 8, no. 4, pp. 359–390, 1976.

[DENN76b] Denning, D. E., A Lattice Model of Secure Information Flow, *Communications of the ACM*, vol. 19, no. 5, pp. 236–243, 1976.

[DIES00] Diestel, R., *Graph Theory*, Springer-Verlag, New York, 2000.

[DIFF76a] Diffie, W., and Hellman, M. E., Multiuser Cryptographic Techniques, *Proceedings of AFIPS National Computer Conference*, AFIPS Press, Montvale, NJ, pp. 109–112, 1976.

[DIFF76b] Diffie, W., and Hellman, M. E., New Directions in Cryptography, *IEEE Transactions on Information Theory*, Vo. 22, pp. 644–654., 1976.

[ELGA95] El Gamal, T., A Public-Key Cryptosystem and a Signature Scheme Based on Discrete Logarithms, *Advances in Cryptology: Proceedings of CRYPTO 84*, vol. 196 of Lecture Notes in Computer Science, Blakley, G. R., and Chaum, D., Editors, Springer-Verlag, Berlin, pp. 10–18, 1995.

[FERR01] Ferraiolo, D. F., Sandhu, R., Gavrila, S., Kuhn, D. R., and Chandramouli, R., Proposed NIST Standard for Role-Based Access Control, *ACM Transactions on Information and System Security*, vol. 4, no. 3, 2001.

[FERR95] Ferraiolo, D., Cugini, J., and Kuhn, D. R., Role-Based Access Control (RBAC): Features and Motivations, *Proceedings of Computer Security Applications Conference*, New Orleans, LA, pp. 241–248, 1995.

[FERR92] Ferraiolo, D., and Kuhn, R., *Role-based access control*, Proceedings of the NIST-NSA (USA) National Computer Security Conference, Gaithersburg, MD, pp. 554–563, 1992.

[FREI96] Freier, A., Karlton, P., and Kocher, P. C., *The SSL Protocol Version 3.0*, Netscape Communications, 1996.

[GLAD97] Gladney, H. M., Access Control for Large Collections, *ACM Transactions on Information Systems*, vol. 15, no. 2, pp. 154–194, 1997.

[GLAS67] Glaser, E. L., A brief description of privacy measures in the Multics operating system, *Proceedings of AFIPS SJCC*, vol. 30, AFIPS Press, Montvale, N. J., pp. 303–304, 1967.

[GLIG85] Gligor, V. G., *Guidelines for Trusted Facility Management and Audit*, University of Maryland Press, College Park, MD, 1985.

[GORD85] Gordon, J. A., Strong Primes Are Easy to Find, *Advances in Cryptology: Proceedings of Eurocrypt 84*, Springer-Verlag, New York, pp. 216–223, 1985.

[GRAN00] Grandison, T., and Sloman, M., A Survey of Trust in Internet Applications, *IEEE Communications Surveys and Tutorials*, vol. 3 no. 4., 2000.

[GRAN02] Grandison, T., and Sloman, M., Specifying and Analysing Trust for Internet Applications, *Proceedings of Second IFIP Conference on e-Commerce, e-Business, e-Government*, I3e2002, Lisbon, Portugal, 2002.

[HARR76] Harrison, M. H., Ruzzo, W. L., and Ullman, J. D., Protection in Operating Systems, *Communications of the ACM*, vol. 19, no. 8, pp. 461–471, 1976.

[HARR78] Harrison, M. H., and Ruzzo, W. L., Monotonic Protection Systems, R. Demillo et al. (eds.), *Foundations of Secure Computations*, Academic Press, 1978.

[HOUS99a] Housley, R., Ford, W., Polk, W., and Solo, D., *Internet X.509 Public Key Infrastructure Certificate and CRL Profile*, IETF RFC 2459, http://www.ietf.org, 1999.

[HOUS99b] Housley, R., and Hoffman, P., *Internet X.509 Public Key Infrastructure Operational Protocols: FTP and HTTP*, IETF RFC 2585, http://www.ietf.org, 1999.

[HOWE03] Howes, A. T., Good, G. S., and Smith, M. C., *Understanding and Deploying LDAP Directory Services*, McMillan Publishing, New York, 2003.

[HOWE95] Howes, A. T., and Smith, M., *The LDAP Application Program Interface*, IETF Informational RFC 1823, http://www.ietf.org, 1995.

[IBMC02] IBM Corporation, *IBM Resource Access Control Facility*, http://www-1.ibm.com/servers/eserver/zseries/zos/racf/, Somers, NY, 2002.

[IBMC03] IBM Corporation, *Websphere Application Server*, http://www-3.ibm.com/software/webservers/appserv/infocenter.html, Somers, NY, 2003.

[KOBL87] Koblitz, N., Elliptic Curve Cryptosystems, *Mathematics of Computation*, vol. 48, no. 177, pp. 203–209, 1987.

[KOHL93] Kohl, J., and Neuman, C., *The Kerberos Network Authentication Service (V5)*, IETF RFC 1510, 1993.

[KOHN78] Kohnfelder, L. M., Toward a practical public-key cryptosystem, B.Sc. thesis, MIT Department of Electrical Engineering, Cambridge, MA, 1978.

[KONR99] Konrad, K., Fuchs, G., and Bathel, J., Trust and Electronic Commerce: More Than a Technical Problem, *Eighteenth Symposium on Reliable Distributed Systems*, Lausanne, Switzerland, 1999.

[KRIS00] Kristol, D., and Montulli, L., *HTTP State Management Mechanism*, IETF RFC 2965, http://www.ietf.org, 2000.

[KUHN97] Kuhn, D. R., Mutual exclusion of Roles as a Means of Implementing Separation of Duty in Role-Based Access Control Systems, *Proceedings of the ACM Workshop on Role-Based Access Control*, pp. 23–30, 1997.

[LAMP71] Lampson, B. W., Protection, *Fifth Princeton Symposium on Information Science and Systems*, Princeton, NJ , pp. 437–443, 1971.

[LAMP73] Lampson, B. W., A Note on the Confinement Problem, *Communications of the ACM*, vol. 16, no. 10, pp. 613–615, 1973.

[LAMP74] Lampson, B. W., Protection, *ACM Operating System Review*, vol. 8, no. 1, pp. 18–24, 1974.

[LAMS01] Lamsal, P., *Understanding Trust and Security*, Department of Computer Science, University of Helsinki, Finland, 2001.

[LIPN82] Lipner, S. B., Non-Discretionary Controls for Commercial Applications, *Proceedings of the IEEE Symposium on Security and Privacy*, Oakland, CA, IEEE Computer Society, pp. 2–10, 1982.

[LIPT77] Lipton, R. J., and Snyder, L., A Linear Time Algorithm for Deciding Subject Security, *Journal of ACM*, vol 24, no. 3, pp. 455–464, 1977.

[LOCH88] Lochovsky, F. H., and Woo, C. C., Role-Based Security in Data Base Management Systems, *Database Security: Status and Prospects*, Landwehr, C. E.(ed.), North-Holland Publishing Co., Amsterdam, The Netherlands, pp. 209–222, 1988.

[MERK78] Merkle, R. C., Secure Communications Over Insecure Channels, *Communications of the ACM*, vol. 21 no. 4, pp. 294–299, 1978.

[MILL86] Miller, V. S., Use of Elliptic Curves in Cryptography, *Advances in Cryptology, CRYPTO'85 Proceedings*, Springer-Verlag, New York, pp. 417–426, 1986.

[MCLE88] McLean, J., *The Algebra of Security*, IEEE Symposium on Security and Privacy, Oakland, CA, 1988.

[MOAT97] Moats, R., *URN Syntax*, IETF RFC 2141, http://www.ietf.org, 1997.

[MOCK87a] Mockapetris, P., *Domain Names: Concepts and Facilities*, IETF RFC 1034, http://www.ietf.org, 1987.

[MOCK87b] Mockapetris, P., *Domain Names: Implementation and Specification*, IETF RFC 1035, http://www.ietf.org, 1987.

[MOFF99] Moffett, J. D., and Lupu, E. C., The Uses of Role Hierarchies in Access Control, *Proceedings of the Fourth ACM Workshop on Role-Based Access Control (RBAC)*, George Mason University, Fairfax, VA, 1999.

[NASH90] Nash, M. J., and Poland, K. R., Some Conundrums Concerning Separation of Duty, *Proceedings of the 1990 IEEE Symposium on Security and Privacy*, pp. 201–207, 1990.

[NEED87] Needham, R. M., and Schroeder, M. D., Authentication Revisited, *ACM Operating Systems Review*, vol. 21, no. 1, 1987.

[NIST92] National Institute of Standards and Technology, *Federal Criteria for Information Technology Security*, Version 1.0, 1992.

[NIST94] National Institute of Standards and Technology, *Digital Signature Standard*, Publication 186, 1994.

[NIST95] National Institute of Standards and Technology, *Secure Hash Standard*, Federal Information Processing Standards Publication 180-1, 1995.

[NIST99] National Institute of Standards and Technology, *Common Criteria*, Version 2.1, 1999.

[NYAN94] Nyanchama, M., and Osborn, S., Access Rights Administration in Role-Based Security Systems, *Proceedings of the IFIP WG11.3 Working Conference on Database Security VII,* vol. A-60, North-Holland, 1994.

[NYAN99] Nyanchama, M., and Osborn, S., The Role Graph Model and Conflict of Interest, *ACM Transactions on Information and System Security*, vol. 2, no. 1, pp. 3–33, 1999.

[OASI02] OASIS Organization, Security Services Technical Committee, *Security Assertion Markup Language*, http://www.oasis-open.org, 2002.

[OASI03] OASIS Organization, Security Services Technical Committee, *Web Services Security Assertion Markup Language*, http://www.oasis-open.org, 2003.

[OSBO02] Osborn, S., Information Flow Analysis of an RBAC System, *Proceedings of SACMAT '02*, Monterey, CA, 2002.

[OSBO97] Osborn, S., Mandatory Access Control and Role-Based Access Control Revisited, *Proceedings of the Second ACM Workshop on Role-Based Access Control (RBAC'97)*, VA, USA, pp. 31–40, 1997.

[OSBO00] Osborn, S., Sandhu, R., and Munawer, Q., Configuring Role-Based Access Control to Enforce Mandatory and Discretionary Access Control Policies, *ACM Transactions on Information and System Security*, vol. 3, no. 2, pp. 85–106, 2000.

[RESN01] Resnick, P., *Internet Message Format*, IETF RFC 2822, http://www.ietf.org, 2001.

[RIVE78] Rivest, R. L., Shamir, A., and Adleman, L. M., A Method for Obtaining Digital Signatures and Public-Key Cryptosystems, *Communications of the ACM*, vol. 21, no. 2, pp. 120–126, 1978.

[RIVE92] Rivest, R. L., *The MD5 Message-Digest Algorithm*, IETF RFC 1321, http://www.ietf.org, 1992.

[RSA99] RSA Corporation, *PKCS #11 v2.10: Cryptographic Token Interface Standard*, RSA Laboratories, 1999.

[SALT75] Saltzer, J. H., and Schroeder. M. D., The Protection of Information in Computer Systems, *Proceedings of IEEE*, vol. 63, no. 9, pp. 1278–1308, 1975.

[SAND88a] Sandhu, R., The Schematic Protection Model: Its Definition and Analysis for Acyclic Attenuating Schemes, *Journal of the ACM*, vol. 35, no. 2, pp. 404–432, 1988.

[SAND88b] Sandhu, R., Transaction Control Expressions for Separation of Duties, *Proceedings of the Fourth Aerospace Computer Security Applications Conference*, IEEE Computer Society Press, pp. 282–286, 1988.

[SAND90] Sandhu. R., Undecidability of the Safety Problem for the Schematic Protection Model with Cyclic Creates, *Journal of Computer and System Sciences*, 1990.

[SAND91] Sandhu, R., Expressive Power of the Schematic Protection Model, *Journal of Computer Security*, 1991.

[SAND92a] Sandhu, R., A Lattice Interpretation of the Chinese Wall Policy, *Proceedings of the Fifteenth NIST-NCSC National Computer Security Conference*, Washington, DC., pp. 329–339, 1992.

[SAND92b] Sandhu, R., The Typed Access Matrix Model, *Proceedings of IEEE Symposium on Security and Privacy*, Oakland, CA, pp. 122–136, 1992.

[SAND93] Sandhu, R., Lattice-Based Access Control Models, *IEEE Computer Magazine*, pp. 9–19, 1993.

[SAND96] Sandhu, R., Feinstein, C. L., and Youman C. E., Role-Based Access Control Models, *IEEE Computer Magazine*, pp. 38–47, 1996.

[SAND98] Sandhy, R. S., and Munawer, Q., How to do Discretionary Access Control Using Roles, *Proceedings of the Third ACM Workshop on Role-Based Access*, Fairfax, VA, USA, 1998.

[SCHN96] Schneier, B., *Applied Cryptography*, John Wiley & Sons, New York, 1996.

[SERB98] Serban, I. G., and Barkley, J. F., Formal Specification for Role-Based Access Control User/Role and Role/Role Relationship Management, *Proceedings of the ACM Workshop on Role-Based Access Control*, pp. 81–90, 1998.

[SHAN02] Shankar, N., and Arbaugh, W. A., *On Trust for Ubiquitous Computing*, Department of Computer Science, University of Maryland College Park, MD, USA, 2002.

[SIMO97] Simon, R. T., and Zurko, M. E., Separation of Duty in Role-Based Environments, *IEEE Computer Security Foundations Workshop*, 1997.

[SNYD81] Snyder, L., Theft and Conspiracy in the Take-Grant Model, *Journal of Computer and Systems Sciences*, vol. 23, no. 3, pp. 337–347, 1981.

[TING88] Ting, T., A user Role-Based Data Security Approach, *in Database Security: Status and Prospects*, Landwehr, C., (ed.), Elsevier North-Holland, New York, NY, pp. 187–208, 1988.

[PARK00] Park, J. S., and Sandhu, R., Secure Cookies on the Web, *IEEE Internet Computing*, pp. 37–45, August 2000.

[POPE74] Popek, G., A Principle of Kernel Design, *1974 NCC, AFIPS Conference Proceedings*, vol. 43, pp. 977–978, 1974.

[USDOD85] U.S. Department of Defense, *Trusted Computer System Evaluation Criteria (Orange Book)*, DoD 5200.28-STD, 1985.

[XNS02] XNS Public Trust Organization, http://www.xns.org, 2002.

[WAHL97] Wahl, M., Howes, T., and S. Kille, *Lightweight Directory Access Protocol (v3)*, RFC 2251, http://www.ietf.org, 1997.

[W3CO99] W3C Organization, *Namespaces in XML*, http://www.w3.org, 1999.

[W3CO00] W3C Organization, *SOAP: Simple Object Access Protocol 1.1*, http://www.w3.org, 2000.

[W3CO01a] W3C Organization, *XML Schema Part 1: Structures*, http://www.w3.org, 2001.

[W3CO01b] W3C Organization, *XML Schema Part 2: Datatypes*, http://www.w3.org, 2001.

[W3CO02a] W3C Organization, *Web Services Architecture*, http://www.w3.org, 2002.

[W3CO02b] W3C Organization, *XML Signature Syntax and Processing*, http://www.w3.org, 2002.

[W3CO02c] W3C Organization, *XML Encryption Syntax and Processing*, http://www.w3.org, 2002.

Index